STEVE GARDENER ON…
A Life in Match Fishing

Steve Gardener and Pat Newman
With a Foreword by Milo Colombo

© Steven Gardener and Patrick Newman

© Design – Mpress (media) ltd

ISBN number: 978-0-9955630-0-1

Designed and published by

Unit 213, Waterhouse Business Centre, 2 Cromar Way,
Chelmsford, Essex, CM1 2QE

For Jeanette, James and Victoria

Contents

Acknowledgements

We are indebted to Milo Colombo, Stewart Cottingham, Trevor Fox, Brian Gay, Dave Harrell, James Lauritz, Steve and Liz O'Rourke, Dave Roberts, Steve and Carole Sanders, Alain Urruty, *Angler's Mail* and *Angling Times* for permission to reproduce photographs.

In the case of a few photographs we have been unable to trace their owners, despite making every effort, and intend no breach of copyright by reproducing them here.

Many thanks, too, go to the following for their help with research: Kenny Collings, Stewart Cottingham, Barbara Durante at FIPSed, John Essex, Dave Johnson, Dave Roberts, Paul Udell and Steve Fitzpatrick and Kevin Wilmot at *Angling Times*. Thanks also go to *Angling Times* for allowing us to reproduce some articles that Steve Gardener did for the publication back in the 1970s and 1980s.

Finally, sincere thanks go to Alain Urruty and Mark Wintle for their invaluable advice, and to Anna Fischel for her unfailing encouragement and the thoroughness of her proofreading.

Foreword
by Milo Colombo

I have been proud to call Steve Gardener *mio amico* ever since we first met, way back in the 1980s. You probably won't believe this, but in those days he had some hair, though perhaps not as much as my favourite band in their 'mop-top' heyday, those other great Englishmen, The Beatles! But to be serious *un momento...*

When England came to Florence for the World Championship on the River Arno in 1985 and beat *Italia* into second place by fishing the waggler, there was an explosion of interest among Italian match anglers in this *tecnica inglese* – and in the years that followed, no Englishman impressed us more with a float rod in his hand than Steve when he burst onto the international scene in the World Championship in Portugal in 1987 on the River Mondego.

Steve quickly proved himself more than just a waggler angler, of course, and soon showed that he was equally *abile* at all methods, from long pole to short pole, from Bolognese to slider. He was the Maradona of match fishing, someone who could have walked into any sponsorship deal that he fancied – but it was Milo who splashed out in the global transfer market and signed him up! That was back in 1990, and ever since then it has been my very great pleasure and privilege to sponsor one of the best English anglers of all time, a man who for so very many years all of us here in *Italia* regarded as no less than the *baluardo*, or bastion, of the England team. In return, Steve has put all his vast knowledge and experience into helping us develop some fantastic products. But more than that, he has been a true ambassador for the sport.

Steve and I have had some wonderful times fishing together over the years – not to mention sharing the occasional bottle of *vino bianco* – and I have learnt so much from him, especially when we fish pairs matches, where we share the same peg. Not only is he *un perfezionista totale*, but time after time he has amazed me with his almost uncanny reading of what is happening beneath the surface of the water. He may be sat on his box, looking at his float, but I reckon he has an extra pair of eyes lurking on the bottom, spying on the fish from a secret hiding place among the weed and stones and reporting back to him everything they are doing!

One day after winning his section in a match on the Arno, Steve came up to me and said in perfect Italian, *"Li ho fumati tutti!"* – "I smoked them all!" I couldn't believe it, I thought all he knew was a few swear words.

That man Steve Gardener simply never ceases to surprise me.

Grazie Steve!

Milo Colombo
Milano
26th July 2016

Introduction
by Pat Newman

When John Waples moved from the South to the Midlands in the mid-1980s and joined Oundle after a number of successful years with the Dorking team, he famously told good friend David Hall, the publisher of *Match Fishing* magazine, "If Steve Gardener ever gets into the England team, they'll never get him out again".

John wasn't far wide of the mark. Calls for the man his one-time Dorking captain Andy Love described in 1988 as "the greatest angler in the South by far" to be selected for his country began as early as 1976 and reached a crescendo in the early 1980s, but for reasons known only to himself Stan Smith, the England manager in those days, totally ignored them. Steve was 'the southerner Stan Smith always forgets', as *Angling Times* put it in 1982. After he finally got his chance in 1987 under new manager Dick Clegg, he went on to represent England in 27 consecutive World Championships, being the one constant in a squad that started off with Kevin Ashurst, Bob Nudd, Tommy Pickering and Denis White as regular members and ended up with Alan Scotthorne, Will Raison, Sean Ashby and Des Shipp as the same, encompassing the international careers of Kim Milsom and Stu Conroy along the way. Along the way, too, Steve won

11 team gold medals, five team silvers and two team bronze. He also won individual silver in Belgium in 1988 and individual bronze in Italy in 2008.

Steve also represented his country in 16 consecutive official European Championships between 1997 and 2012, winning four team golds – in Portugal in 1998, England in 2000, Holland in 2003 and Hungary in 2004 – five team silvers and two team bronze.

In the Dick Clegg era, when his team became known abroad as 'the English professionals', Steve won gold with England in World Championships on his debut in Portugal in 1987 and subsequently in Belgium in 1988, Hungary in 1991, England in 1994 and Croatia in 1998. On day two at Holme Pierrepont in 1994, when Dick and his team were under maximum pressure after finishing third on day one, Steve was the only one in a line of 20 anglers in his section to catch a fish – there were five blanks one side of him, 14 the other – and without that one fish, a perch, England wouldn't have won. Dick Clegg said in 1997 that in trials the two England anglers who consistently stood out above the rest were Bob Nudd and Steve Gardener. On another occasion he said that Steve was always the first name on his team sheet.

Mark Downes and Mark Addy took over from Dick Clegg in 2001, and that year England scored a famous victory in the World Championship on French soil, beating the host nation in their own capital, on the River Seine in Paris. Steve rates that as one of the greatest weekends of his career. Further World golds followed in Finland in 2005, Portugal in 2006, Italy in 2008, Spain in 2010 and Poland in 2013. Of these, 2008 stands out for Steve, for it was the first time in his international career, and the first time since 1985 – Dick Clegg's second year as England manager – that England had beaten Italy in their own country in a major international tournament.

Dave Harrell was in Italy in 2008 covering the event on the Spinadesco Canal as Editor of *Match Fishing* magazine, and had this to say: "I sat behind Steve Gardener for the whole of the match on day two and witnessed a masterclass in decision making. It would have been so easy for him to have fed too much bait at the wrong time and killed his swim, as other anglers around him were doing, but instead he kept his cool and his concentration and coaxed out every last fish that he could, on his way to third overall. It was a performance of the highest quality and one of the best I've ever witnessed at this level."

Steve was the 'Mr Consistency' of the England set-up. In 2006, in a list of the top 20 international anglers based on average daily penalty points scored in the previous five World Championships – 2001 through to 2005 – Steve came out top with a score of 4.9. Stu

Steve Gardener in action for England. (Image courtesy of Angling Times*)*

Conroy was second with 5.2, Alan Scotthorne eighth with 7.1 and Will Raison 13th with 8.5. According to my own calculations, over his entire England career, based on the days he fished, Steve had an average daily penalty points score of only 5.9 in World Championships and only 4.6 in European Championships.

When Steve's international career did finally end, in 2014, Mark Downes released the following official statement: "This year one of the most difficult decisions me and Mark Addy have ever had to make was to leave out Steve Gardener. Steve has had an amazingly long and prolific international career and has played a major part in building Team England's success. However, we now feel that the time is right to give the next generation the chance to develop their own long careers. We both wish to thank Steve for all of the hard work he has afforded the team over the 13 years we have been co-managers and the part he has played in helping us secure six gold medals during that time."

Here's what Dick Clegg had to say: "It is not difficult for me to summarise what Steve's contribution to the team has been in all those years – dedication, team spirit, ability, professionalism and above all his willingness to put team success before individual glory. In other words he has been the ultimate team professional. Mark Downes and Mark Addy, England's management pairing, feel that to continue with their tremendous winning record then changes need to be made, and unfortunately Steve will have to stand down to make way for the youth. It must have been particularly difficult to make a decision to leave him out, but I totally agree with their reasoning, although I sympathise tremendously with Steve. I personally would like to thank Steve Gardener for being part of England's winning formula and congratulate him on 27 years as a member of the world's most successful coarse fishing team."

Steve was 62 at the time, and wasn't bitter about the decision – "After all," he told me, "It had to happen at some point, didn't it?" – yet there were those who were bitter on his behalf, ostensibly because they felt he still had more to offer, but largely, I suspect, because they had so dearly wanted him to be individual World Champion and it had

Dick Clegg, who in 2008 named his all-time England squad as Kevin Ashurst, Bob Nudd, Denis White, Alan Scotthorne, Will Raison – and Steve Gardener. (Image courtesy of Angling Times)

never happened. But neither does Steve dwell on not ever winning the individual title, for the simple reason that he has always been a team man first and foremost, whether with England or with Dorking. "The best angler never to win the World Championship" is how Kevin Ashurst and others have described him, and no one would argue with that. But the fact that he never won it is just a quirk of fate. As multiple winners Alan Scotthorne and Bob Nudd have both said, you need a bit of luck to win, and Steve never had that. Better, then, simply to state for the record that Steve Gardener is indisputably one of the greatest match anglers of all time.

David Hall once said that the great thing about match fishing, unlike any other sport, was that anybody could get to the top if they really applied themselves. Later he said that he had changed his mind, having realised that the best match anglers are a breed apart. This is the harsh reality that the majority of us sooner or later have to accept. Yes, we can get better if we really apply ourselves, but no matter how technically proficient we become, no matter how much knowledge and experience we acquire, we will never, ever be as good as the best.

The reason for this, I believe, is that the best match anglers have vastly superior 'angling brains', by which I mean they have the ability to read a water, to assess the conditions and to understand fish behaviour – the way fish react in any given situation – so much better than the rest of us. Moreover, this is something they demonstrate, or rapidly acquire, from the moment they take up fishing. As a result, they get those two key elements of success – bait presentation and feeding – correct so much more of the time.

That doesn't mean the rest of us should give up, for one of the great things about match fishing is that, in most cases, so long as you do make the effort you need never stop learning, never stop improving, and you can gain great satisfaction and enjoyment from that, just so long as you are ready to accept, without rancour, that you won't ever reach the top. (There will always be a few who, for whatever reason, never seem to learn or improve.) And two of the other great things about match fishing are that anyone can take on the best in an open, and almost anyone can win on the day if they draw the right peg. I can't think of any other sport where the same is true.

Steve Gardener shot to prominence in 1969, when he was still only 17, by winning two big matches on the River Arun in the space of a week followed by two more on the River Mole. After his second victory on the Mole, when he more than doubled the weight of second-placed Pat Richardson – a legend of the southern match scene – *Angler's Mail* had this to say: "Steven is only in his second season of senior match fishing but has earned a terrific reputation and is known as 'the man who never sits down', preferring to crouch throughout matches."

Steve Gardener in typical 'crouching' style, seen here in action in the 1973 Angling Times *Winter League final in Ireland, on the River Blackwater in Fermoy, County Cork. (Image courtesy of* Angling Times*)*

These were the days of willow tackle baskets, not seat boxes, and of fibreglass float rods, not long carbon poles, and it was his prowess at floatfishing with a rod that earned Steve his reputation. His restless style is a trademark feature of his fishing, reflecting his

15

constant quest to get the best out of his peg. I was lucky enough to do a feature with Steve on the tidal Thames at Richmond – one of his favourite venues – for *The Art of Fishing* in the early 1990s, and what struck me most that day was his phenomenal work rate when it came to feeding the swim and finding the best way to present his hookbait. At one point he decided he needed to set up another rod, and he asked me to keep feeding the swim for him with hemp and maggots while he tackled the rod up. It only took him a few minutes, but he must have asked me at least three times, "Are you keeping that feed going in?" I had watched him feed the swim all morning, and thought I was doing it right. Obviously not.

The other thing that struck me that day was how modest and friendly Steve was. He had no airs and graces and was genuinely interested in my own fishing. When I occasionally saw him on matches on the Thames after that he would always make a point of saying hello. Our paths then didn't cross for many years, but when I approached him earlier this year about doing this book I found he hadn't changed, and was just as friendly as all those years before. He was also just as modest. There are no display cabinets full of trophies and medals at his home. It's almost as if it embarrasses him to have won them. He has also never sought publicity for his achievements, and was anxious from the moment we embarked on this project that he didn't want to be seen to be blowing his own trumpet. That seems to be a trait of genuinely top-class anglers. I can certainly think of a number of much lesser match anglers who would benefit from showing the same level of humility.

Back in the early 1970s the southern match scene had been hampered for years by size limits and was regarded as a bit of a joke by match anglers in the Midlands and

Kenny Collings, Steve's friend and fellow superstar. (Dave Roberts)

North. Steve Gardener and his close friend Kenny Collings, another brilliant match angler in his own right, helped change all that, especially when they fished for the South against teams from the North, West and East in the Ladbrokes Super League in 1976 and won the league outright in front of an appreciative crowd in the last round on the Warwickshire Avon at Evesham.

Steve and Kenny, along with another old friend of Steve's, Steve Sanders, will also forever be associated with the Dorking team, a team that will go down in match fishing history as one of the all-time greats. Dorking first made their mark by reaching a succession of *Angling Times* Winter League finals in the 1970s, and showed they had firmly arrived when they scored their first win, at Coombe Abbey Lake, in 1978. After Dorking's fifth Winter League final win, in 1989, when they surpassed Cofton Hackett's record of four wins in the competition, the then Editor of *Angling Times*, Neil Pope, said: "The most refreshing part about Dorking's run of success has been the way the team have conducted themselves. While some outfits have moaned about venues and draws, the Surrey squad have gone about their business in a professional way." Dorking's great strength – apart from the ability of their anglers – has always been that they are a tight-knit unit, a team in the full sense of the word. They went on to win the *Angling Times* Winter League a record nine times, completely dominated the Drennan Super League in the 'noughties', and in 2012 became only the second team, after Birmingham in 1976, to win successive Division One Nationals.

Right from the start, Steve was regarded by his fellow Dorking team members as an indispensable asset. When Dorking reached their first Winter League final, in 1972, it clashed with him being away on an already booked and paid for holiday in Majorca. The rest of the

Some of the Dorking squad in 1976. From left, at the top are John Tullett, Dave Taylor, Mike Bartlett, Peter Shepherd, Steve Sanders, Bob Evans, Les Collins, George Harrison and Mark Spring, at the bottom Dave Roberts, John Moriarty, John Benham, Terry Wright and Steve Gardener. (Image courtesy of Angling Times*)*

team desperately tried to raise the money between them to fly him home at short notice, and pooled £38, which was about the average weekly wage at the time. Unfortunately for them it wasn't enough.

Right through the 1970s, 1980s and 1990s, Steve won seemingly everywhere he went, from the Rother to the Thames, from Old Bury Hill Lake to Willow Park, gaining him legendary status on the southern match circuit,

Steve with a bream and a tench he caught in a match on the Lea in the early 1970s. (Image courtesy of Angling Times)

where – like John Allerton and Dave Harrell on their own respective circuits – he became known simply as 'God'. Further afield he set a new match record for Coombe Abbey Lake in 1980 with over 100lb of bream on the waggler, and won the individual Courage title at the August Bank Holiday festival at Evesham on the stick float in 1983, among a great many other triumphs in major contests. On into this century he continued to win regularly on a variety of venues, not least commercial carp fisheries, and over the course of his whole career he won no fewer than 13 individual and team medals in Nationals, including being crowned individual Division One Champion in 2011.

Towards the end of 1989 Steve won six out of seven matches – all of them on the Thames, which was 'on fire' that year – including five in a row. The run started with a win in an open on the tidal river, followed by victory in Dorking's Scandinavian Seaways quarter-final tie against Banstead on the same venue. Next came a win in a midweek Silstar Top 40 match on the lower Thames at Molesey in which he set a new venue record with 33lb 7½oz of dace. Win number four came in the annual open for the coveted Marlow Rose Bowl, and win number five in a round of the Winter League at Medley, where he drew on the canalised Channel stretch, fished a maggot feeder and landed a 7lb 7oz barbel two minutes from time to add to a smaller barbel and several pounds of perch and just beat Banstead's John Smith 19lb to 17½lb. In his next match, a midweeker at Wallingford, his 20lb wasn't enough to make the frame, but he came good again in match number seven with a stunning 40lb 12oz winning bag of whip-caught dace back on the tidal Thames.

All of this prompted *Angling Times* to publish a letter from fellow southern match angler Stewart Lister jokingly suggesting that rather than ban bloodworm, it was Steve Gardener who should be banned.

Stories about Steve abounded, many of them promulgated in *Match Fishing* magazine by Andy Love, his Dorking team captain in the 1980s and early 1990s. Andy, who often referred to Steve as 'Obi-Wan Kenobi', recalled in February 1991 how, on a typically hard round of the Winter League on the Wey Navigation Canal, bank runner Robin Morley came up to him three hours in, said the rest of the team had all caught, then asked if he had caught anything himself. "No I f---ing ain't!" Andy replied. "Mind you, I reckon I've as much chance of catching a chub as I have of catching a gudgeon." At this, Robin said, "I tell you what, Stevie's in the next section. I'll go and ask him what he thinks." A few minutes later he was back. "Stevie says that you've as much chance of catching a chub as you have of catching a gudgeon – and to tell you the pressure's on now!"

Steve enjoyed great success everywhere from Old Bury Hill Lake to Evesham from the 1970s onward. (Images courtesy of Angling Times*)*

It was that very month that Steve won Dorking's Winter League semi-final on the Nene in quite spectacular style with 42lb 9oz of roach from a swim known ever after as 'Gardener's peg'. With about an hour to go, the bank runner for one of the teams pegged next to Dorking came up to Andy and said, "Andy, my mate next to Stevie Gardener has just found out why Stevie fishes for England and he don't!"

A few months after that, according to Andy, John Raison was walking around during a match at Willow Park and when he got to Steve at his peg he found him even more agitated than usual. The ensuing conversation went like this:

"What's the matter, Stevie?"

"Did you see that?"

"What?"

"That heron's just flown down and caught a perch in my peg."

"Whereabouts?"

"About nine metres out."

"Well," John said, "You haven't caught all the fish in your peg, then."

"Mind you," Steve said matter of factly, "I ain't fished that far out yet."

Going back to that Scandinavian Seaways tie between Dorking and Banstead on the tidal Thames, I can remember the buzz it caused in the London area, with everyone talking about it in the preceding weeks whenever you walked into a tackle shop, and both teams practising for it at every opportunity. The match was held down at River Lane at Richmond, and drew quite a crowd. Andy Love had told Banstead's Simon Duke the night before that the contest was a bit unfair, really, as Dorking had nine men to Banstead's eight – the difference being Steve Gardener. After Steve had led Dorking to victory, Andy found himself signing autographs alongside Steve. "God knows

Andy Love, who captained Dorking to numerous victories and was always amusing in his monthly Match Fishing *magazine articles. (Image courtesy of* Angler's Mail*)*

why they wanted mine," he said. "I just fill in the team sheet." He added that if he could be granted three wishes, one of them would be "the ability to get inside Steve's brain – it'd be a revelation to a mere mortal". In the same vein, Milo Colombo is only half joking when he says that Steve must have an extra pair of eyes under the surface of the water when he is fishing, observing everything the fish are doing.

Steve signs an autograph for a fan at the 1993 World Championship in Portugal. (Image courtesy of Angling Times)

Andy is just one of many over the years who have joked, too, about Steve's supposed supernatural ability at the draw bag. "Look very closely and you can see 666 tattooed on the top of his head," he once said. "Not a lot of people know this but his middle name is Damien." (In fact it's James.) Calling Steve 'The Great One', Keith Arthur said in *Angling Times* in 1994, "It is legend that when Steve draws, a glow appears through the bag, and his hand turns into a cloven hoof".

In 1995, Steve was driving to a pairs match at Gold Valley when he spotted a number plate with the number 112, which happened to be the peg from which Simon Gould had won the previous match at the venue. When he got there, he scribbled the number down on the palm of his hand before getting out of the car. His pairs partner Will Raison drew for them both but before he could say anything Steve showed him the palm of his hand. A dumbfounded Will handed Steve his draw card: peg 112.

Steve says that because there are always more bad pegs than good ones he prefers to draw last, to reduce the odds of drawing a bad one. But then others like to draw first while the good pegs are definitely still in the bag.

Luck is important, yes. Back in 1971 Steve entered a close season pike match run by the Twickenham Piscatorial Society at Littleton Lane Lake in Shepperton, the aim being to

An early 1970s portrait of Steve, always a demon at the draw bag. (Image courtesy of Angling Times)

move the pike to their Hithermoor fishery near Colnbrook. Steve had never fished for pike before, but it was a chance to go fishing, so he thought, why not? Another 244 anglers fished that day, most of them experienced pike men. It was a six-hour, 'roving in sections' affair, and Steve chose a shallow, weedy swim near the sailing club. On the whistle he cast out his gudgeon bait under an Avon float and as the float hit the water it kept on going, so he struck, and found himself attached to an 11lb 6oz pike. When he got the pike in he saw that it had a small bream stuck halfway down its throat. An hour before the end he added a jack to weigh in 15lb 13½oz, enough for first place. If that first pike had regurgitated the bream at any point, he would have been second.

In the end, though, skill counts for everything. It was sheer chance that Steve Gardener was never individual World Champion, but it was skill tantamount to genius that got him into the England set-up in the first place, and it was that, coupled with his total dedication to putting the England cause before his own, that kept him there for the best part of three decades and helped make England so fantastically successful. And who else has 11 team golds?

Forever England – Kevin Ashurst, Mark Downes, Steve Gardener, Bob Nudd, Denis White, Tommy Pickering and Dick Clegg sport their England caps in the early 1990s. (Image courtesy of Angling Times*)*

CHAPTER ONE
In the Beginning...

In 2013, for the first time in my international career, I stepped down from an England squad – the squad for the European Championship in Serbia – so that the management team of Mark Downes and Mark Addy could give someone else a go. I knew then that I would have to impress in future World Championships to stay in the World squad. To cut a long story short, I felt I might have done enough in practice for the World Championship in Poland later that year to be in the team, but for the first time in 27 years I found myself running the bank on both days. So I suppose it was no real surprise not to be picked for the squad for the World Championship in Croatia in 2014, even though the fast-flowing venue would have suited me, as I'd fished many similar venues. It was Mark Addy who rang to tell me I wasn't in, but I know how difficult it must have been for both him and Mark Downes to make that decision, and I shall always appreciate the backing they gave me in the years I fished for them – just as I shall always be grateful to Dick Clegg before them for picking me to fish for England in the first place.

Knowing my England career was over, I decided there and then to retire not only from international duty but from top-flight team fishing altogether, to leave the Dorking team as well after four glorious decades with them, and just do my own thing, just please myself. And that's exactly what I have been doing these past couple of years. People ask me all the time, "Don't you miss fishing for England?", but I honestly don't, because I'm over all that now. And now that I've moved on, I've had time to reflect on my whole long life in match fishing, to think back to how it all began, way back in 1968, when I first joined Dorking at club level at the tender age of 16.

But to begin at the very beginning... I was born in Hampstead on 4th March 1952, and a sister, Sally, followed a couple of years later. My father was a bricklayer, my mother a housewife, and we lived in various parts of London before I was five, when we settled in a council house in Tadworth, near Epsom Downs in Surrey. There was a small pond only a hundred yards from our house in Marbles Way – Marbles Pond, it's still there – and that's where it all started, though it seems I always had the bug. My grandad on my dad's side told me that on a day's outing to Hampton Court when I was three some people fishing on the Thames there tied some line to a stick so that I could 'fish' alongside them. Apparently I sat there for ages just thrashing the water, not knowing what I was doing. My dad wasn't interested in fishing, but wherever we went I was always drawn to water. At the seaside I would happily spend hours playing in rock pools, and on walks along the Thames and Mole

I was always looking for bits of lost fishing tackle.

In Tadworth my parents helped me make 'rods' out of garden canes, and I would 'fish' in Marbles Pond without any chance of catching anything. Then I got my first proper rod, a 6ft solid-glass American affair with a short handle and a finger crook for one-handed casting, and with that I caught my first fish, a little crucian carp, on bread paste, when I was five. I can remember the bite to this day, the way the garish little float went dib-dib-dib for ages before finally going under. I took the fish home to show everyone and put it in a bucket of water on the coal bunker in the back garden.

Steve Sanders, the current Dorking captain and a lifelong friend, lived even nearer Marbles Pond than I did, and in summer we would get

All wrapped up, ready for my first Winter League!

Gardener family outings often involved riverside walks and picnics – combined with a spot of fishing. Here I'm having a dabble with my sister Sally on the Pevensey marshes in Sussex when I was about eight.

up at dawn to fish before school. The pond was chock-a-block with weed, and every year we'd have to clear a swim. Even then we had to stand out in the water on milk crates to reach holes in the weed. There were a few small carp in there, but mostly it was little crucians. Our set-ups were pretty crude, and the float might bob away for 15 minutes to the tugging of a fish while you waited for a proper bite. Mainly we used a paste made out of custard powder, flour and water, which we kept in tobacco tins. It would go rock hard on top, but underneath it would be perfect for moulding around the hook. In the close season we'd see who could catch the most newts – not with hooks, I hasten to add, but simply by tying worms to the end of the line. Sometimes we'd get two newts at a time, one on each end of the worm.

Loads of my other friends growing up went

Here I am, standing on a milk crate to fish Marbles Pond when I was about five, while my Uncle Charlie looks on. On the other side of the pond is De Burgh School, where I was later a pupil.

Steve Sanders (in the dark top) and myself (bottom right) were both keen footballers. I was a striker, and played for a local club on Saturdays after I left school, until one Sunday I woke up to find my feet were too swollen and bruised to get my wellies on to go fishing.

fishing too, when we weren't all playing football or cricket. Things were very different then, there weren't all the amusements you've got today, and if you wanted to talk to a friend about going fishing or having a kick-about you cycled round his house and hoped he was in. We all cycled everywhere, and though we still fished Marbles Pond, as we grew older we started fishing slightly further afield, on bigger ponds like Mere Pond in Walton on the Hill and the pond at Burgh Heath.

Someone else who fished Burgh Heath pond was future carp record holder and renowned angling writer Chris Yates, who lived in Tattenham Way, but being four years younger than Chris I never really knew him as such, though I knew his brother, Nick. We called Chris 'Herbie' for some reason, and he was a bit eccentric even then. While Chris would pay a shilling to fish the pond from the tea gardens, my friends and I would climb out and fish for free from the branches of an old willow tree that had been struck by lightning at some point and fallen in the water, or even wade out and fish from the island in the middle. We used to catch all sorts there – roach, rudd, perch, small carp, even gudgeon – and I once caught quite a big goldfish, which I took home and kept in a tank in the back garden. Then one day I went out to feed it and it was gone. I knew exactly which 'friend' had taken it, so I went round his house when he wasn't there and took it back.

Being so shallow, Burgh Heath suffered a big fish kill in the Big

Chris 'Herbie' Yates as we all know him now. It's fair to say that his angling career and mine took very different paths. (Image courtesy of Angler's Mail)

Freeze of early 1963, but in time, happily, its stocks recovered. Sadly, fishing is now banned there – and at Mere Pond, for that matter – which is a sign of the times, I'm afraid.

As we grew older still, my friends and I started cycling as far as the Mole, which meant going down Box Hill, which in turn meant going back up it at the end of the day, and that was a nightmare, because it's so steep. I got all the way down to the river one day and my bike fell over, snapping the rod strapped to the crossbar, so that was it, I couldn't fish. Disaster!

One Christmas my grandad on my dad's side bought me a Japanese cane combination rod. It came in a wooden box and had multiple sections, all with metal ferrules, so that you could make up a float rod, a fly rod, a boat rod, whatever. It was a rod for every occasion. He didn't fish himself, but my other grandad did a bit of sea fishing, and when I was about seven he took me to Littlehampton to fish in the estuary there. All we caught were a few crabs, but that didn't matter, it was my first sea fishing trip and I got to spend the whole day with him.

I used to get a bit of pocket money, but my friends and I all did things like paper rounds as well to pay for our fishing. The first place I ever bought hooks and line from was Burgh Heath Corn Stores, but the main place for such items was a local newsagents, which sold hooks to nylon with the line whipped and glued to hooks with no spade ends, just straight shanks. I remember wondering what the loop on the end of the line was for, and always cutting it off then tying the line to my reel line with a granny knot.

Frank Peacock, my grandad on my mum's side, who introduced me to sea fishing. After serving in West Africa, he returned to England in poor health and died when he was only 56 and I was eight, before I had the chance to really get to know him.

Getting some practice in on the Barge Walk stretch of the Thames at Kingston with my friend Alan Clarke (seated). Note the centrepin reel – we never fished very far out in those days! In later years the Barge Walk became a regular match haunt for me, but sadly I lost touch with Alan once I left school.

Posing on Brighton's West Pier, which later fell into disrepair, was closed in the early 1970s, burnt down in 2003, and has since disintegrated. Meanwhile fishing is no longer allowed on the Palace Pier, but on the bright side fishing has been available on the newer Marina since 1977.

Not long before I started at senior school – De Burgh School, handily sited right next to Marbles Pond, but now long since pulled down – my mum and dad split up, and as I stayed in Tadworth with my dad the only way my mum could see me really was if she took me fishing. I remember her saying, "Come on, I want to see you, I want to see you! I'll take you fishing!" I went a few times with her, and she'd buy all the maggots and everything, even the time I brought my friend Alan Clarke along to fish on the Thames at Kingston, on the Barge Walk stretch. I'll never forget that.

Another outing that sticks in the memory was one boiling hot Sunday in the summer of 1966, when I was 14 and went with another friend, Terry Wright – who later fished with me in the Dorking team – as a guest on one of the Banstead club's fortnightly coach outings. This was to Speringbrook Sewer, a tiny drain – a ditch, really – near Snargate on Romney Marsh, and I fished next to Chris Yates, who the Banstead secretary, Fred Jones, had recruited to the club some years earlier when he fixed the electrics at Chris's house. (Years later, Fred did all the electrics for Kenny Collings and me in our tackle shop in Sutton.) Anyway, all my maggots and worms died that day, it was that hot, and neither Chris nor I caught very much, though I know Chris caught more than me – a few rudd, I think. In fact I'm not sure I caught anything at all, nor do I recall Terry catching much. What I do recall is going as red as a beetroot when Fred boarded the coach afterwards, held up a bag containing all the rubbish that I'd left on the bank and demanded to know whose it was. But I learnt my lesson, and never left litter again. CALPAC – the Central Association of London and Provincial Angling Clubs, to which Banstead still belongs – have that water to this day, thanks no doubt to men like Fred.

In winter and the close season some of us sometimes went sea fishing. I used to get 10 shillings a week for my paper round, and that would have to pay for my whole day. We'd get the bus to Redhill, then the train to Brighton, buy some lugworm from a little tackle shop in Kensington Street called Sid & Don's, and fish on either the West Pier or Palace Pier.

Mostly we caught the usual rockling, pouting, flatties and mackerel, but one day I went with two brothers, Roger and Ronnie Wood, and there was great excitement when what looked like a double-figure cod took one of their baits. After much heaving they had the fish wallowing on the surface, but while we were frantically trying to sort out a drop net the hook pulled and the fish got away. Oh, the agony!

Another time we fished from the harbour wall in Shoreham, and I had so many flounders stuffed into a plastic bag that on the train home the inevitable happened and the bag split. The fish shot everywhere, across the aisle and under the seats, and much to the amusement of the other passengers, my friends included, I had to crawl around on my hands and knees gathering them all up, then take them to the toilet to wash them off in the sink. When I got home I gave them all away.

Much more appetising were the little plaice I caught each day on holiday in Newquay in Cornwall with my sister and dad when I was about 11. I would take them back to our lodgings and the proprietor would cook them up for me for breakfast.

So keen were my friends and I that even when heavy snow disrupted the train service one time we set out undaunted and finally made it to Brighton. The snow was two-foot deep all along the front, and the piers were closed, but the waves and tide had washed the beach clear of snow and we basked on the shingle all day in the sun. And we caught some fish.

Winter or spring, by the time we got back to Redhill after a day's sea fishing we'd have just enough money left for our bus fares home, but we'd also be starving hungry. There was a bakers next door to the station so we'd go in there and buy some bread pudding, and that'd be our bus fares gone. We'd then have to try to hitch a lift home, but often we had to walk the whole five or six miles. Can you imagine kids doing that these days? But back then we all did things like that all the time.

With my mum gone, and having no interest in school, I used to play truant quite a lot to go fishing, and one day when I was about 15, at a time when many of my friends, including Steve Sanders, were losing interest in fishing, even if only temporarily, I got to know a guy called John Benham, who was in his twenties at the time and lived just down the road. John was into his match fishing big time at club, association and open level, so following his example I joined the Dorking club and started going with him to matches. He had a white Ford Anglia, and he'd pick me up and drop me back home. He was a quiet, stay-at-home sort of guy, and match fishing was his life, until much later when he got married. From the start his total dedication to the sport made a lasting impression on me.

John Benham in the 1970s. (Image courtesy of Angling Times)

I did no good at all that first, 1968/69 season. The first match I ever fished, as I recall, was a club match on the Mole when the river was in flood. I think it was autumn, but it could have been summer – the Mole floods at the slightest bit of rain. I fished the upstream end peg at Puddenhole and I remember sitting there with two gudgeon in my

CENTRAL ASSOCIATION OF LONDON AND PROVINCIAL ANGLING CLUBS

Hardy Cup Competition

Open to members of C.A.L.P.A.C. only

**To be Fished on Sunday, 6th July 1969, in the River Arun
at Pulborough on the Association's Waters**

PEGGED COMPETITON IN SECTIONS
ASSOCIATION RULES AND CONDITIONS TO APPLY

All coarse fish in season to count including Pike, Pope and Bleak
as provided in amended Rules.
SEE GUIDE BOOK

The draw for Sections will take place at

THE CATTLE YARD, at 8.15 to 10 a.m.
(outside Pulborough Station)

Competitors must show Privelege Ticket at the Draw

Starting Instructions: Draw your Section and Peg number at Headquarters.
Proceed to the start of your section, report to the Steward, then go to your
peg and tackle up and wait for the start.

Starting Whistle: Commence fishing at 10 a.m.   Cease fishing at 4 p.m.
Stewards will be at starting points until 10.30 a.m.   Late starters **must** find
a Steward before starting.

For Prizes **see** Guide Book.

5/- each

(Under 16; 3/-)

Competition Secretary: **R. BRIDGER**
72 Holmesdale Road, Selhurst, London SE25
Telephone: **01-653 7660**

*Dave Roberts is a real hoarder of memorabilia. This is his actual ticket for the
1969 Hardy Cup. I probably left mine in John Benham's car. (Dave Roberts)*

keepnet thinking I was doing quite well and even wondering if they
could be enough to win. Two gudgeon!

I left school that summer with one 'O' Level, in metalwork, and
was taken on straight away as one of a hundred or more first-year
apprentices by the British Aircraft Corporation in Weybridge. Trouble
was, most of my £5 a week went on fares, so after six months I left there
to work as an apprentice toolmaker with a small family firm, JA & MF
Engineering, in Lower Kingswood, which was only a shilling bus ride
away. I ended up staying with them until 1988, when I went into the
tackle shop business with Kenny Collings.

The 1969/70 season was the breakthrough one for me, in large
part thanks to John Benham. We were both mad keen, and with the
usual big CALPAC matches that summer on the Arun at Pulborough,
starting with the prestigious Hardy Cup, we fixed up a practice session.
The night before, I fished with some friends on the Thames at Canbury
Gardens in Kingston, by the hot water outfall from the power station
that was there in those days. This was always a popular spot, and all
you had to do was fish over the railings, straight down under your rod
tip. We caught mainly bream, but one night, I remember, someone
had a big tench on a legered dead bleak intended for eels. When we
got too tired to carry on, we'd kip in the roof space of the open-fronted
building where deck-chairs were stored, then start fishing again at

first light. Anyway, on this occasion John thought nothing of driving the 15 miles or so from Tadworth to pick me up from Kingston early in the morning, then driving all the way back past Tadworth and another 30 miles on to Stopham, near Pulborough, just so we could practise swingtipping bread on the Arun, swingtipping being all the rage back then. The river is semi-tidal here, and to counter the sluggish flow we weighted our swingtips with lead wire. (In later years we also used the stiffest of those angled rubber connectors that came in packs of three.) We fished on a stretch where the river widens out to about 20 yards, casting across with flake, and caught a lot of skimmers.

By this time I had the standard match angler's kit for the period, namely a willow basket and a canvas rod holdall. Having a short, fixed 'foot' at each corner, the basket rested at whatever angle the bank was at, and you sat on it as best you could – if you were sensible, you strapped a foam cushion to the lid to prevent the dreaded 'basket bum' – or you just stood to fish. The basket had a leather strap for slinging over one shoulder, and typically contained a towel, a wooden float box, a couple of rod rest heads, and another box for bits and pieces like hooks, line, two metal disgorgers (in case you lost one), and lead plummets, Arlesey bombs and split shot. Also in your basket would be your reels – an open-face Mitchell reel for legering and either another Mitchell or a closed-face Abu reel for floatfishing, all of which were like mangles. Some anglers had a separate bag for their nets and bait, otherwise you strapped your knotted landing net head and keepnet to your basket, and crammed your various bait boxes, a bag or two of brown or white crumb, a small mixing bowl, and your flask and any food inside with all your tackle. The holdall, meanwhile, which you slung over the other shoulder, held the obligatory green umbrella, a telescopic landing net handle (metal or fibreglass), a few bank sticks, and two heavy, floppy hollow fibreglass rods, namely a two-piece, nine or 10ft rod for legering and a three-piece 13ft rod for floatfishing. And with that little lot we fished everywhere, river, lake or canal. And we would readily carry it all a mile or more – and back again – though primitive folding trolleys were beginning to make an appearance around then.

Anyway, come the day of the Hardy Cup match, which was a 200-plus pegger in early July, I was delighted to draw Stopham, and couldn't wait to see my peg, but when I got there I found I was in this really narrow bit only about eight yards wide. But I was determined to swingtip bread regardless, and I remember saying to myself, "I'm going to do it, I'm going to do it!" There was an overhanging tree opposite, and I threw my groundbait straight into the branches, so that it fell into the water below, then underarmed a pinch of flake under the tree. And it worked! By the end of the six-hour match I had a tench, a small carp and a handful of skimmers nestling in my keepnet, and they weighed something like 5lb 15oz – enough, anyway, to win.

There were many more youngsters on the match scene back then, and another 17-year-old, Dave Roberts, was second that day, with 19-year-old Nigel Venters third, each including a decent chub in their catches. Sadly for them, Dave and Nigel didn't enter the pools, a mistake they were careful not to repeat a few weeks later when they each went one place better in the Championship Challenge on the same venue. In the years that followed, Dave became a Dorking team mate and friend, and in 1992 he captained Banstead when they ended

Dorking's 18-year winning run in the Surrey division of the *Angling Times* League (or the Winter League, as it's commonly known).

Dave Roberts, aged 17. (Image courtesy of Angling Times*)*

The Saturday after the Hardy Cup I was back on the Arun for the 72-peg Pulborough & District Carnival Open, drew the Hardham Straight and, once more fishing bread, caught two skimmers on the tip then five more on a crow quill Avon for about 7lb to win again. And then the next day I won a typically low-weight club match on the Mole – though, as was usual then, I would have to wait for the club's AGM before I got my hands on my prize money, and only then in the form of a postal order. So I had three wins on the bounce – one an association match, one an open and one a club match – and I'd never even framed before.

Later that same season Dorking held two opens on the Mole and I was lucky enough to win both of those as well, with low double-figure catches of roach and dace on floatfished caster. The vital thing I'd learnt with John was that on such a small river you had to nurse your swim, feeding really lightly and resting it after every few fish, to keep the peg alive as long as possible. It also helps to draw an out-and-out flyer, and in both of those matches I drew spot-on. In the second one, for instance, I more than doubled the weight of second-placed Pat Richardson – a legend on the southern circuit – and that is something I can only put down to the draw.

Looking back, I had an unbelievable run at the draw bag that season. They were big matches in those days, and you simply could not compete from most pegs. You were beaten before you'd started. The luck of the draw played a huge part, and I realise now just how fortunate I was to have such a string of flyers. If you draw well repeatedly, it breeds confidence, but also you learn so much more, because you are catching fish. Mostly you learn from your mistakes, especially when it comes to feeding the swim, because you can gauge how the fish react to what you do. The more you draw well, the better you become, and I've had more than my fair share of good draws over the years, I'll admit. (It's not true, by the way, that I once picked out the only white maggot from a gallon of bronze when blindfolded. Kenny made that one up. It is true, though, that when we raffled a Normark rod in the shop, I bought one 10p ticket and won.) But if you analyse any top match angler's career, including mine, how many matches of 100-plus pegs have they won? Very few. And in the old days, on the big matches, if you were unlucky, and never drew well, you never got the chance to learn, so you never got any better. When you are on a bad peg catching little or nothing there isn't much you can learn. That's why, if we weren't doing any good, John and I wouldn't just sit there going through the motions; we'd go and find someone who was catching, and watch them. In my first season in match fishing, especially, I may have done no good, but I learnt a hell of a lot just by watching, and put what I had learnt to good use the following season.

Equally, in my breakthrough season I recall Kenny Collings and John McCarthy – who at the time I knew only by reputation, really, as established CALPAC stars – both watching me in matches, no doubt wondering who this upstart was. They would both have been 23 at the time. In subsequent years I fished alongside them with Dorking and CALPAC and they became my lasting friends. Kenny and I were in business together for many years, and he and Johnny Mac both came to my daughter Victoria's wedding in 2008.

At a Dorking club prize-giving evening with Syd Fuller, whose family have had a tackle shop in the town since 1892.

Other CALPAC 'big hitters' back in 1969/70 were Peter Burton, Dickie Vetterlein and Ray Mumford – but especially Ray Mumford. Kenny fished with Ray, Chris Love and Albert Batting under the Tonkers banner – a 'tonker' being a big dace – until 1971, when Kenny joined forces with Johnny Mac, Dickie, Mick Thill, Billy Hughes and Andy Partridge to form the modestly named The Team. The Team met every Monday evening in The Sun in Splendour pub in London's trendy Portobello Road, and were the first southern outfit to really make midland and northern match anglers sit up and take notice when they won the Trent Championship in their first year.

Like that other giant of the southern scene, Jim Randell, Ray had already blazed an individual trail beyond the southern circuit, but whereas Jim was always easy-going and approachable, Ray was totally focused and dedicated. He was never a team man, despite captaining CALPAC at the time, and there was always something that stopped you from getting close. He was in his own world, I suppose, and was just different from everyone else, like the way he always wore a jacket and tie when he fished. He would talk to you, but you could never sit down and really chat about fishing with him. Well, I couldn't, anyway. Like Kim Milsom much later, I found him a difficult guy

Mick Thill, who 'Women's Angle' in Angling Times *in 1972 described as a trendy body-builder and former South of France DJ "now working in a London disco". Readers voted him southern match fishing's "biggest heart throb" ahead of Ray Mumford – "that suave lady-killer and playboy of the Thames valley" – and John McCarthy, "who dazzles the girls as he drives around London in his sports car". (Image courtesy of* Angling Times*)*

to get to know. But like Kim he was a fantastic angler, definitely the best in the South at the time, and he led the way with pole fishing. It was mainly because of Ray – his great success and high profile – that so many young blokes in the South started match fishing. I would go so far as to say that he essentially created the southern circuit as it is today, because sadly we've all grown old together, with fewer and fewer youngsters on the scene – but that's another story.

Anyway, I travelled to matches with John Benham for several years, and that was crucial to my development, because going with someone of equal or greater knowledge and experience is the best way to learn. You learn on the way to the match and then again on the way home. It can't help but make you a better angler, as long as you take it all in. At some point – it could be next week, it could be next year – what you learn could well come in handy, so remembering things is key. It helps to start when you are young, though, like I did, because the older you are when you take up anything new the harder it is to learn.

I've always been naturally highly competitive – I don't think that's something you can teach anyone – but what John did teach me was the need to prepare thoroughly for a match, something he had learnt in turn from the example set by the likes of Ray and Kenny. Like them, we knew we couldn't expect to win unless we made at least the same effort as everyone else. All our tackle and bait had to be spot on. We didn't see it as a chore – quite the opposite, in fact. We wanted to do it.

Like almost every serious match angler in those days we bred our own gozzers, thinking they caught more fish. Nowadays we know different, but back then gozzers were considered essential. John would do the actual breeding, with pigs' hearts, adding annatto paste to dye the maggots yellow, and I'd sit there picking the maggots out of the mess one by one on the way to the match in his car. You can imagine the smell, but in our minds they gave us a better chance. Anything we felt would give us an edge, we did. So, we'd drive all the way to East Sheen just to get caster maggots from George McCarthy's shop, because they were bigger and fatter – 'elephants', we called them – than elsewhere. Or we'd go all the way over to Dells in Battersea just to buy certain float-making materials that we couldn't get anywhere else.

When it came to floats, John and I were heavily influenced by Ray Mumford, whose own home-made floats – not to mention float and seat boxes – were beautifully crafted and famously immaculate. We made everything from peacock wagglers to balsa and crow quill Avons and porcupine quill 'sticks' – we cut the porcupine quills down flat at their fattest point, then put tiny eyes in the side near the top – and painted and varnished them all to the highest possible standard we could. 'Animals', we called them. For the shallow Mole we made special floats, carrying

Ray Mumford (left) shows one of his home-made floats to his brother Vernon. (Image courtesy of Angling Times)

some 2½BB, out of 1½-inch balsa bodies and 1½-inch crow quill tips, and fished them top and bottom in the slower glides, and bottom end only in the faster, really shallow bits, for a clean, splash-free strike.

We also made our own swingtips, the lightest ones we could, in various lengths, out of cane. For swingtipping we soaked our reel spools overnight in washing-up liquid to ensure the line sank quickly, but were always careful to replace the line after only a couple of outings before the washing-up liquid could rot it. Everything had to be right. John was a perfectionist in everything he did, and I was the same. At work as a toolmaker it was all about tolerances – if something wasn't right I wasn't happy, and it has always been the same with my fishing, be it my tackle or tactics. A fair few top match anglers have been from an engineering background – Bob Nudd, for one – while Ray Mumford was in the printing game and John Benham was originally an electrician. I think that inner, almost compulsive need for things to be just so is something we all had in common.

Even the close season couldn't stop John and I practising. We'd go to Pippingford Park in Ashdown Forest where there's a chain of stream-fed lakes with a little waterfall and a bit of stream between each lake. The lakes were full of chub – you could see them cruising around, the water was that clear – and we'd catch them on the waggler, then trot the bits of stream, catching little brownies and chub. We weren't supposed to be there, but for some reason whoever ran it turned a blind eye.

I'm jumping ahead a bit here, but I remember one Saturday in October 1973 we drove all the way to Norwich – a mere five-hour journey in those days, before the M25 or M11 were even built – just to fish a four-hour afternoon open on the Wensum there. That's how keen we were. But it was worth it in that John won the match. What I mainly recall about that day, however – and I relate this as a strictly unbiased Chelsea supporter – is that Norwich were playing Spurs at home, and some drunken Spurs hooligans in make-up came rampaging along on their way to the match, threw several anglers' tackle in, and then pushed a 50-year-old guy called Bert Good into the river eight feet below 'for a laugh'. Thank God they didn't pick on me, because I can't even swim. Bert went under several times before he could be hauled out with the help of a couple of landing net handles. An ambulance took him to hospital, and thankfully he was okay.

Going back to when I first knew John, there was a club match one summer on the Mole that we both wanted to fish, but John's car had broken down. No one was able to take us, so John said, "Right, we'll walk". Now this was some walk, the best part of 10 miles. John borrowed his mum's shopping trolley, and off we set, into the fog, at 4am. When we got to where the road zig-zags its way down Box Hill we looked at it and thought, we can't do that, we'll go straight down, so we did – straight through all the trees where there'd been a recent hill fire, slipping and sliding our way through filthy wet ashes and soot. When we got to the river, we simply waded across, because the nearest bridge was half a mile or more away, and put up with wet feet for the rest of the day. But it was all worth it, as John won the match. Moreover we were able to cadge a lift home – well, most of the way home, anyway.

Some of the actual matches in those days were marathons of another kind, for it was nothing to fish a six-, seven- or even eight-hour match. The Hardy Cup was a mere six hours, but the same summer I won that match John and I fished an eight-hour Saturday open on the estate lake at Petworth Park, a fabulous place near Pulborough with a great big stately home and lawns sweeping down to the lake, all landscaped by Capability Brown – the sort of place you really look forward to going to. This was a 180-pegger, and I managed 20lb of small roach on the waggler – hard enough work with a hollow glass rod over five hours, never mind eight – for fourth place, just ahead of Kenny and the up-and-coming Paul Udell, and not far behind the winner Pat Richardson, with Stephen Guy second and Dickie

Pat Richardson was best known for his mastery of the Medway, but in July 1969 he beat around 180 others, including myself, with this winning 20lb-plus bag of roach at Petworth Park. (Image courtesy of Angling Times*)*

Vetterlein third. John missed out that day, but made up for it by coming second in the big match there the following month, with a couple of tench as I recall. In subsequent seasons John and I both enjoyed further success in Petworth Park opens – in August 1972 we were second and third respectively behind Johnny Mac in the 200-peg Bank Holiday open there – but they stopped running those matches after a few years, which was a real pity, as they were great days out.

A few weeks after my 1969 Petworth success – and no doubt it was John's idea – we

Ade Scutt was known for his prowess at catching bleak. (Image courtesy of Angler's Mail)

entered a match actually advertised as a 10-hour 'mini-fish marathon' on the Lea at Waltham Abbey, and run by Ade Scutt. Ade was a bit of a character, larger than life, and like Ray Mumford was always campaigning for southern match anglers to get the recognition he felt they deserved, especially when it came to bleaking. He was a debt collector, so you didn't mess with him, but he was okay, he was alright. Anyway, he organised this match in protest against his club, Leaside AS, deciding to ban bleak in their opens. When we got to the draw, at a pub called The Old English Gentleman in Cheshunt, sanity prevailed and, following a show of hands, the match was reduced to 'only' seven hours. Ade duly won it with just under 4lb, then I was second and John third. I seem to recall John and I both won silverware that day. (If so, the cup'll be in my loft somewhere, along with all my other trophies.)

Not all of our ventures afield were a success that year. In the autumn John, Dave Roberts, Nigel Venters and I all fished for the losing 12-man CALPAC team in the annual challenge against the LAA – the London Anglers Association – on the LAA's stretch of the Great Ouse at Tempsford, near Roxton in Bedfordshire.

This was a roving match, as many matches were in the South in those days. You'd draw a number, then you'd be called 'away' in order, "Number one!" first and so on, and off you went to choose a swim. (If the organiser was fishing, then whoever was unlucky enough to draw the highest number had the job of doing the calling out.) An hour into the match if you wanted to you could move to another spot. You carried any fish you had caught with you, in water, in a waterproofed canvas

CENTRAL ASSOCIATION OF LONDON & PROVINCIAL ANGLING CLUBS.

COMPETITION SECRETARY-
R. Bridger,
72 Holmesdale Road,
Selhurst.   S.E.25.
Tel 653 - 7660.

30 July '69.

Dear MR ROBERTS

You are invited to fish in a representative match -
C.A.L.P.A.C. Vs L.A.A. - which will take place on Saturday 20th Sept '69
on the Bedford Ouse at Roxton. Fishing from 10 a.m. to 4 p.m. followed by a
Buffet and "get together" at the Anchor Hotel, Great Barford. The
Associations will each be represented by two teams - one a Matchmans Team
and an Officers and Committee Team.

It is proposed to run a Coach for this match leaving West
Croydon Station at 6.45 a.m. and making a pick-up at London Bridge Station
at 7.15 a.m. This will cost approx 15/- each for the return journey.

Will you please complete the form below and return to me as
soon as possible,

Yours sincerely

Competition Secretary.

*Every competitor chosen for the CALPAC team in the annual match against
the LAA received an official invite. Needless to say, Dave Roberts kept his.
(Dave Roberts)*

bucket that fastened at the top to stop the fish jumping out. And at the
end, everyone with anything to weigh in carried their fish – along with
all their gear – back to a single set of scales at the point where the draw
had taken place.

Inevitably, stroke-pulling was rife in roving matches. In theory you
weren't supposed to overtake anyone ahead of you. In practice on big
matches there would be chaos, with people taking no notice of their
number and rushing off to grab a spot. People would also 'save' swims
for their mates. I can remember on many occasions walking ridiculous
distances, a mile or more, sometimes by choice, but sometimes just to
find a vacant swim.

John Benham and I fished next to each other that day on the Ouse,
but it didn't do us any good – the LAA team hammered us 23lb 8oz to
4lb 3¼oz, because they knew the venue and we didn't. Being an LAA
affair, it was fished to standard Thames size limits, which were 12 inches
for bream and chub, 10 for tench, nine for perch, eight for roach and
rudd, seven for dace and five for gudgeon. The bleak were like piranhas,
but they didn't count, and we tried everything to get through them, even
throwing in the bread from our sandwiches in the hope they'd follow
it away downstream. When you did get through the bleak you caught
undersized roach and skimmers. I must have had 20lb of fish I couldn't
weigh in that day. Maurice Woodyard did best for us, catching a few
'goer' roach on blackfly caster, which the small fish couldn't crush. The

LAA guy who won it – Brian Gent – had five small tench and a roach on stewed wheat, of all things, for about 8lb. Altogether the LAA team weighed in 40 sizeable fish – 29 roach, eight tench, two chub and a dace – to CALPAC's 12 roach and a perch. Still, we had a slap-up buffet after the match before the long coach journey home.

Another guy who fished for CALPAC that day was Gary Cowlam, and I remember going over to Gary's place in Croydon just to watch him use a hook-tying machine he'd acquired. I'd always tied my hooks by hand, but in due course I bought a Delco Sidewinder, the forerunner of the Drennan hook tyer, and practised with it until I could tie hooks on the bank in a flash, much faster and more efficiently than I could tie them by hand, especially with cold fingers. That way, if I felt I needed to change my hook, I wouldn't hesitate. Indeed, my whole mentality when fishing since those early days has always been that if I think I should change something – my shotting, my float, anything – I'll do it straight away. It's no good going home after the match thinking, "I should have done this, I should have done that". If I think trying something different might work better, I'll listen to that voice in my head saying "Do it – do it now!" But on a river, especially, you must never, ever stop feeding while you make the change. That's vital, to keep the rhythm going.

Going back to John Benham and the importance of preparing properly for a match, it wasn't just about tackle and bait. It was about planning too, about knowing the venue, and how to approach different pegs, better than anyone else, so you knew what to do whatever number you drew. It was never a case of just turning up on the day and hoping for the best.

So, with roving matches in mind, in the close season John and I would walk the banks of the Mole and the Thames and look at loads of different swims, so that we'd have an idea which would be good ones to pick when the river was low and which would be better when the river was up. We both learnt from the example of Ray Mumford, too. When it came to big roving matches on the Thames, Ray would practise on the venue in the week, and come up with first- and second-choice swims. Often the latter was a swim no one else would think of picking, so that he would be confident of it being free even if he was one of the last 'away'. We often saw Ray practising on the tidal Thames at Ham, for instance – you'd know he was there, because you'd see his black Jaguar in the car park – and then went and watched him. (Maureen Anderson, his girlfriend, often accompanied him, and she was no mean match angler herself.) The way Ray fished was as meticulous as his tackle, and impressed us deeply.

I remember one match at Ham, a Duke of Gloucester open in January 1970, when the river was up and coloured and there were

180 entrants. Downstream of the car park was the place to be, as it turned out, but I'm not sure the draw mattered that much the way the river was that day. I was third behind Tony Karby and Ray Mumford with two or three pounds of gudgeon. I found a little slack in the trees just above River Lane, a hole in the sloping rocky bank where some rocks had gone, and legered maggots – not with a quivertip, but with a method that John and I also used on the Mole, which was to use a float rod, so that you could reach out and fish directly under

Tony Karby, who later became a successful pike angler, as I recall. (Image courtesy of Angler's Mail*)*

the rod tip. The gudgeon bites were little dink-dinks, but every now and then you'd get a snatchy, bigger bite that you couldn't hit, the sure sign of a quality roach or dace spitting the bait out. If you then went straight back in with a little redworm, the same roach or dace would take the worm and hang on to it. Tony Karby had a couple of roach that day at Ham, to go with his gudgeon, and they made all the difference. (The same method worked on the Mole with tiny bits of bread on the hook in conjunction with marble-sized bits of groundbait. John was brilliant at this, and could catch up to 8lb of gudgeon on the method – I couldn't.)

Well, I could go on, but that's how it all started for me really, more than 40 years ago now. Looking back, I can't help wondering whether, had I not done any good that second season, I would have had the drive to carry on with match fishing – or the money, for that matter, because I wasn't earning much as an apprentice, and in 1970 when I turned 18 I left home and moved into a flat in Epsom with Steve Sanders and another guy, so then I had rent to pay. But I'd won enough to pay for me to carry on – I won nearly £100 from the two Mole opens alone, which was a lot of money in those days – and that's all you can ask for, in the end, in match fishing, that you win enough to cover your costs. Anything else is a bonus.

CHAPTER TWO
Back in the Day

Summer or winter, carp or silvers, we take double-figure catches for granted on today's commercial still-water fisheries, but in the days when most of my match fishing was done on rivers you were doing well if you weighed in double figures three or four times in a whole nine-month season. People talk fondly of 'the good old days' of river fishing as a time of bulging keepnets, but the reality was that the fishing was terrible most of the time. In summer on rivers like the Medway you typically caught all your fish – little roach, mostly – in the first hour, then that was your swim empty and you were left fishing for eels. In winter in bad conditions – frost or flood or both – things were even worse, and blanks were commonplace. I can't remember the year, but one time in the 1970s on the Loddon at Sindlesham Mill we got there and found it was flooded, it was a horrible day too, and I thought, that's it, I'll put the brolly up and fish the lobbie – not just the tail, but a whole big worm, something that was almost unheard of then – and hope for a bream or chub. Towards the end of the match I hadn't had a bite and I was bored out of my brains, so I went for a stroll – stupidly leaving my rod to fish for itself. I met up with the organiser, Dave Sweet, who blew the whistle for the end of the match and walked back with me to start weighing in. As we passed my peg I said, "Hang on a sec, Dave, you've got to see what bait I've got on here," picked my rod up to wind my rig in – wondering vaguely why the line had gone slack – and found a great big bream hanging on. I couldn't believe it, it would have got me in the frame, maybe even won me the match. That was definitely a day for sticking it out, not going walkabout.

In the early 1970s, especially, I think it was widely accepted that the standard of match fishing was lower in the South than it was in the Midlands and North, but also there simply wasn't an abundance of fish in many of the rivers in my area. On the Mole, low single-figure catches won many a match even in summer until chub took a hold in the late 1970s – after, rumour had it, someone slipped some chub they'd caught on the Thames into the river, to provide new breeding stock. There were pegs named after anglers who had caught double figures from them – like 'Yonkie's peg', after a guy in the Dorking club who once had 13lb of dace out of it. There were very few chub, and only small ones at that. Going back to my club match days, one July on one of the slower stretches, after catching nothing for a couple of hours I thought, this is no good, I'm going to have something to eat, so I put my rod in the rest with the float just over the bed of lilies in front of me and started munching my sandwiches. All of a sudden the float was gone, I grabbed the rod and whatever had hooked itself shot all over the river. When I got it in it was a mirror carp and it weighed 1lb 2oz. There was a trophy for the biggest fish caught each season in a match on the Mole, and that carp was it right up until the last weekend, when someone had a 1½lb chub. I was gutted!

Even in opens, low single-figure catches were often enough to win on the Mole. Sometimes you were best off targeting the minnows. In August 1974 I fished an open on the river and when I got to my peg I saw that it was solid with minnows all the way across. So I started feeding little bits

Andy Partridge took the prized Marlow Rose Bowl on the lower Thames in October 1972 with this fabulous bag of skimmers and clonking great roach on the float, but take it from me, such catches were very rare indeed in river matches 'back in the day'. (Image courtesy of Angling Times*)*

of groundbait close in, to gather them all under my rod tip, and fished for them there for the best part of four hours, until I couldn't catch any more. Then I went across and was able to snare a pound or so of dace on caster. I ended up with 5lb-something, and that was top weight out of 60-plus anglers.

Jumping forward a decade, the Mole was a very different river, one dominated by big chub. In September 1986 in the Tuborg Cup Dorking had a home draw against the holders Essex and we decided to take them to the North Bank stretch of the river. They were a strong pole team, with the likes of Bob Nudd in their ranks, and being the away side had the choice of pegs, odds or evens, so we came up with a cunning plan and, as best we could, alternated the horrible-looking, fast, shallow swims – where we knew the chub liked to be – with the more attractive-looking but actually less productive glides, thinking Essex would be sure to pick the latter. Trouble was, a few days before the match Thames Water went down there to electrofish the stretch to remove some of the pike, and that evening the Dorking club chairman rang me and said, "You're not going to believe what's happened, Steve." Apparently, as the electrofishers worked their way upstream, the disturbance they made in the shallow water drove all the fish in the river ahead of them until the whole lot, big chub and all, ended up turning over in a cattle drink at the top of the stretch. I thought, well now, bang goes our cunning plan. On the day, Essex chose the slower pegs as we thought they would, and I remember getting to my peg, which was dead shallow, and worrying if there were even going to be any fish in it. But as it turned out all the fish were back in their usual swims, and our plan worked perfectly – and that taught me a lot about fish behaviour. I then understood why, back in the old days of roving matches when all the fish were taken to one central set of scales and put back in one spot, that spot was never any better than anywhere else the next time around. The fish had all gone home!

Going back to the early 1970s again, one vivid memory of the same stretch of the Mole wasn't a match, but a day one winter when Steve Sanders and I first shared the flat in Epsom and Steve was just getting back into fishing after packing it in for a few years. Neither of us could drive at the time, but we fancied a day's fishing by the sewage outlet – a noted spot – and that meant going by train and bus. We eventually got there and Steve promptly fell straight in, headfirst. It was a freezing cold day, but it was sunny and the roach were biting so we carried on and he dried out a bit – but he didn't half pong on the bus and train home.

Sometimes in those days when Steve and I wanted to go fishing, Steve's girlfriend Carole, now his wife, dropped us off and picked us up again in her Hillman Imp. That was a tight enough fit, with all our gear, but when we went with John Moriarty, who worked with Steve at a bakers in Twickenham and couldn't drive either – well, he could, but he'd lost his licence – then John would get his wife to take the three of us and all our gear, and *she* had a Mini. One day she came to pick us up again, from the Thames at Walton, but we weren't ready, we were still fishing, and she went mad. The next time she took us she pointedly turned up with John, his gear, their Labrador, their baby boy – and the biggest white rabbit you've ever seen. By the time Steve and I had squeezed inside with all our gear, with this rabbit jumping about our ears, the car was almost scraping the ground. It must have been about this time that Steve and I decided enough was enough and both learnt to drive.

Rabbits are one thing, but in our ground-floor flat it was rats we had to worry about. They raided the kitchen at night and sometimes even got into the bedroom, where we kept an old chair leg handy just in case. The place was a bit of a tip, to be honest. The telly was always on the blink, and we once watched a whole England football game through a crack in the door because we had jammed a screwdriver into the back of the set to get it to work and were afraid that it was about to blow up.

Another occasion when we lost our bottle was Christmas Day 1970 – a rare white Christmas – when we thought we'd take the opportunity to poach a private stretch of the Wey at Send. There was no one around when we started, but before long the banks were swarming with people out for a walk and we chickened out, packed up as fast as we could and legged it.

In our first two years in the flat we paid our rent direct to the landlord, a guy named Siegfried, or 'Siggy' as we called him, until one day, sadly, he was killed when he crashed his Porsche on a visit home to Germany, and an agent started collecting the rent instead. But we never got a rent book, and after a while we became suspicious, so we stopped paying, while putting the money aside just in case. No one ever came round for it, and after a few months of this we thought, this ain't right, so we did a runner. First, though, there was the matter of the electricity bill, which was in my name. Quite a few local racing stable lads lived in the block and our pre-pay meter was for ever being broken into for the coins. When I went to settle up, the electricity board said, "It's £100, Mr Gardener." I told them I only had five pounds, and they said, "We'll take that then." I can't imagine getting away with that now.

For a brief while I moved back in with my dad, then my boss, Jan Bohacek, very generously let me have the flat above the office at work rent-free for the next couple of years. Around that time Jan also branched out into making industrial cleaning equipment, under the name Jani-

Jack, and took Steve on as a van driver, after Steve had left the bakers and had a brief spell as a milkman. Steve and I then worked alongside each other in Lower Kingswood until in 1988 I left to join Kenny Collings in his tackle shop in Sutton – KC Angling, formerly Roberts Brothers. Steve stayed on, eventually becoming Jan's UK sales manager, then in the mid-1990s when Kenny wanted a change Steve bought Kenny out and joined me in the shop. But that was all in the future…

Steve Sanders (third from left) and myself (far right) back in the early 1970s at the wedding of our good friend and sometime Dorking team mate Terry 'Bennie' Wright and his wife Susan. (Steve and Carole Sanders)

Fishing wasn't the only thing Steve and I got up to in our years in Epsom, and we did as all young men do and had a good time on Friday and Saturday nights. It was shortly after moving to Epsom that I started going out with Jeanette, my wife. I'd known her by sight from when I still lived in Tadworth and my friends and I all used to get the bus into Epsom on a Friday or Saturday night to hang out in the pubs before going on to a disco somewhere, like the old Ebbisham Hall. (David Bowie played there once, I remember, but I was always more into Motown.) By the time we were going out together Jeanette had moved with her mum and dad in the opposite direction, from Epsom to Tadworth. It all started when I offered to see her safely home on the bus one night, walked her to her front door and asked for her phone number. We didn't have anything to write it on, so I pulled a leaf off a plant and scribbled it on that – I can remember it now, 58317 – then I walked the three miles back to Epsom, as I'd missed the last bus. I was 18, she was 16, and that was that. Later, thanks to Jan's generosity, we were able to save up the deposit on a house in Redhill – and on 17th July in the long hot summer of 1976 Jeanette and I got married at St Mary's Church in Burgh Heath.

Jeanette's never minded me going fishing, which is just as well because I did more and more of it as the years went on, fishing matches most Saturdays and Sundays during the river season. I did promise her that when we were married I would 'only' go once a week, but the way it panned out, I was making a bit of a name for myself and doing a few articles for *Angling Times*, and that was the excuse, really, to keep going both days at the weekend. I've taken Jeanette for granted a bit at times over the years, I must admit. In August 1979, a month or so before our first child, James, was born, she accompanied me to an open at Rowfant lakes near Copthorne – where a young Geoff Vallance was so often in the frame – got up to adjust her chair halfway through and fell straight in. I pulled her out and she went and sat in the car for the rest of the match. And when our daughter, Victoria, was born, in February 1982, Jeanette went into labour the night before the southern semi-final of the Winter League on the Thames at Oxford. Dorking reserve Mark Richardson was all set to stand in for me, but after she finally gave birth in the hospital at four in the morning, Jeanette said, "There's nothing you can do here, you might as well go fishing." So I did – and fished with a freezing northeasterly in my face all day for very little reward.

We're a selfish bunch, match anglers, it's not easy being a 'fishing widow', and I take my hat off to Jeanette for putting up with me all this time, especially in those early years when neither she nor the kids saw very much of me. At JA & MF Engineering I worked from eight to seven Monday to Thursday, and all I used to think about all week was where I'd be fishing at the weekend. Then on Friday afternoons, when we knocked off early, I'd be straight down the tackle shop in Sutton to chat with my mates for hours about where we were going fishing on the Saturday and Sunday. The shop was in the opposite direction to Redhill, so it would be the middle of the evening by the time I eventually got home.

The circuit was very different back then, we fished matches all over the place, especially in summer, and they were nearly all big, one-off events where the luck of the draw determined your fate before you'd even wet a line – if you won four or five matches a season you were doing well, believe me. Take the day in July 1974 when John Benham and I made the 200-mile round trip to fish a 120-peg open on the Lark at Prickwillow near Ely, hoping for a nice fair roach match. The roach proved absent, and the winner, fellow toolmaker Geoff Cushing from Cheshunt, had 30lb of bream on the waggler, more than double everyone else's weight put together, while John snared two bream in two casts for 4lb-odd and second place. A lot of competitors that day wisely stopped fishing and went to watch Geoff in action.

Jeanette and I with (we think) the trophy awarded to the overall individual winner in the 1980 National Benzole Kent Summer League. (Image © Derek Davis)

Fellow competitors watch winner Geoff Cushing on the Lark at Prickwillow in July 1974. When you aren't catching yourself, watching someone who is helps you learn how fish react to the way a swim is tackled and fed. (Image courtesy of Angler's Mail)

Be it a river down in Sussex one day or a lake over in Kent the next, you saw the same old faces everywhere you went, week in, week out, including a few women who more than held their own on the open circuit. I've mentioned Maureen Anderson, but a couple of other women who did consistently well in my area were Sylvia Kemp, wife of top London matchman Eddie, and Jenny Harrison from the Canterbury area in Kent. One baking hot day when Kenny drew next to Jenny on the Medway at Tonbridge, she stripped off to her underwear and plunged into the river at the end of the match, so Kenny – always a keen swimmer – immediately followed suit.

In 1973 Sylvia got through to the Woodbine Challenge Final – *the* big individual competition in those days – in the regional qualifier on Waller's Haven on the Pevensey marshes, the last time they used 'the Wallers' for that match following howls of protests about how peggy it was. But it was even peggier in the annual Southeastern Open held by the Eastbourne club, the Compleat Angler FC. This was always a several hundred pegger, and every year the organisers placed a steward at either end. Not only that, but the stewards knew their pegs the night before. In 1969 one of these stewards was Lew Nightingale, later of the mighty Isfield team, and he won the match – and the same thing happened when I fished the match in 1972 and one of the end-peg stewards walked it with a bag of bream. Afterwards there was a right rumpus as Ray Mumford, Kenny and a few others confronted the organisers.

Jenny Harrison was a regular competitor on the Kent circuit in the 1970s, travelling to matches with her husband John. (Image courtesy of Angling Times)

Backed up by George McCarthy (left) and Kenny Collings (centre), Ray Mumford tells Compleat Angler FC match secretary Joe Eastes a few home truths following the Southeastern Open on Waller's Haven in August 1972. In those days I wouldn't have said boo to a goose. (Image courtesy of Angling Times*)*

Sylvia Kemp needed only 3lb 8½oz of skimmers to finish seventh out of 92 in the regional Woodbine Challenge qualifier on the Wallers in September 1973. (Image courtesy of Angler's Mail*)*

Only eight anglers broke 5lb that day. In another match on the Wallers, an open in October 1973 at Middle Bridge, the winner had one bootlace eel, someone else had a 2oz skimmer, and that was it, while my Dorking team mate Peter Knight had one bite, missed it and fell in. One stretch of the Wallers was known by some as the Dead Mile, which says it all really. The Wallers did fish better in later years, especially at the Boreham Street end. On hot days the skimmers would often be right up in the water, but when they got heads down and grubbed around on the bottom their mouths were stained a bright orange-brown – "chocolate lips" we called them. But the Wallers was always notoriously patchy, with some horrendous walks and stile after stile to get all your gear over. And I did win there once, a Kent summer

From left to right, fellow 1973 Woodbine qualifiers Chris Love – who went on to win in Denmark – Dave Harris, Alan Harrington, Chad Palmer, Dickie Carr, Terry Harrison, Roger Young, Barry Wilson and Derek Stripp congratulate Sylvia Kemp on the banks of the Wallers. (Image courtesy of Angler's Mail*)*

league match at Boreham Street in 1982. (Confusingly, rounds of the Kent, Sussex and Surrey summer and winter leagues were often held on venues in neighbouring counties.) I could see rods bending and a few slabs being caught several pegs away – my old friend and Dorking team mate Nick Aplin was getting a bit of the action – so I filled my swim in and went to have a look. When I came back I started catching some myself, and everyone said I'd walked them back to my peg. Sadly my catch wasn't enough to stop Johnny Mac's DELCAC side beating Dorking to the league title, the first time any team had done that. Another day I got all the way to Iron Bridge for a match and realised I'd left my keepnet at home. Kenny said, "I know what, I'll cut mine in half." Neither of us had a bite that day so he sacrificed a perfectly good keepnet for nothing. No, the Wallers was never my favourite venue.

Much more to my liking was a venue I've touched on already, the tidal Thames, from Teddington Lock down past Ham car park, River Lane and Richmond Bridge to Richmond Lock (which is actually a half-lock). I loved that place – as did Kenny. It was always an exciting venue, because you knew, nine times out of 10 – in summer and autumn, at any rate – that you were going to catch wherever you fished, if you did it right, and it regularly attracted match entries of 100 or more in the early 1970s.

Kenny Collings on the tidal Thames at Richmond, one of our favourite venues and one where Kenny and I both did well in matches right through the 1970s and 1980s. (Image courtesy of Angler's Mail)

In bad conditions in winter in those days a few pounds of bleak sometimes won matches on 'the Tidal' for the likes of Chris Love and Ray Mumford, but that wasn't my game. The venue was renowned primarily for its 'goer' roach and, above all, its herring-sized dace. In good conditions in autumn and winter you could catch them on the waggler or, more usually, the stick, but in summer things weren't so straightforward. The old school, LAA way of fishing the Tidal then, which Ray Mumford favoured and which dated from the days when throwing-sticks and catapults weren't allowed anywhere, was to lay on close in with a crow quill – a 'Jim Crow' – while lightly feeding hemp and caster, by hand or with a bait-dropper, and waiting for the roach and dace to come to you. That was the trouble, though, you had to wait, sometimes for two hours or more, because they lived out in the main flow. But so did the bleak – swarms of them – and if you fished a light float further out you never got through them to the roach and dace below. One answer, used by the likes of the 'the Dangerous Brothers' – the Vincent twins, Mick and Dave – was to fish crude block-end feeder and bucket-of-maggot tactics, with a single maggot on a meat hook and a two-inch hooklength – a bit like the method feeder, really – but I thought, there must be a better way, so I developed a very different approach to beat the bleak.

When the tide drops below Teddington Lock the river races out until the half-lock at Richmond is lowered to maintain a navigable depth. The river then backs up for a few minutes until it starts flowing over the half-lock at a steady rate. What I started doing, therefore, was to take a gallon of hemp and caster and then, when the half-lock was down, ladle it in every cast with a catapult, gradually feeding shorter and shorter to draw the fish in closer and closer. To get through the bleak I fished a big bulk-shotted Avon with a no.4 dropper. The roach usually pulled the float straight under, but many of the dace bites were no more than slight lifts, which were very hard to hit. What with them and the bleak, which were impossible to avoid altogether, the float would be in and out of the water like a yo-yo.

In July 1974 I fished a 40-peg open at Richmond and thought I had it won, having topped Ray Mumford's weight with 9lb 15oz on the float, only for Dave Vincent to weigh in this 11lb 11oz bag taken on the block-end. *(Image courtesy of Angler's Mail)*

I used the same heavy feeding style on the lower, non-tidal Thames above Teddington Lock as well, at places like Walton and Laleham, to get at least some bait past the hordes of bleak that infested the river there too – until the late 1970s, at least, when both the bleak and the gudgeon seemed to vanish into thin air. Ray Mumford didn't like it, and accused me of ruining the river for the traditionalists.

Tidal or non-tidal, below Staines the Thames has always been free fishing, which is why matches there were always rovers in the old days. With so many people pleasure fishing the river back then – and there were loads and loads, believe me, especially in the school holidays – pegged-down matches would have been impossible. We did have pegged-down matches in later years, when there were fewer pleasure anglers on the river, but you still had to start at the crack of dawn to be sure of making them work, and in winter you'd be drawing your peg in the dark.

I mentioned in the previous chapter the chaos of walk-offs, with people overtaking those ahead of them, but on the Tidal, where in most places you had to scramble down steep, slippery stone and concrete banks to stand all day on a precariously narrow ledge, this was inevitable, as people would keep stopping and then spend ages looking for a safe way down – holes and cracks in the bank that gave you some sort of foothold – while those behind them grew ever more impatient. "Come on, come on!" they'd say, "We haven't got all day! Are you going there or not? Right, we're going on ahead!" That happened a lot.

Sometimes on rovers there'd be pleasure anglers in noted swims who'd all too readily agree to pack up when certain people approached them. You could never prove it, but the suspicion was that it had been prearranged, or that money changed hands. Some of the best swims on the Tidal were the steps just above Richmond Bridge – but you could never be one hundred per cent sure which spot would be good on any given day. One match in January 1971, on a freezing cold foggy day, I had one bite, one fish, a bream on the waggler from the entrance to the marina about halfway between Ham car park and Teddington Lock I was so high up that I had to lift the fish almost out of the water to get it in the landing net – and that was enough to pip Jim Randell, who organised the match, for first place. Another time, I started off on the steps, after walking all the way down from Ham, had one foul-hooked dace, and thought, forget this, so I put the fish in my bucket of water and carried it, plus all my gear, all the way up to the marina entrance again, but did no good. I can't believe how far I walked, it's miles. Mind you, John Benham once carried 12lb of bream in his bucket along with all his gear all the way back from Teddington Lock to win one match.

In later years, much more sensibly, there would be more than one set of scales, and they would come to you. But we still had size limits until 1978 – right about the time the bleak and gudgeon disappeared, ironically enough – and some scales stewards were stricter about enforcing them than others. Like everyone else, I carried an aluminium measuring stick – a kind of ruler with a lip on one end which you put the nose of the fish up against – but if you caught a fish that was borderline you just put it in your net and hoped the scalesman wouldn't be too strict about measuring every single fish you had caught. One match, I was standing behind a friend we'll call 'X', at River Lane – he was one of the few anglers catching that day – and he caught a clearly undersized chub. (There have always been a few chub on the Tidal.) One of the scales stewards was watching too, and he said, "You aren't going to try to weigh that in, are you?" 'X' said, "No, no, but I'll just keep it in my net for now, I don't want to muck up the swim by putting it straight back." Later, 'X' was waiting to be weighed in, and he could see the same scales steward approaching from one direction and another scales steward approaching from the other. Luckily the second man, who knew nothing about this chub, got to 'X' first and didn't bother to check his fish. As a result 'X' won the match, with something like 3lb.

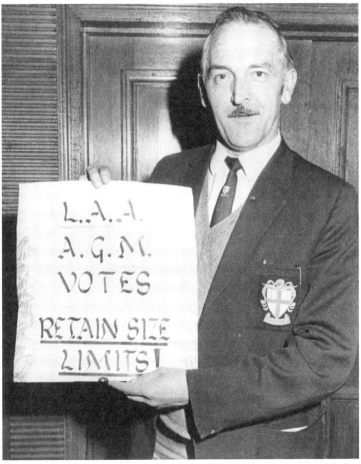

Every year until 1978 the traditionalists in the London Anglers Association would solemnly vote to keep size limits in place, despite most match anglers in the capital wanting them to be abolished. (Image courtesy of Angler's Mail*)*

Right through the 1980s – the days of the first carbon rods and poles – the Tidal gave us some fabulous catches of dace in winter on both the stick and then also the flick-tip pole, or whip, to hand. Simon Wheeler was the first in a five-hour open to break 40lb, in February 1989. (In August the same year, when Nick Howell had 55lb 13oz of bream on the feeder above the town, I told him that bream didn't count.) Conditions had to be spot on for big catches of dace, and you almost always had to draw in the town. Some days whole sections not in the town blanked. Even on the favoured pegs you could go an hour, two hours, without a bite – scaling down made no difference, and it was pointless using anything smaller than double maggot on an 18 – but you had to keep the maggots going in (whites were best, and you needed plenty of them!) then suddenly the dace would turn up or switch on. One match my Dorking team mate Alan Wood was drawn outside the White Cross pub below Richmond Bridge, got fed up waiting and went into the bar for a pint with his apron full of maggots still around his waist. God knows what the other customers must have thought.

The Tidal fished best on a big spring tide, which coloured the water up nicely, but sometimes we got caught out. One match in January 1983 on a big tide Steve Sanders had the first ever 30lb bag in a five-hour open but at the end when the tide came in again the river came right up over the footpath, several feet deep, and when we got back to the bottom of River Lane all the cars left there, Steve's included, were half under water, with everything floating around inside them. (Banstead's Jason Ahrens couldn't blame the tide, though, the time in 1989 he roared down to the slipway at the end of River Lane in his brand new hot hatch to spy on a Dorking practice session for our Scandinavian Seaways quarter-final tie, somehow forgot to stop and ploughed straight into the river.)

River specialist Alan Wood, a regular in the Dorking team in the late 1970s and early 1980s, with the sort of catch that was common when the tidal Thames was at its best. (Image courtesy of Angler's Mail)

Sometimes we had the opposite problem. Once a year, every winter, repairs carried out to Richmond Lock meant the river above it ran right out and down, just like below it, and then in places you had to follow the water out across the riverbed, and you'd end up halfway out to the middle, among all the old mattresses and other stuff dumped in the river over the years. Trouble was, if the water became too shallow where you were, your fish just vanished.

In January 1983 I drew sock-on outside the Three Pigeons pub above Richmond Bridge and had 29lb 3¼oz of dace on the stick float and maggot on a day when 25lb only took sixth place. (Image courtesy of Angling Times)

To digress for a moment, another tidal river where I ran out of water once was the Kentish Stour between Grove Ferry and Plucks Gutter, in a summer league match in 1976. I was drawn handily and started catching bream on the float, but because I was on the inside of a bend I had to stand on my box on top of my trolley in the mud, and as the river ran out it fell further and further away from me until my keepnet was almost out of the water. I thought, what the hell am I going to do now? Then I saw that there was a ditch full of water in the field behind me – so I moved my keepnet over to that. Every time I caught another bream I had to dig it out of the mud with my landing net then scramble up the bank with it and take it across the field. The bloke with the scales couldn't believe it when he came to weigh me in and I directed him over to the ditch. Luckily we could reach the water a bit further along to put the fish back in the river, about 30lb of them in all.

Going back to the Thames, the biggest matches of all 'back in the day' were on the non-tidal river. On the lower Thames – broadly speaking from Marlow down to Teddington – the Hammersmith Open every autumn between Kingston and Walton was always a big event with several hundred people fishing it in the old size limit days. Ray Mumford won it three times over the years – over the decades, I should say – but the best I ever did in the old days was in 1971 when it was an eight-hour match and I was fifth with 5lb-odd. The match kept going as a big roving event even after size limits were abolished, and in the early 1980s both Dave Vincent and Andy Love, my Dorking team captain at the time, got their hands on the coveted old trophy awarded for winning it by topping a string of double-figure weights of float-caught roach and dace.

Andy Love. When he won the Hammersmith Open in 1983 he said it was the fulfilment of a lifelong ambition. That's how much it meant to him. (Image courtesy of Angler's Mail)

It was the numbers of dace especially in the lower Thames that made it such a good river to fish in the early 1980s, for they made for fair matches, with plenty of bites for all and the best anglers winning. It could be a nightmare in summer, what with all the boats, but autumn was a different matter. A favourite stretch was the Barge Walk at Kingston, where I fished as a boy. The dace bites on the waggler took some hitting up in the water, and among the hardest guys to beat both on the lower river and on the Tidal were Andy Rogers, Clive Gingell

Andy Rogers, always a danger on his beloved lower Thames. (Image courtesy of Angler's Mail)

and 'the Andersons Octopus' Glen Fleet, so-called because of his all-action style.

So good was the dace fishing on the lower Thames in the early 1980s that in September 1982 Warlingham match organiser Dave Harper ran the first ever Lower Thames Championship, a 180-pegger won by 18-year-old Dorking team man John 'Bullet' Merritt, who headed loads of double-figure dace weights, and it was a similar story when Kenny's then business partner Charlie Taylor won the following year, and Andy Rogers the year after that. Then in 1985 the dace just seemed to vanish. I recall in July that year Omri Thomas of Normark, my sponsors at the time, bringing a group of smartly dressed Japanese businessmen down to the Barge Walk to see me fish an open, and I had something like 14lb of dace on the waggler to finish second. Come September you could hardly catch a dace, and Johnny Mac won the Lower Thames Championship with around 15lb of chub and perch from Laleham on the maggot feeder. The following year, in 1986, Graham Dack won the match with bream and only 5lb got you in the frame, and that was the last time the match was held until Dave Harper revived it in 2008.

Moving upstream, on the middle Thames in the mid-1980s, at places like Goring, Mapledurham, Reading and Wallingford, it was much the same story, with the roach seeming to vanish, leaving

Charlie Taylor, who won the Lower Thames Championship in 1983 with 19lb 10oz of dace on the waggler, a day when my own double-figure bag got me only fifth place. (Image courtesy of Angler's Mail)

you fishing the maggot feeder across for chub and perch, and making the matches ultra-peggy. The colour dropped out of the water and the flow seemed to increase unnaturally, I don't know why. Whatever was going on, you couldn't catch small fish, not during the day at any rate. I think they all shoaled up somewhere safe and only fed at night. And then in the late 1980s the dace fishing was good again on the lower Thames and the roach fishing good again on the middle reaches. In one round of the then Sundridge-sponsored Super League in the autumn of 1989 – Drennan took over sponsorship of the competition in 1991 – there were loads of double-figure weights of roach, headed by DELCAC's Paul Greest with a fantastic 53lb bag, all caught on the waggler. Often, though, for some reason I could never fathom, at places like Wallingford the roach would feed well in midweek matches like the Southern Top 20 but not at weekends.

On Saturday 2nd October 1982 I was lucky enough to win the £1,000 first prize in the rain-soaked Middlesex Angling Centre individual league final on the middle Thames at Goring with 22lb 2¼oz of chub on the maggot feeder, just beating Dorking team mate John Waples. Chris Love was third that day with nearly 20lb of roach and over 13lb was needed for 10th place, which shows just how well the river was fishing then. A year or two later I was lucky enough to win the same match again in similar fashion. (Images courtesy of Angler's Mail)

The same thing had happened in the late 1970s, when the Thames went clear and the dace and roach were scarce. Before that, in the long hot summers we had in the mid-1970s, the algae bloomed and the Thames held colour, despite standing almost still, and Chris Love and Mike Gilbert cleaned up on the waggler. Midweek matches then – which I was never able to get the time off work to fish – were known as 'Chris Love's pay-day opens'.

Moving even further upstream, the Thames Championship, on the upper river above Oxford, was always a 700-plus pegger, and the likes of Chris Love, Dave Roberts and Ray Mumford were all lucky enough to win this prestigious event in the old size-limit days with nets of mainly float-caught big chub. For the rest of us it was the usual maddening case of

Chris Love with a typical net of Thames fish. (Image courtesy of Angler's Mail)

having to put back most of what we'd caught, because you caught loads of chub that were just short of the 12-inch size limit.

After size limits went in 1978, some of the Birmingham and Nottingham stars started fishing the big matches on the upper Thames, and I remember Clive Smith's Cofton Hackett team, which included the likes of Ivan Marks, Max Winters, Ken Giles, Tony Scott and Stan Piecha – Dad's Army, Kenny called them – cleaning up in the

Thames Championship. They found Medley in Oxford particularly to their liking, as did I in later years, even though, being an almost 200-mile round trip, it was just a little bit too far for me to go quite as often as I would have liked. Medley has always been stuffed with bream, but the best matches – the fairest matches – when I used to fish it were in autumn and winter on days when the bream didn't show and

Chris James, later a Dorking team mate, catches a typically undersized chub in the 1971 Thames Championship won by Ray Mumford. (Image courtesy of Angling Times)

you needed a nice bag of stick- or waggler-caught roach, plus maybe a chub or two, on the maggot or even breadpunch to frame or win. The river is no more than six-foot deep, with a clean gravel bottom once you get past the marginal weed, making it ideal for floatfishing. 'Black Jack's' was always a favoured spot, on a bend where the flow pulled away from you and out across the middle, but there were many pegs and areas you could win from. Despite some long walks, loads of university rowing boats ploughing up and down and – on some days – trouble from roach-grabbing pike lurking in the marginal weed, it was always a lovely place to fish. Lovely on the right day, that is, with a gentle southwesterly off your back – not a freezing facing easterly like the time my daughter was born – plus a steady flow and just a tinge of colour. But how often do you get such days on any river?

Wednesday October 7th 1992 saw me catch 21lb 1oz of mainly roach on stick float and maggot to win the first round of that year's Keenets Southern Top 20 at Medley, pipping Tony West and Darren Davies who also had 20lb-plus roach bags. Happy days! (Image courtesy of **Angler's Mail***)*

Moving on, another favourite river back in the day was the Rother near Rye, from Blackwall Bridge down to Iden Lock. The first time I ever went there was in November 1976 when I drew next to Newbridge, fished a waggler across and had just under 20lb of roach – they were all shoaled up there, I'd drawn bang-on – and I thought, I like this river! I fished it a lot after that, though mainly in summer. It was like a Wallers with fish in it. Both venues are about "3AAA waggler wide", as Kenny put it, run down to the sea and, unlike similar waters in the Fens, are only accessible from road bridges. There aren't many of those on either venue, so there are some long walks on the Rother the same as on the Wallers, but the Rother was always a much fairer venue in my day. Okay, every now and then someone had a big haul of bream. Steve

Sanders held the river record for a while, with around 80lb of slabs, sharing a huge shoal spread over several pegs – until Rye's Tony Curd went and blitzed it one day when he had the fish all to his own and put a three-figure haul on the scales. But when the bream didn't show – and that was most of the time – you could frame from most areas, so wherever you drew you felt you had a chance. Kenny liked to feed little puffs of groundbait across to catch small skimmers and roach up in the water, whereas I liked to feed casters across for chub and eels. Either way, 4–6lb was a good weight on most days – enough to win you money, anyway, if not always the match.

A typical Rother bag back in the day. I can't remember what match this was, but I do recall catching those chub right across where the fence goes down into the river top left. (James Lauritz)

Sometimes it was too windy on the Rother for the waggler – the float just skidded through, and you couldn't feed across – so you had to fish the straight lead, but I always loved fishing the river, especially the two-day festivals that Dave Bird ran every year, with a pairs match on the Saturday and a teams of four match on the Sunday. Dave always got great sponsorship for these events, they were always brilliantly organised, with big pay-outs, and people came from all over the country, driving for hours, just to fish them. They made a real weekend of it, staying over, having a good time, and there were always sore heads on the morning of each match after a session

Rye DAS stalwart Tony Curd was always a danger on the Rother when he was drawn anywhere near any feeding bream. (Dave Roberts)

in the Globe in Rye the night before. The Trentman team in the shape of Don Slaymaker, Roy Toulson, Wayne Swinscoe and Pete Palmer cleaned up in the teams of four match in 1980 fishing wagglers and spraying big bronze maggots – 'Dorman's Donkeys', much bigger than any maggots you could ever get down South – for anything that swam. It was Mark Downes, though, who started the trend, when he came down for a week's holiday at the beginning of the river season in 1977 – him and a couple of other Starlets, Paul Dennis and Pete Hobson – to suss out match fishing down our way, fishing the Rother on the Saturday and the Medway the day after. Raiding visitors didn't always clean up in the Rother festivals. Dorking and other local anglers had more than their fair share of success in them. One year Kenny and I won the pairs match despite Kenny going for another of his swims – an involuntary one this time – and having to be pulled out by Michael Wood, later of top East Sussex team Polegate.

It was on the Rother in 1977 that Johnny Mac, who'd always modestly styled himself 'The King', as in Elvis, got labelled 'Brawling John McCarthy' in 'Snide Rumours and Dirty Lies' in *Coarse Fisherman* magazine. It was the first round of the Surrey Winter League, Sunday 4th September, and we were back at the bridge at Iden afterwards waiting for Dave Harper to tot up the results – Dorking had won emphatically – when Johnny's then girlfriend, Julie, came running over yelling, "Steve, Steve, they're fighting!" Johnny had Ray Mumford pinned to the ground and was laying into him, while Ray's Molesey team mate Mick 'Moggy' Beard, aka 'The Beast', was giving Johnny a right kicking. And all the while Johnny was calmly

I couldn't resist putting this one in (above), of Kenny Collings, me, Terry Harrison and Mark Richardson looking like flowerpot men. God knows where those hats came from. This was July 1979, and we'd just won the Rye Super Four, sponsored that year by Dictamite. (Image courtesy of Angler's Mail) *Another Dorking man, George Harrison, set a new river record that weekend, so the following year the sponsors, Daihatsu, offered this jeep for anyone doing the same. Neither Kenny nor I nor anyone else came anywhere near winning it.*

going, "One at a time! One at a time!" It took three of us to pull Moggy off him. How it all started was that Ray was catching a few bleak while Johnny at the next peg was getting big skimmers, and every time Johnny caught one he taunted Ray with it. They settled their differences in time, but Johnny's reputation was made.

It was on the Rother, too, one Saturday in September 1980, that I qualified for the first time for the Embassy Final – formerly the Woodbine – by winning down at Iden, then the next day I was on the old River Lea at Fishers Green for an invitation match arranged by Dickie Carr, who was a driver at the time for the sponsor, St Albans Sand and Gravel. Each of the 40 invited 'stars' – and they came from all around – was paired with a junior partner. My partner for the day was a certain G. Thomas, in the next swim down, but when I saw my peg I thought, that's it, we've no chance. It looked barren, it was about 25-foot wide and only 18 inches deep, and from the top of the high bank you could see the bottom – which was solid with weed, apart from a bare patch with an old tyre in it – all the way across to where someone had cut all the branches off a big willow tree. Under the tree, in a hole in the bank, was a tiny patch of dark water, but that was it. Ken Giles stood with me looking at it and said straight away, "That's a joke, Steve, you can't fish that. I'd ask for another draw if I was you." So I thought, I've got to find Dickie. I found Dickie alright, he came along to look, and as soon as he saw it he said, "But that's a good peg, Steve!" Just then this other chap who had come along to watch and who was lying on top of the bank said, "There's two chub in your peg, Steve, I can see them!" so I said to Dickie, "Fair enough, I'll fish it." As I was tackling up, the chap watching said, "There's five of them there now!" I couldn't see anything from where I was, down below, but as soon as the whistle went and I began firing out casters more and more chub appeared as if from nowhere to take the bait on the drop. They must have all been hiding in that dark hole under the tree. I ended up taking nearly 30lb of them shallow on the waggler, my partner added a hard-earned 14oz and together we won the pairs quite easily.

That was certainly a memorable weekend, but a week or so later venue regular Chris Hacknett from Welwyn Garden City showed how to do it when he fished the same peg with meat for barbel – the stretch was noted for them, it turned out – and had over 60lb of chub. Meanwhile I went and won an open at Longford Lake near Sevenoaks, and so I was flying – Kenny joked that customers in his shop were asking for "Steve Gardener draw bags" to practise drawing flyers. But then came news that brought us all crashing down to earth.

Kevin Zanocelli and David Taylor, two popular young men who only that year had broken into the Dorking team, were killed when they crashed into a tree near Lingfield when out celebrating Kevin's 19th birthday. David himself was only 21. Their loss hit everyone who knew them, and took a lot of coming to terms with. Later that year there was a big turn-out for the first of what became an annual memorial match, for charity, on the Rother at Iden – one of David and Kevin's favourite venues – with Rye DAS waiving all pegging fees. I felt honoured to win the event the following year, and the year after that the money raised went towards the first of two fishing platforms for disabled anglers – 'The David and Kevin Peg' – at Newbridge, sturdy platforms that are still there to this day.

In subsequent years we lost a number of other team mates, but the one that hit me the hardest was the death of Nick Aplin from cancer at the age of 31 in 1983. Nick was another old friend from school, in fact he was my best friend, and I miss him still. The annual memorial match held in his name on the Mole was another match we'd all rather we never had to fish. No matter how clichéd it may sound, such losses really do make you appreciate all the more how blessed you are to be alive, to have your health, your family, your friends and the chance to carry on enjoying this wonderful sport of ours as long as you possibly can. They put things into perspective, for sure.

To get back to happier memories… I've talked about the Thames and the Rother, but another favourite venue back in the day was Old Bury Hill, a 12-acre estate lake near Dorking where I still fish matches now. I first saw it one summer evening in the late 1960s, when we had a club match there, and straight away I thought how idyllic it was. In those days the water was clear and dark, there were lily pads everywhere, and it had a low, natural stock of pike, tench and blackspot-covered roach and rudd. Then Graham Rowles, who'd skippered a charter boat out of Newhaven at one time, bought the place and piled in the fish – bream, crucian carp, pike, zander, the lot – turning it into one of the country's first ever commercial coarse fisheries, really, a place that was years ahead of its time. He ran it until the early 1990s, when he sold it to David De Vere, the current owner, who has made it even better.

Back in Rowlesy's day we'd have 150-peg opens there, sometimes even bigger matches, and to cram everyone in the pegs were barely five paces apart. (Big Petworth Park matches were a bit like that, come to think of it.) There were even six pegs on the island, and if you drew one of those you were rowed across and that was it, you couldn't pack up and leave early if you weren't doing any good, you had to stay to the end and wait for them to come and get you. When pleasure fishing at Old Bury Hill in the old days you caught as soon as you started feeding – roach, skimmers, everything, even close in with one of those 14ft fibreglass poles we used to use with 18 inches of elastic dangling from an aluminium crook. But in a match, with everyone so close together, when the whistle went and everyone started feeding and fishing at the same time, God it was hard – the fish just scarpered.

Rowlesy was a big guy, with a big Alsatian always at his side, and in the middle of a match he'd bellow out "Hot pies! Hot pies!" – which wasn't much help if you were stuck on the island and wanted one. He could be a bit of a dictator, but he was always up for a challenge, like the 16-peg Glebe Invitation event in June 1979, when Ivan Marks came down with an eight-man 'All Stars' team of himself, Stan Piecha, Clive Smith, Edgar Purnell, Ken Giles, Tommy Pickering, Denis White and Ian Heaps to take on a Dorking outfit of myself, Terry Harrison, Johnny Mac, Kenny, John Benham, Dave Whitehouse, Mike Bartlett and Mike Ewin in a head-to-head contest. Denis said he'd never been so far south in his life. Fishing on the favoured front bank – always a good bet for bream, even today – in front of a few hundred spectators, from well-spaced pegs this time, everyone had double figures that day, and while I managed top weight with 31lb-something of mainly big skimmers on the waggler, Ivan's 'All Stars' just pipped us on total weight.

Me looking serious, Clive Smith playing a tench, and Ivan Marks with a typical netful at the Glebe Invitation at Old Bury Hill in 1979. (Image courtesy of Angling Times*)*

Back in the 1970s the angling papers made a big thing of the rivalry between match anglers from the South and those from the rest of the country. In 1973 Ivan Marks so incensed Johnny Mac with comments he made in his column in *Angling Times* that Johnny challenged him to a £100 winner-take-all square-off on the Thames. Ivan declined. In truth, though, it was only friendly banter in the main, and there's no doubt we were playing catch-up in the South, both individually and teamwise, but catch up in due course we did. The first big invitation match I fished, on the strength of being top points scorer in the Surrey

Winter League the year before, was the Gladding Masters in June 1973, on the Warwickshire Avon at Luddington. That was one to forget. The river was up and coloured – it was racing through – and I was one of nine DNWs, in fact I think I blanked. Then in 1976 I was one of five who fished for the South in the Ladbrokes Super League, against teams from the North, East and West, and we won, despite being 4/1 outsiders. Elthorne and England's John Wilkinson was our captain and from an initial squad of five others he picked Elthorne team mate Del Root, me, Kenny and Ray Mumford.

John Wilkinson (left) captained the South in the 1976 Ladbrokes Super League, while his Elthorne team mate Tony Bloomfield (right) was the unlucky sixth squad man who John left out of the team. (Images courtesy of Angler's Mail)

The idea was to have one round in each region. The first round, at Ecclestone Mere near St Helen's in July, was a good match, with plenty of skimmers and roach, and a fair few people watching. Robin Harris won it for the East, Kenny was second for the South and we were second overall behind the North. We came second again at Coombe Abbey Lake, where Benny Ashurst, Clive Smith, Robin Harris and myself were pegged in a line on swims cut out of thick beds of lily pads only the day before and all blanked, while Lloyd Davies, Del and winner Kevin Ashurst shared a huge shoal of spawning slabs, foul-hooking loads. Third time lucky we then won the round at Leisure Sport's Larbourne Farm gravel pit, near Iver in Buckinghamshire, with our skipper topping the field (not that there were many spectators at that one – I don't think anyone could even find it!). That set things up nicely for the final round, on the Warwickshire Avon at Evesham.

Kenny and I got there early, and after parking up in Crown Meadow we walked onto the road bridge to look at the river,

John Wilkinson on his way to winning the third round of the 1976 Ladbrokes Super League at Larbourne Farm with 8lb 11oz of bream and skimmers. (Image courtesy of Angler's Mail)

as you do. Looking over from the upstream side we saw a shoal of chub hanging in the flow. "Get some casters, get some casters!" Kenny said, so I dashed back to the car and fetched some. We threw them in and the chub all bolted. "Get some maggots, get some maggots!" Kenny said. When I came back with the maggots – bronze ones – the chub had all come back again. We threw the maggots in and the chub leisurely ate every single one. We decided there and then to fish maggot, even though caster was THE bait there in those days. The top weights that day, headed by Max Winters, were indeed taken on caster, but Kenny and I both won our sections, Ray won his section too, and the South were crowned Ladbroke's Super League champions in front of 2,000 people. That was a turning point, I think, for top southern match anglers gaining recognition nationwide.

Del Root, John Wilkinson, Kenny Collings, myself and Ray Mumford after winning the 1976 Ladbrokes Super League. Ivan Marks was top scorer over the four rounds, Kenny second and Ray third. Flash bulbs often made me blink at the critical moment. (Image courtesy of Angler's Mail)

Evesham has always been a special place to fish on such days – it always draws big crowds, and the fish don't seem to mind the disturbance – but it was even more so at Dick Derrington's August Bank Holiday festival, with its carnival, family-friendly atmosphere. Invitation matches at Coombe Abbey, with its majestic, stately setting, always had a special atmosphere too when big crowds turned out to watch, as they often did. Both venues provided me with some of the high points of my career over the years.

Coombe Abbey was always regarded first and foremost as a swingtip water, but I liked to fish it much the same way I did Old Bury Hill when I could, with the waggler. Ivan Marks used to fish for bream almost everywhere he went with a 20s hook, because in his own mind the small hook gave him more and better bites, but I was always more in the 16s and 18s camp. I found you got just as many good bites, you could get the fish out quicker, and there was less chance of deep-hooking them. It's all a question of confidence in the end. Back in September 1980, that memorable month when I was flying, I fished a 12-a-side Midlands versus South challenge match at Coombe Abbey, an invitation event organised by Gerry Casey, and drew what was normally a pretty mediocre peg near the car park. But that day the swim happened to be full of big hungry bream, and I had 25 of them for 102lb 4oz, all on the waggler, to set a new match record for the venue. (Appropriately enough, Freddie Mercury and Queen were in the charts at the time with 'Another One Bites the Dust', and the song played in my head every time I netted a fish.) For some reason there was only a ridiculously small bucket for the weigh-in, with silly little scales that only went up to 8lb, so it took quite some time to weigh me in – but the fish all went back okay.

As for Evesham, in 1983 I was lucky enough to win the individual Courage title with 14lb 15½oz on the stick float, then the following year Kenny won the individual title with a fantastic 12lb 14oz of mainly bleak on the waggler and I won the team match the next day with 16lb 7oz of dace, roach and chub on the waggler from the same peg. And I think it was those two results, winning on the stick and waggler in front of big crowds, that ultimately brought me to the attention of the England manager, Dick Clegg.

The 1980s and on into the early 1990s was a time of transition for match fishing in the South. As sport on rivers in general and the Thames in particular became ever less consistent, more and more anglers looked elsewhere to get their string pulled on a regular

Collecting the spoils in the Courage festival at Evesham.

basis. One day in the 1980s Jeanette and I took the kids to a pick-your-own fruit farm called Nutfield Priory down the road from us in Redhill, and I couldn't help noticing a couple of on-site lakes, Priory and Hungerford, that looked to be full of fish. I asked the owner what the score was, and he said a little club called Faulkners was allowed to fish there on certain days but that he wasn't averse to the idea of me running a few open matches and giving him a bit of extra income. For three or four years I ran opens including two-day festivals there every summer, and people came from all over – from as far afield as Birmingham, Bristol and Essex – to fish them, because the lakes were full of carp and it was a new and exciting

Another good match for me at Coombe Abbey was in a round of the Ladbrokes Super League in 1977, when I had this 51lb 9oz bag on a day when 17 of the 20 anglers fishing had double figures in front of 1,000 spectators. (Image courtesy of Angler's Mail*)*

game catching such hard-fighting fish on the waggler. The only other places like it at the time, really, in the whole country were Bolingey and Shillamill down in Cornwall.

On Priory Lake you fished across to the island, and when you got a bite you had to strike and pull like mad to keep the hooked fish from leaping out of the water and 'climbing the trees'. Well do I remember my waggler rod smashing in half in my hands, much to everyone's amusement, when I pulled just a little bit too hard one day! On Hungerford Lake you could spray maggot – 'spray and pray' – leave the rod in the rest with the tip at right angles to the float and let the fish hook themselves, much like fishing the method.

Nutfield Priory gave the Dorking team a head start when it came to match fishing for carp – something that gave us a massive advantage in several Winter League finals, which is something I'll be talking about in the next chapter. Two of the best at the game in those early days were Johnny Mac and John 'Lasher' Larraman. Just about the funniest thing I've seen in all my years of match fishing was Lasher diving in after a big carp that flipped out of his hands back into the water. He managed to grab hold of the fish, but being face down in the lake he was well and truly stuck, and had to let the fish go in the end.

Sometimes in those early days of match fishing for carp you were limited to a gallon of maggots each, and if you asked Simon Gould how much he'd fed, he'd say, "A big gallon". Maggots were so much cheaper back then, so you could afford to take loads.

John 'Lasher' Larraman was a real pioneer in the early days of carp matches, someone at the very forefront of this branch of the sport. (Image courtesy of Angler's Mail*)*

In autumn and winter especially, many anglers in the London area in the 1980s, like the Vincent twins and Clive Gingell, turned increasingly to matches on the capital's canals for more consistent sport than you got on rivers. Weights might have been low and the venues not the most scenic, but the matches were fair, in the main, and you usually got plenty of bites, especially when and where bloodworm and joker were allowed. As for me, I took to the long pole and bloodworm and joker relatively late. When Dick Clegg first picked me for the England squad for the 1987 World Championship, he said it was because the venue in Portugal, the River Mondego, was a waggler one, and that I wasn't in the running for the 1988 squad as the venue that year, the Damme Canal in Belgium, looked like being a long pole and bloodworm and joker job. So I knew I had to work on my long pole and bloodworm and joker fishing – and that was the best decision I ever made, the way things worked out.

The very last time the Hammersmith Open was held, it was as a pegged-down match on the Regent's Canal in October 1987, the weekend before the Great Storm that devastated so much of southern England. I hadn't long been back from the World Championship in Portugal, and I phoned my Dorking team mate Robin Morley to see where all the lads were going, assuming it would be somewhere on the Thames as usual. "No, mate," Robin said, "We're all going on the Regent's Canal." I said, "But I haven't got any bloodworm and joker," and he said, "Don't worry about that, I've got a spare match pack." Come the morning of the match, when I got to my peg and opened up my match pack the joker was cut 50/50 with peat, and I thought, what am I gonna do now? I was used to getting a bit of neat joker that you separated with dry leam and fed neat in little balls. I couldn't do that because of the peat. The only way to feed my swim would be to mix the whole lot, joker and peat together, in groundbait, but I hadn't brought any of that to the match as I hadn't expected I'd need it. Another Dorking team mate, Lennie Goodwin, was only a few pegs away, so I went along to see him and luckily he had a couple of spare bags of groundbait. Exactly what they were I forget, but they were Van den Eynde. So I knocked some up, stirred in some joker and peat, and on the whistle lobbed a few balls in. And for about four hours I caught one little roach after another. I ended up winning the match with 10lb 7½oz, while Keith Arthur was second.

It isn't often you get one over on Keith, by the way, in fishing or anything else. The man's like a walking encyclopaedia. I remember once finding an ancient tin of some sort of powder in the room above the tackle shop in Sutton. It must have been there for donkey's years. I forget the name on the label, but the small print said that it was ideal for making 'junket', whatever that was. I thought, right Keith, I've got you this time. When he next called in the shop I held it up to him, already tasting victory. "Junket powder," he said. "Makes a kind of blancmange. Mind you, I haven't seen *that* particular brand in years."

But going back to that last Hammersmith Open, I honestly believe that the match was a big turning point in my international career, because the following year when Dick went to look at the Damme Canal with some of the guys he had picked, they found that there were fish to be caught on the waggler after all. I remember reading about it, and him saying that he was thinking of taking another angler as well as his original squad of six, which was Kevin Ashurst, Alan McAtee, Dave Roper, Vinnie Smith, Bob Nudd and Dave Vincent, and me thinking, Tommy Pickering, Denis White, Ian Heaps, they all fished the previous year, it's sure to be one of them. Then Dick rang me up and said he wanted the extra man to be me, that he knew I'd been working on my bloodworm and joker fishing since Portugal.

It was fate that I had even fished that last Hammersmith Open in the first place, and fate worked in my favour. That's the way it is sometimes. As for the trophy, I've still got it somewhere. I never knew who, if anyone, to give it back to!

My old nemesis and friend 'Keefy' Arthur. It was hard enough beating him off the next peg, never mind catching him out! (Dave Roberts)

one meeting him having a go at me about something or other and Peter Knight stepping in and telling him, "You'll have to go through me first!" Ray and the Dorking members never saw eye to eye. Kenny Collings missed out getting in the team for the 1971 National on the Severn when one of his weight cards from the trials went 'missing'.

I didn't get into the CALPAC National team in any of the next three years after 1970, in fact I'm not even sure I tried to. I was sharing the flat with Steve and having a good time, and while I took my own fishing and Dorking Winter League fishing seriously I wasn't that bothered about trying to qualify for a one-off annual match somewhere miles away with CALPAC. The trouble with the trial system was that it never produced the best team. At least CALPAC fished their trials on the actual venue for the 1970 match. Sussex County had all theirs, every year, on the Wallers – even for the 1969 National on the Trent, when perhaps not surprisingly they came last. And for the 1971 National one of the CALPAC trial matches was the 1970 Welland Championship – as won by Ivan Marks – when the 1971 National was on the Severn! Even so, CALPAC came a respectable 15th out of 116 teams in that one.

The first ever Division One National, on the Bristol Avon in 1972, was something of an embarrassment for CALPAC. In the run-up to it, Johnny Mac won two opens on the river while in another open, at Claverton, Johnny, Dickie Vetterlein and Ray all framed, Ray breaking the Bristol Avon barbel record with a 9lb 11oz fish in the process. So CALPAC went into the National full of confidence and as one of the favourites. They drew

CALPAC Invicta Shield contest winner Steven Gardener.

Although I didn't fish for CALPAC in Nationals in the early 1970s, I continued to fish in various CALPAC matches, like the Invicta Shield, which I won in December 1972 on the Grand Union at Hayes with this 3lb 12¼oz catch of roach on waggler and caster – I could take you to the exact swim now. Second that day, only 2oz behind, was Dave Vincent of Leatherhead – not to be confused with Dave Vincent of 'the Dangerous Brothers'. (Image courtesy of Angling Times*)* next to the mighty Birmingham outfit, Johnny blanked on the peg next to Clive Smith and despite Billy Hughes winning his section CALPAC slumped to 21st out of 80 while Birmingham stormed to victory.

This was the first points National, and the NFA had the bright idea of doing it on penalty points, with one point for a section win and so on. This meant that if, say, 25 anglers in one section caught, while in another section 50 anglers caught, then all those who blanked in the first section got 26 penalty points, while all those who blanked in the other section got 51 penalty points. So you could get fewer penalty points for blanking in one section than someone in another section did for catching!

Not surprisingly, the more sensible points system we're all used to now was introduced the following year for the match on the Witham. Arguments within the CALPAC set-up meant that anglers of the quality of Ray Mumford, Johnny Mac, Kenny Collings, Andy Partridge, Mick Thill, Chris Love and Billy Hughes – all of whom had fished at least one of CALPAC's two previous Nationals – didn't even try to qualify for the team, which came 66th out of 80, narrowly avoiding relegation.

More in-fighting saw Peter Burton leave the set-up ahead of the 1974 National on the Welland. In trials, 30 selected contenders were whittled down to 24, and Ray, back as captain, had to choose his 12 from the 24. It was a step in the right direction toward what we all now accept is the best system, giving one man the power to choose what he thinks is the best team.

Anyway, having made a concerted effort to get back in the team, I was picked to fish and took it into my head to book

CALPAC's Peter Burton – he was with the Grebes outfit – was one of the best match anglers in the South in the 1970s. In fact, Keith Arthur rates him the most innovative match angler he ever knew. (Image courtesy of **Angling Times***)*

a week's holiday that September – the match was at the end of the month – in sunny Crowland. Jeanette was happy to come along and sit with me each day, but any thoughts she might have had of topping up her tan on the river bank went out the window the moment we got there. It was bleak, it was windy and it was cold! I fished a different bit of the match length each day, and despite the water being gin clear caught loads of roach up to 1lb-plus everywhere I went. I remember thinking, this is going to be some National, not realising that on the Welland, as on so many venues, you could bag up in the week when on your own, then come a big match the roach would disappear.

Jim Randell had to walk seven miles to his peg in the 1974 Division One National. Luckily he was able to borrow a trolley. Unhappily for Jim, he blanked. (Image courtesy of Angler's Mail)

The night before the National there was a hard frost, and on the day the wind was freezing. The match was terrible. Loads of people never had a bite – 3½oz won one section, and there were 80 teams fishing! – and for most competitors it was a day to forget. That day the NFA were also absurdly officious about the section coaches leaving Spalding at nine o'clock on the dot, with or without you. Jim Randell was famously one of several who had no choice but to walk miles to their pegs – they'd have been disqualified if they went by car – and start the match halfway through.

I was one of the very few lucky ones that day. I hadn't a clue about my peg at Four Mile Bar, but I did what almost every other competitor did on bream waters in Nationals in those days, which was to put some groundbait in across as soon as the whistle went. Depending on the ambitions of your team, you then either sat it out for bream and, most likely, blew out – and in truth this is what most people did – or you started off scratching close in for a few small 'team' fish before chancing your arm. I caught a few small roach early on just over the weed fringe, then I went further out past the middle with a big waggler, Ivan Marks style – and caught seven bream.

Eventually the wind became too strong for the float – the rollers were really ripping through – and I had to change to the bomb, but I didn't catch any more bream after the switch. They'd moved upstream to the guy chomping on a big cigar two pegs to my right, Percy Anderson – like Bryan Lakey, a

Here I am with a bream safely in my landing net in the Welland National in 1974. It was a bit blustery that day! (Image courtesy of Angler's Mail)

Cambridge angler – and he really hammered them on the swingtip in the last hour to win the section and the match with over 40lb. No one fished the feeder for bream in those days, remember. You fed by hand or with a catapult. Percy said afterwards he'd fed 12 pints of casters in his groundbait, but I don't know about that. It's possible, I suppose, but it takes some doing. I do know that he kept unwrapping foil parcels and adding something to his groundbait, and I sat there thinking, what's he doing? I think now it was chopped worm – redworms from a muck heap, most likely, for this was long before you could get farmed dendrobenas. Anyway, I ended up second in the section and eighth overall, with just under 21lb, and that got me a solid silver medal for finishing in the top 12.

Percy Anderson on his way to winning the 1974 Division One National. Note the foil packets in the grass by his side, which I'm sure contained pre-chopped worm, though I could be wrong. (Image courtesy of Angling Times)

Angler's Mail wrote that I was one of several anglers Percy "slammed" that day, which was a bit harsh, though I agree he would probably have won off my peg, the way he fed so heavily when the fish weren't in front of him. He had the greater knowledge and experience of bream fishing. The guy in between him and me had nearly 15lb, the guy to my left a couple of bream, and Percy later said in an article in *Angling Times* that none of us to his left fed enough that day, which was probably true. But here's the thing. Percy's team went into the match as one of the favourites but had five blanks and finished 66th, not far off relegation. The CALPAC team of Ted Allen, John Benham, Kenny Collings, Reg Cook – who later emigrated to Canada, where he still fishes bass tournaments – myself, Freddie Gladwin, Peter Knight, Dick Lloyd, Chris Love, Ray Mumford, Dickie Vetterlein and Dennis Wells had only one

Blinking again! Here's me with one of the bream I caught in the 1974 National. I remember ordering the ex-Navy jacket I've got on. I was glad of it, too, on such a cold day. (Image courtesy of Angling Times*)*

blank and finished seventh. It was a good scratching side, that.

The following year, 1975, the National was on the Nene, and I recall going up with John Benham to practise on the exposed North Bank and fishing like the locals with home-made peacock wagglers up to 18 inches long to try to beat the wind. On the day, I drew Splash Lane at Castor, but again my peg meant nothing to me as I'd never even seen the river there before, but as it turned out I was on another flyer, in an area noted for bream. Being on a bream water, I did much the same as the year before, only this time after catching a few bits I went over on the bomb with worm and caster. Quite a crowd gathered behind me as I started catching, and after I'd weighed in another 'lucky seven'

Sussex bream ace Roger Izzard was also second in his section in the 1974 Welland National, with his 24lb 7oz bream bag enough for fifth place overall. (Image courtesy of Angling Times*)*

When your luck's in, it's in. I'm playing a bream or chub here in the 1975 Nene National. I lost one big bream that day that would have got me third place ahead of John Essex of the Leicester 'Likely Lads'. (Image courtesy of Angler's Mail*)*

Time to smile after weighing in at the end of the 1975 National. Angler's Mail *said I admitted to being unnerved by the crowd behind me that day, but that's not how I remember it. The crowd spurred me on! (Image courtesy of* Angling Times*)*

With Angling Times *Editor Bob Feetham pouring the champagne, the bulk of the Birmingham squad, led by Clive Smith holding the cup, celebrate victory on the Nene in 1975. Note a young Mark Downes on Clive's left. Out of shot are Ken Giles and Kevin Ashurst. (Image courtesy of* Angling Times*)*

slabs – the biggest 5lb 9¼oz – plus four chub, for 35lb-odd, I recall that Charlie Townsend, who I used to see on Thames matches and was watching that day, came up to me and said, "I'm not going to say nothing, Steve, but I think this could be a very special day for you". Then he wandered off. He must have thought I'd won the match. Alas not, but I did come fourth and win my section, so I went home with two solid silver medals this time.

Angling Times gleefully announced on its front page that southern teams had "disappeared under an avalanche of anglers from the North and Midlands", a rout led by Birmingham. The paper later went so far as to call CALPAC's performance in finishing 22nd "dismal", but that was a bit strong, and certainly not fair on someone like Maureen Anderson, who was fishing her first National, I believe, and was by no means the team's lowest points scorer.

Birmingham won again the following year, on the Trent, to become the first team to defend the Division One title. While some of us scored good points, CALPAC finished 38th out of 79, despite the team being hand-picked this time, as I think it was. The line-up certainly looks like a river team, being John Benham, Les Collins, Reg Cook, myself, Billy Hughes, Peter Knight, Chris Love, Johnny Mac, Rob Mittens, Ray Mumford, Andy Partridge and Steve Sanders, in his first ever National. That's a strong line-up, one easily good enough to have done much better. But that was CALPAC's problem – it was a group of talented individuals, not all of whom were pulling in the same direction. You also have to consider that, historically, Nationals were held almost anywhere except the South. The Thames couldn't be used because of size limits. Putting in any meaningful practice was therefore a big issue for southern teams when the venues were usually so far away.

And there the CALPAC story ends for me, because early the following year, 1977, CALPAC were barred from fishing the Division One National on the Welland and automatically relegated to Division Two for failing to ensure that someone attended the required minimum two out of four regional NFA meetings in 1976. Over the years many clubs around the country fell foul of this ruling. It tended to happen when the person who usually attended was unable to go, and the person who promised to fill in for them then let everybody down. For a team the consequences could be devastating, and in CALPAC's case in 1977 this meant they lost most of their best anglers at a stroke, as they went their separate ways and joined other teams.

I didn't rush off and join another team, however, because I wasn't that desperate to fish a National just for the sake of it. My loyalties lay firmly with Dorking, who would soon become members of the NFA in their own right and would fish their first ever National in 1979. With Dorking, everyone worked together for the success of the team. The reason for this was simple – the Dorking team were all friends. The likes of Steve Sanders, myself, Terry Wright and Nick Aplin all went to school together, all grew up together, while the older team members like John Benham, Doug Gregory, Roger Paul and Peter Knight were popular local anglers who we looked up to and admired. There was no clash of egos, no fighting to be top dog.

The Dorking story begins with the forming of the 'Alliance of Croydon and District Angling Clubs Surrey Winter League' in October 1970. Alan Lathwell was the organiser, and Dorking, Warlingham, Leatherhead, Croydon, Englefield, Duke of Gloucester and Twickenham all entered teams of six for a series of four matches. I must admit I remember very little about any of them! The first round was on the Wallers at Boreham Street, of all places, on Sunday 25th October, with Doug Gregory, Peter Knight, Roger Paul, 16-year-old John Tullett, myself and Bert Coombes turning out for Dorking. I imagine I travelled down in Doug's van. Young John Tullett had the distinction of winning that historic match. Subsequent rounds were on the Kentish Stour at Cut End, a flooded Thames at Chertsey, and Desborough Cut. In the fourth round Dorking entered a 'B' team of John Benham, Bob Sharp, John Monk, K. Youngs, S. Stephens and Steve Sanders. Dorking A won the first two rounds and did enough in the last two to win the league by a narrow margin from Twickenham.

The Surrey Winter League became part of the *Angling Times* League the following season, and I'm proud to say that Dorking won the Surrey Winter League every single year in the four decades or more of its existence with the notable exception of the 1973/74 season, when we were third behind winners Leatherhead and runners-up Twickenham, and the 1992/93 season, when we were second to Banstead. Highlights along the way included winning one round, on the Grand Union Canal at West Drayton in 1990, by a record score of 115 points out of 120 – there were 10 teams of 12, so there were 10 points up for grabs in each section – having set the old record of 113 points ourselves way back in 1977.

So how do I explain Dorking's success over so many years?

Right from the start, we had the better anglers. You can put that down to coincidence, I suppose, but if you start off being slightly better and start winning, then momentum, confidence and team spirit all build, and you become even harder to beat. The best anglers around want to join you, be part of the success, and so it snowballs. But it doesn't just happen of its own accord. You can have the best anglers, but unless they put the team first that means nothing. You need a captain who everyone respects – at Dorking over the years we variously had Doug Gregory, John Benham, Peter Knight, Kenny Collings, Andy Love, Steve Champion and Steve Sanders – and you need anglers who embrace running the bank no matter how disappointed they are not to be fishing. There's no place for divisive prima donnas, moaners or sulkers. Everyone must also be able to take the necessary time off work for practice.

Looking back at the venues, the water conditions, the weather,

ALLIANCE of CROYDON & DISTRICT ANGLING CLUBS.

SURREY WINTER LEAGUE.

To All Member Clubs,

The result of the first match fished at Boreham Bridge, Pevensey on Sunday 25th October was as follows:-

DORKING A.S.
D.Gregory 3-14-0
P.Knight 1-3-12
R.Paul 11-12
J.Tullett 4-8-4
S.Gardener 3-3-0
A.Coombes 13-00
14-5-12

WARLINGHAM 'A'
D.Pooley 1-3-0
P.Jerron 2-8
A.Jopling 9-8
G.Tuck 1-12-8
B.Kennedy 3-11-0
M.Knight 6-4
7-12-8

WARLINGHAM 'B'
R.Kennedy 1-9-0
G.Cousins 1-6-0
D.Simmonds 5-0
C.Wood 1-1-0
P.Cousins 2-11-0
P.Norris 4-8
7-4-8

ENGLEFIELD 'A'
L.Whittington 1-3-0
D.Roones 0-0-0
M.Matthews 4-5-8
P.Evans 1-1-8
J.Loveridge 0-0-0
..Sherwood 8-12
7-2-12

TWICKENHAM
P.Issott 0-0-8
A.Edwards 2-7-0
F.Meads 0-0-12
W.Irvine 2-3-8
W.Peare 1-10-0
M.Anoss 4-0
6-9-12

LEATHERHEAD 'A'
F.Fritchard 0-4-8
M.Welling 0-5-8
N.Kenward 1-13-8
R.Clarke 2-7-0
R.Vetterlein 7-0
R.Nursery 4-4
5-9-8

CROYDON 'B'
D.Davis 1-8-0
M.Borroff 2-8
R.Hobbs 1-0
L.Evans 6-0
.Varndell 1-8-8
..cent 0-0-0
3-10-0

ENGLEFIELD 'B'
E.Harrington 0-1-8
J.Alloway 0-0-0
D.Parker 1-4-0
E.Batley 15-0
E.Sherwood ..8
J.Sherwood 12-0
3-4-12

CROYDON 'A'
W.Worrell 1-13-0
P.Harriss 10-8
D.Roberts 5-4
G.Hodson 2-8
W.Hunt 0-3
G.Hobbs 2-8
3-1-15

LEATHERHEAD 'B'
..McDonald 0-15-12
..techman 0-0-0
..Wells 2-8
..Vincent 0-0-0
..Bishop 1-0-12
..aine 5-8
2-8-8

Duke of GLOUCESTER
A.Lathwell 0-1-12
L.Lathwell 0-0-0
J.Stagg 0-0-0
R.Wells 4-8
C.Tong 0-0-0
J.Gerry 1-4-0
1-10-4

SEEBOARD.
P.Pittman 0-0-0
R.Letts 0-0-0
P.Smith 0-0-0
F.Smith 0-0-0
T.Toombs 0-0-0
A.Lee 0-0-0
0-0-0

..Nicolle WADAS 1-6-0
..Brown WADAS 0-0-0
J.Ball WADAS 0-5-8
..Jerrom WADAS 3-6-8
5-2-0

RESERVES
G.McCarthy Twick 4-6-0
J.Turner DGAS 0-0-0
K.Williams Twick 2-4
A.Reading Twick 1-10-4
W.Goss SEEB 0-0-0
F.Coomber SEEB 0-0-0
5-12-8

With reference to Day permits, I now understand that these are 3/- per head, will all clubs please render this money to me at the next meeting of the League.
It would be appreciated if clubs intending to fish the Individual at Ham Car Park this Sunday, would bring along their scales.

Yours Sincerely,

The results sheet from the first ever round of the Surrey Winter League. Dave Roberts turned out for Croydon and Dickie Vetterlein for Leatherhead. Seeboard – South Eastern Electricity Board – did get on the points board in the next round, but then left the league. (Dave Roberts) then to keep going and give it your all when it's lashing down and the rain's straight in your face, and when you're on a bad bit of somewhere like the Wey Navigation Canal and it's dirty with mud and you're scratching for a few gudgeon, you need total commitment and a tremendous will to win, a refusal to be beaten. I used to love it, I always relished the challenge, and that's the mindset you need. All the Dorking lads I fished with over the years were of the same mind – we were all ultra-competitive – though it's not everyone's cup of tea, I know. For my own part, it gave me a grounding in what it takes to succeed as a team, and that helped me later in my England career, I'm sure.

12/11/75

DORKING & DISTRICT ANGLING SOCIETY
(Founded 1905)

Dear Sir,

Your attendance is requested at a ~~Committee/General~~ *TEAM* Meeting of the above Society, to be held at *WESTCOTT VILLAGE CLUB* on *19th* day of *NOVEMBER* 1975, at *8.45* pm. *(WEDS)*.

Agenda:

WEY NAV. COMP.
YOU HAVE BEEN SELECTED TO FISH.
SOME OF US ARE HAVING A PRACTICE SESSION THIS SUNDAY. MEET ANCHOR PUB, PIRFORD LOCK 9.00 A.M.

Yours faithfully, *John Benham*
~~Hon. Secretary.~~

John Benham was a conscientious captain, notifying team members in writing of meetings and practice sessions. (Dave Roberts)

I say 'scratching', and it may surprise a lot of people to know that the famous 'Dorking bagging machine' of later years was once better known as 'the Dorking scratching machine'. With rounds of the Winter League on venues like the Mole, the Wey and Broadmead Cut, Wraysbury Number Two and the Wey Nav, there were often blanks galore, so one fish could be worth a lot of points. You weren't there for a day's fishing. If you drew a good peg and won or framed, great, but that wasn't why you were there either – you were there solely for the sake of the team. Most of the time you were on a peg you couldn't possibly win or frame from, anyway, so you had to take the utmost care not to destroy it at the start by trying to make it into something it wasn't. You had to feed cautiously and fish carefully for every last bite. The fish soon told you if by chance you were on a few. Half the time anyone sensible would have stayed at home, the weather was that awful, the venue so horribly out of sorts, but the satisfaction of defeating the elements, contributing precious points to the team total with maybe a handful of sticklebacks or minnows or even a single stone loach – as was often the case on the Mole – then that feeling kept you coming back for more. And if you had a bad day, either individually or as a team, you had to be able to put it behind you – not brood on it – and 'go again' in the next round.

ANGLING TIMES LEAGUE SURREY DIVISION

Results of the Sixth and Final Round Match fished on the R Mole at Cobham on Sunday 1st February 1976.

DORKING(4)
```
J Tullett    0- 3- 8(10)
M Bartlett   0- 0- 0
P Knight     0- 4- 0( 5)
S Gardener   0- 5-12( 9)
J Moriarty   0- 0-12( 9)
L Collins    0- 1- 8( 7)
J Benham     0- 0- 0
M Spring     0- 7-12(10)
P Shepherd   0- 0- 0
T Wright     0- 4- 0(10)
G Harrison   0- 0- 0
R Evans      0- 4- 8( 9)
             1-15-12(69)
```

Leatherhead(7)
```
R Boychuk    0- 0- 4( 8)
J Errett     2-12- 8(10)
I Eastwood   0- 5- 4( 6)
R Nursey     0- 0- 8( 8)
M Rollins    0- 0- 0
D Harris     0- 0- 0
D Gregory    0- 0- 0
T Hiscock    0- 6- 0( 9)
D Vincent    0- 1-12(10)
N Kenward    0- 1- 4( 9)
M Errett     0- 0- 8( 7)
C Stechman   0- 0- 0
             3-12- 0(67)
```

Cobham Court(9)
```
A England    0- 0- 0
D Wesley     0- 3- 0( 8)
S Newton     2- 9- 0( 8)
H Notley     0- 0- 0
R Turley     0- 0- 4( 8)
A Cornock    0- 3- 4(10)
C Palmer     0- 0- 0
A Long       0- 0- 0
B Chubb      0- 0- 8( 9)
M Cobbett    0- 1- 0( 8)
F Pritchard  1- 1- 0(10)
P Norrington 0- 0- 0
             4- 2- 0(61)
```

Godalming(8)
```
D Waddy      0- 0- 0
P Stephens   0- 7- 0( 9)
P Cannon     0- 9-12( 7)
F Sherlock   0- 0- 0
D Bridger    0- 0- 4( 8)
S Gray       0- 2- 0( 8)
W Butcher    0- 0- 0
K Gray       0- 0- 0
R Holland    0- 0- 0
I Covey      0- 0- 0
B Butt       0- 1- 8( 8)
D Lake       0- 0- 0
             1- 4- 8(40)
```

Twickenham(2)
```
D Woolgar    0- 0- 0
R Baker      0- 0- 0
B Price      0- 2- 0( 9)
P Adams      0- 0- 0
K Harbour    0- 1- 4(10)
J Henning    0- 3- 0( 9)
J Nicholls   0- 0- 0
P O'gorman   0- 0- 0
A Love       0- 0- 8( 9)
P Issott     0- 0- 0
H Edwards    0- 0- 0
M Bennett    0- 0- 0
             4- 6-12(37)
```

Six Bells(3)
```
D Walton     0- 0- 4( 8)
R Newnham    0- 0- 0
S Cummings   4-15- 0(10)
P Shirley    0- 0- 0
P Brice      0- 0- 0
W Wicker     0- 0- 0
S Langley    1- 6- 0(10)
M Woodyard   0- 0- 0
P Warne      0- 0 -0
G Lockwood   0- 0- 0
D Norris     0- 0- 0
L Herve      0- 0- 0
             6- 5- 4(28)
```

Banstead(0)
```
T Jones      0- 2- 0( 9)
C Taylor     0- 0- 0
-------      0- 0- 0
M Ewin       0- 0- 0
P Norris     0- 0- 0
-------      0- 0- 0
D Devere     0- 0- 0
G Tuck       0- 0- 0
-------      0- 0- 0
D Jones      0- 2- 8( 9)
A Wood       1- 9- 8(10)
             1-14- 0(28)
```

Englefield Green(1)
```
A Harrington 0- 0- 0
M Batchelor  0- 0- 0
R Young      0- 0- 0
P Gaff       1-10- 0(10)
D Macleod    0- 0- 0
J Macleod    0- 0- 0
W Irvine     1- 4- 0( 9)
A Rogers     0- 0- 0
B Evans      0- 0- 0
D Young      0- 0- 0
G Kidd       0- 0- 0
J Turani     0- 0- 4( 8)
             2-14- 4(27)
```

Molesey(6)
```
R Leadbeater 0- 0- 0
B Darragh    0- 0- 0
T Enticknap  0- 1- 0( 4)
B Rawden     0- 0- 0
---------
J Arndt jnr  0- 0- 0
P Davidson   0- 0- 0
R Mittins    0- 0- 0
C Evans      0- 0- 0
D Powell     0- 0- 0
K Collins    0- 0- 0
R Cook       0- 0- 0
             0- 1- 0( 4)
```

Warlingham(5)
```
Nil
```

Points for the Day
```
Dorking           10
Leatherhead        9
Cobham Court       8
Englefield Green   3
Godalming          7
Banstead           5
Molesey            2
Twickenham         6
Six Bells          5
Warlingham         0
```

115 fished   42 weighed in   Total Weight 26-11-8

A typical Surrey Winter League score sheet from way back when. Was it worth the effort? You bet it was! (Dave Roberts)

A lot of the time in Winter League matches you were fishing for one bite, be that from a gudgeon, a roach or even a chub. In very cold conditions, after a hard frost the night before, often if you were going to get that bite it would be from a chub, so you had to stay alert for it. You might not get a second chance, because if you struck and missed you often spooked the fish, and that would be that if there was only one chub there. I remember one round in December 1973 on a frosty but flowing Wey Nav trotting a little stick float down the middle all day for one bite and one 2lb 5oz chub, which got me third place overall, but more importantly got me the section and helped Dorking to a narrow win on the day. That was with a fibreglass rod too, bear in mind. Pick one of those up now and they're horrendous, you wonder how we ever fished with them, but we did. (I also remember Godalming's Reggie Holland at the next peg to me one year in one round on his club's stretch of the Wey putting a little crayfish on the scales. Reggie said, "Well, I caught it, and it's a fish, ain't it?" – and the scalesman let him have it!)

In a lot of the river matches I fished in winter when I was younger, not just Winter Leagues either, on the Mole, the Wey, the Thames, or wherever, you fished for one chub bite. If you got it, and caught the fish, then you fished for another, and if you got more than one chub, great, you were probably going to win the match. Often as not you were on the tip, and you couldn't take your eyes off it for a second, because in that second a chub could spit the bait out and be gone. Chub don't often hang themselves, as you know. So you got yourself set, and you concentrated like mad for the whole five hours for the slightest indication.

Lasher and I had many a discussion about this on the way to and from winter river matches, we were both well into it. We used to look for chub liners as well. People laugh at this – "Liners on rivers? Leave it out!" – but on a rock-hard day we'd cast to different spots, and sit there with our eyes glued to that tip, until all of a sudden on one cast we'd spot the tiniest slow pluck, like a leaf had gone into the line, and we'd say to ourselves, "Whoa, there's one there!" After all, they had to be somewhere, didn't they? The fish wasn't necessarily feeding, but it was there, in your swim, and you'd found it, so now you had a chance of catching it. And on places like the Wey Nav, which is shallow across and moves only slowly, the fish merely had to brush your line for you to see a movement on the ultra-fine quivertips we used on such venues in the old days. It was common practice to make or adapt your own quivertip rods and to rub the tips down as fine as you dared, because it was difficult fishing, and you often had to search your peg for that one fish. But when you found it, and caught it, you got a real buzz out of it, much more than from bagging.

Andy Love with a brace of hard-won chub. (Image courtesy of Angler's Mail)

I travelled with Lasher quite a lot in the late 1970s and through the 1980s, Lennie Goodwin too in the late 1980s. Lasher used to drive me mad. I hate not being on time, but he used to do a bread delivery round first thing and was nearly always late picking me up. Having said that, I couldn't always be relied upon either, because I recall that after one match on the Wey at Godalming I had just got back home to Redhill when I remembered I was supposed to have taken Mark Richardson home to Dorking first. I raced all the way back to Godalming and found him standing on the platform at the station with all his gear, waiting for a train – on a Sunday!

Going back to this business of fishing for one bite at a time and how immensely satisfying it can be, I was talking to Will Raison about it recently – we talk a lot on the phone – and he reminded me of the day he sat behind me on a round of the Winter League at Medley. I was drawn on the Channel, which is a length of the Thames that is artificially constricted into half its normal width as it flows out of Portmeadow and into Oxford city centre. I set up three different rods that day – a waggler, a straight lead and a Bolognese – and I caught one chub from one bite on each rod as I worked my way through the card, and ended up framing. On days like that it's a case of reading the swim correctly, working out whereabouts in your peg the fish are likely to be given the particular water conditions, then feeding carefully for one bite at a time and being totally confident in what you are doing, no matter how long you go without that first bite. It's fatal to panic after two, three or even four hours without a bite, then mess your peg up by blasting in bait here, there and everywhere. The last hour's so often the one when you get that one bite.

Talking tactics before a match in the early 1980s with team mates John Merritt (left), Steve Sanders (centre) and Alan Wood (right). (Dave Roberts)

It was never easy winning the Surrey Winter League. For many years Weybridge were our main rivals – they were another good scratching side – and in 1986/87 we beat them by only half a point. Then the following season they tied with us on points – 529 points each – and only lost out on overall weight. It was ironic, therefore, that it was Banstead and not Weybridge who eventually became only the third team, after Leatherhead and Twickenham in 1973/74, to beat us, in 1992/93, and that time it was our turn to lose out by only half a point – and I'm talking final scores of 556.5 and 556 points here, the finest of margins.

That Banstead team was Kenny's project, although Dave Roberts was nominally captain when they beat us. After several successful years as Dorking captain, in 1983 Kenny had stepped down from the team for a well-earned rest, but after I joined him in the tackle shop a few years later he felt refreshed enough to take on the challenge of beating his old team. But I must stress, there was never any needle, it was all in good part! The team he assembled – 'the Banstead Bandits', as they were known – was a right rogues' gallery, with the likes of Keith Arthur in its ranks, although Keith preferred to call it "a team built on a foundation of youthful exuberance and worldly experience". Seriously,

they put a massive effort in to beat us – even going so far as to hire Essex ace Pete Vasey to coach them in the finer points of bloodworm fishing before the last round, on the Grand Union Canal at West Drayton – got their deserved reward, and almost went all the way in the competition, getting through to the final on the Trent where they finished an unlucky second.

Getting through an *Angling Times* Winter League semi-final was never easy, such was the strength of the opposition – and it got stronger every year. All told we fished 38 semi-finals, got through to the final 21 times – and ended up winning an unrivalled nine titles. But it took us a few attempts to win that first one.

Banstead's Geoff Hough, Darren Davies, Bob Clampitt, Jason Ahrens and John Smith get a lesson in bloodworm fishing from Pete Vasey ahead of the last round of the 1992/93 Surrey Winter League. (Dave Roberts)

I can't remember who we beat or where we fished to get through to our first final, on the Dolphin Meadow stretch of the Great Ouse at St Ives, in 1972 – they had 'regional eliminators' to decide finalists in those days – but I know we ultimately came third, behind Chester and Crawley. John Tullett was also third individually, with 8lb 6oz of skimmers on the waggler. Unfortunately for me I missed that final, as I was foolishly on holiday in Majorca at the time.

In 1973 we were up against Dartford and Linton in the regional eliminator, which was on the Beult, a tributary of the Medway, at Hunton. I remember that match well, for it was my 21st birthday, and I was second overall with 6lb 4oz of bleak, all caught on the waggler. More importantly, we won through as a team, Dorking weighing in 29lb 1oz to Dartford's 18lb 10½oz and Linton's 6lb 1oz. (Right up until 1991, Winter League semi-finals and finals alike were decided on total team weight.)

Individual 1972 Winter League final winner Norman Randles helped his Chester team to victory with this 27lb 5½oz bag caught legering with a butt indicator. (Image courtesy of Angling Times)

Bleak kept me busy on the waggler in the regional eliminator on the Beult on my 21st birthday in 1973. (Images courtesy of Angling Times)

The final that year was in Ireland, on the Blackwater at Fermoy in County Cork – *Angling Times* billed it as the 'Battle of the Blackwater' – but there was disappointment for a few people in each of the eight teams that got through when *Angling Times* decided that only nine anglers from each team could fish, not the usual 12. When I got there with Steve Sanders, just about the first thing we saw was a pipe from the hotel toilets emptying straight into the river, which otherwise looked lovely. Doug Gregory was Dorking captain for the second year running, the rest of the team being John Benham, Les Collins, Bob Evans, myself, Peter Knight, John Monk, Steve and John Tullett. I had another good day, chucking across to the main flow with a 'ducker' – a bodied waggler – to come third overall with just under 15lb of dace, but of the rest of the team only John Benham and Les drew on any numbers of fish and we slumped to fifth, Rotherham taking the title, with Johnny Lipscombe of fellow southern finalists and runners up Causton taking the individual title.

Johnny Lipscombe was only 24 when he won the Winter League final on the Blackwater with 20lb 9oz of roach and dace. (Image courtesy of Angling Times*)*

Rotherham's Mick Hartley with part of a 12lb 4oz catch that helped his team to victory in the 1973 Winter League final. (Image courtesy of Angling Times*)*

In the 1975 regional eliminator we squared up to Holmesdale and the overall 1974 Winter League champions Saints on the tiny River Lod, a tributary of the Western Rother, at Lickfold in West Sussex – and when I say tiny, I mean barely a rod length wide. This was the sort of venue – the Cole at Lechlade was another – that was right up John Benham's street, he loved the challenge of really small rivers like this where more often than not 5lb of small roach was a very good weight.

John was very good at winkling fish out of them, they suited his style, which was to be very methodical and precise, very careful with his feeding. I preferred bigger rivers myself, as they gave you more scope. Too often on those tiny rivers you caught a few fish for an hour, then that was it. But this was a team match, not an open, so it was the match that mattered, not the fishing, and it turned out to be a proper competition, not a dip, with gudgeon and little roach to be caught on pinkie or big maggot in almost every peg. Top weight was only a little over 3lb. John was captain by this time, and with him, Peter Knight – on his 40th birthday – Terry Wright and John Errett all finishing in the top six we won comfortably, totalling 14lb 13oz, more than twice what Holmesdale and Saints caught between them.

Wielding a fibreglass pole, Dorking pal 22-year-old Terry Wright plucks a roach from the Lod in February 1975 towards 2lb 10½oz and third place. (Image courtesy of Angling Times*)*

With the final at Coombe Abbey being only a few weeks later, on the last day of the river season in fact, there was precious little time to practise, and while we were second on the day we fell way short of Crawley on the peg next to us, with 26lb 8oz to their 44lb 7¼oz, Crawley providing the first three

The Dorking mob for the Lod semi. From left, at the front are Mike Bartlett, Peter Knight and John Benham, in the middle Mick Errett, me, Les Collins, Dave Roberts and Terry Wright, and at the back Doug Gregory, John Errett, Steve Sanders, Bob Evans, John Tullett, Peter Shepherd and George Harrison. (Image courtesy of Angling Times*)*

individuals to boot in Ken Sheath, Terry Sneyd and Jim Coles. Clive Smith's Cofton Hackett were pre-match favourites, but slumped to fifth. The lake was heavily coloured from rain, and towing like mad – my swingtip was stuck out almost straight, even with a stiff angled rubber, and a load of lead wire near the end ring – and it was a day when one bite, one fish, be it a skimmer, roach or bream, was a good return, but there weren't many blanks. I was drawn near the entrance, and I remember when I finally got a bite out of the blue and struck into a bream thinking, hooray, I've got one! It weighed 4lb 10oz and won me the section. But Crawley in those days fished a lot more still waters than we did, so they knew better on the whole how to fish the place on the day. We were basically a team of river anglers then.

Crawley's 19-year-old Ken Sheath took the honours at Coombe Abbey in March 1975 with 8lb 15oz (left), while my young Dorking pal Mick Errett had this bream in his 4lb 12¼oz bag (above). (Images courtesy of Angling Times*)*

That was the first of three Winter League finals at Coombe Abbey for Dorking, but the next wouldn't be until 1977, for in 1976 we blew out big time in the southern semi-final on the Wey. In the build-up to the match, *Angling Times* news editor Peter Maskell wrote, "Southern matchmen, being southern matchmen, never lack confidence in their own ability," and the paper then 'quoted' me as saying, "We will be at Coombe and we will win", which is something I would never have been so bold as to claim! On a cold and clear, chub or bust river, we came last of the 10 teams, while Crawley stormed to victory ahead of Dickie Carr's ABC rabble, who were next peg to us. All in all, it wasn't our finest hour.

The great Crawley side of the 1970s, seen here after their 1976 Winter League semi-final victory on the Wey. From left, at the front are Graham Self, Brian Coles, Bruce Barnett, Ray Valance and Ken Sheath, in the middle Derek Sneyd, Roy Steele and Terry Sneyd, and at the back Terry Harrison, Bob Whittle, Tony Spurdle, Don Garner, captain Stan Parsons and Nigel Self. (Image courtesy of Angling Times*)*

Alan Brown of ABC helped his team into second place with a 3 lb 5½ oz catch, which included this near 3 lb chub.

No wonder Alan Brown's smiling – he's on his way to the 1976 Winter League final at Coombe Abbey. Dorking managed a paltry team total of 2lb 2¾oz in the semi on the Wey. (Image courtesy of Angling Times*)*

The 1976, 1977 and 1978 Winter League finals at Coombe Abbey were all held early in the season, and each time the bream were more intent on spawning than feeding. Cofton Hackett won in 1976, but weren't there the following year, when Dorking got through after a tough semi-final on the Thames at Dorchester. On the day we drew next to Dick Clegg's Barnsley. I was next to Tommy Pickering, and we had liners all day. We each had two bream and a hybrid, but his fish were slightly bigger than mine and he weighed in 9lb 3¼oz to win the section while I weighed in 6lb for second. Barnsley won the title, Starlet Steve Webb was individual champion with a splendid 61lb 5oz of bream to over 6lb, and Dorking finished down in sixth.

In 1978 Peter Knight took over as Dorking captain, Kenny Collings joined the team, and it was third time lucky at Coombe Abbey for us as we

These two slabs helped Dorking's Peter Knight to 31lb 9oz and sixth place in the 1977 Winter League final. (Image courtesy of Angling Times)

were at last crowned Winter League champions for the first time. But it was our performance in the semi-final in February that year that epitomised what the Dorking team of the 1970s was all about. The match was switched from a flooded Medway to Brooklands Lake at Dartford, and on the day the water was partially frozen over. A real scratching job ensued. We didn't win – we were second to Dickie's lot, on weight, with Catpack, who included Bob Nudd in their ranks, third – but we were the only team without a blank. Our plan was to start close in on the pole (short fibreglass ones, remember), then move further out on the waggler and bomb until we found a fish – any fish. I had one bite for one skimmer weighing 7¼oz. Dorking weighed in only 12oz more than fourth-placed Greenwich 279 – only the first three teams qualified for the final – so every Dorking man contributed to the result that day, even though Kenny and Mark Richardson were the only two of us to break 1lb.

Most of us spent the close season practising feeding and casting at Old Bury Hill. This was in the days before groundbait feeders were widely used for bream fishing, and it takes a lot of practice to feed groundbait accurately and confidently at long range with a catapult and

Kenny Collings plays a slab on the swingtip on his way to 46lb 4¾oz and second place in the 1978 Winter League final. (Image courtesy of Angling Times)

then land your bomb on top of it – especially in the pressured situation of a big match, and especially with a swingtip dangling from the end of your rod! We also practised hard for four days solid at Coombe Abbey just before the final. Unfortunately for Johnny Mac he couldn't take the time off work to join us, and so was left out of the team on the day. Sadly he took it badly and left Dorking shortly after.

In a match where there were loads of double-figure weights – the nine teams weighed in 1,034lb 8¼oz, reckoned *Angling Times* (though I haven't checked that myself!) – Dorking came out on top with 169lb

6¾oz, ahead of Cofton Hackett on 151lb 15½oz. Cofton had the individual winner in Ken Giles, who had most of his 60lb 15½oz of bream on the waggler, while Kenny managed second for us. Sadly for long-time Dorking servants Peter Knight and John Benham they both blanked, but their winners' tankards that day were richly deserved reward for a decade of loyal and sterling service to the team. Along with the likes of Dave Roberts, Terry Wright, Mike Bartlett and Les Collins, both would shortly make way for such fresh blood as Terry Harrison, Lasher, John Waples, Andy Love and Gary Shotnik, and a new captain in the charismatic

Dorking's Bob Leadbetter had a good day at Coombe Abbey in the 1978 final. Sadly, he quit the sport altogether at the end of 1979 after a disastrous run at the draw bag shattered his confidence. (Image courtesy of Angling Times*)*

The victorious 1978 Dorking Winter League final squad. From left, at the front are Mike Bartlett, Steve Sanders, Peter Knight and Terry Wright, behind them Dave Taylor, Rob Mittens, Les Collins, Alan Wood, myself and Johnny Mac, then behind them Bob Leadbetter, Nick Aplin and someone I don't recognise (!), and at the back Kenny Collings, Keith Mills, John Benham, Dave Roberts and Mark Richardson. (Image courtesy of Angling Times*)*

and highly respected form of Kenny Collings would take Dorking to another level.

Under Kenny's leadership, Dorking joined the NFA so that we could fish the 1979 Division Four National, the aim being to see if we could not only gain promotion to Division One in just three seasons, but also win at least once along the way. Kenny was nothing if not ambitious! The 1979 match was on the Trent, where I'd fished my last National with CALPAC in 1976, and of that CALPAC team John Benham and Steve Sanders were the other two surviving Dorking lads now turning out for their club. I had a dream of a match personally, winning my section on the float and finishing seventh overall. I drew at Winthorpe, if I remember rightly. I'd never been there before, so I just fished my peg as I saw it and caught a few roach on the waggler then some chub on the stick closer in. But Dorking ended the day a disappointing third, and while

I had three medals to take home with me this time, this was the year the NFA switched from solid silver to cheaper silver-plated ones. Billy Knott's Cornish raiders Marazion won the match from downstream end peg, with Marazion's Geoff Salisbury winning the individual title at Holme Marsh, while Smithies from Barnsley were second. Among those promoted that day were 279 – Dave Roberts's new team – and Defiant Mobile, with 'the Dangerous Brothers' Mick and Dave Vincent in their ranks, so it wasn't a bad day for the South, although Isfield missed promotion by one place for the second year running.

Geoff Salisbury battles a chub on the end peg above the weir at Holme Marsh on his way to winning the 1979 Division Four National with 34lb 6oz. (Image courtesy of Angling Times)

The Division Three National the following August was on a horribly up and coloured Ancholme where 1lb scored mega-points in every section. Wisbech had three section winners, including Bryan Lakey, to win, leaving Billy Knott declaring himself "pig-sick" that Marazion could only manage second this time. As for us, we were fourth, so at least we got promotion, along with, again, Defiant Mobile and 279. Kenny had a cunning plan that we should each take a couple of bricks to our pegs to put in our keepnets to create a slack from which we might winkle out a few sprats. Andy Love had to walk something like 130 pegs with his bricks and all his gear to reach his peg, only to find a huge pile of bricks behind the peg when he got there. Then, when he threw his keepnet out complete with bricks, it landed with an almighty splash in only three inches of water! As for myself, what can I say? I fished for bits from the off, as per the team plan, but after three hours had only had two tinies, so when the bloke one side of me caught a slab on the tip I had to try for them. I caught four, on worm and caster, won my section for the second year running, and finished third overall – with less than 10lb.

It was around this time, following a short piece that ITV's *World of Sport* did on an 'All Stars' match at Weir Wood Reservoir in Sussex, I think, that the programme's presenter Dickie Davies famously described match anglers as looking like a bunch of pig farmers, which wasn't far off the mark,

Billy Knott (left) doesn't look too "pig-sick" as he collects the spoils from fellow bookie Jim Wooding after the 1980 Division Four National. (Image courtesy of Angling Times*)*

in truth, but Dorking under Kenny were one of a number of teams making an effort to smarten up their appearance. In January 1981 our 'manager', the ever enterprising Dave Bird, managed to secure us a bit of sponsorship from Dartex, the waterproof clothing manufacturer. Part of the deal involved me going up to Nottingham to meet up with Dick Clegg, Tommy Pickering and Denis White for a photo shoot for a Calverton Sports Calendar with a topless 'mermaid', a charming young lady from Leeds called Sue Key. I remember thinking, if that's all she's got on in January, what's she going to be wearing come December? It's a hard life being a sponsored angler sometimes, but someone has to do it...

When Bob Cheeseman from the Essex team enquired in the Angling Times *letters page whether our wives minded us featuring in this calendar, Jeanette wrote straight back saying how proud she was! (Image courtesy of* Angling Times*)*

In the main, 1981 was a very good year for Dorking. In the southern semi-final of the Winter League, on a dire Bristol Avon at Newbridge, we qualified for the final on the River Skjern in Denmark by finishing second to Isfield, despite having seven blanks, including me. We'd missed out on the previous year's final on the Skjern, and were all chomping at the bit to get there this time, as the venue was basically a bagging river for dace and roach and so looked to be right up our street, given our experience on the tidal Thames. And although only 12 anglers could fish the actual match, we were determined that everyone should be involved and make the trip, so we had a whip round to cover the extra cost of the whole squad making the journey. We also badly wanted to win for the sake of young team mates Kevin Zanocelli and David Taylor, who had helped us get to the semi before tragically being killed just a few months earlier.

The Skjern is a fast-flowing but shallow river, and in practice we found that feeding hemp and caster in groundbait at the start, then loosefeeding heavily with bronze maggots for the rest of the match, helped hold the fish in front of you. Even so, the water was so fast and so shallow – about 4ft deep – that the maggots didn't reach the bottom until the next peg down, and the vast shoals drifted in and out of your peg all the time and took some pinning down. We found it was important to catch as many fish as you could, as quickly as you could, early on, as in most pegs there came a point when the fish said, "Enough's enough", and moved off. When that happened it was a case of searching for the odd fish on the far side of the river with a bouncing bomb – so you went from bagging one minute to scratching the next.

The previous year the weights had been lower than expected, and the consensus afterwards was that the anglers themselves had been largely to blame for charging along the bank in their eagerness to get to their pegs, so this time the teams all agreed to stay behind the

Rob Mittens about to weigh in, and Steve Sanders on his way to 35lb 12oz and fourth, at the Winter League final in 1981. (Images courtesy of Angling Times*)*

high flood-bank on their way to their sections and then approach their pegs carefully. As match anglers we're all guilty sometimes of ignoring basic watercraft. The final was a six-hour match, and come the end of it Dorking put 266lb 8oz on the scales to top the six-team field and finish more than 50lb ahead of our nearest rivals, Leeds. Rob Mittens led the way for Dorking, winning the individual title with exactly 59lb of roach to 12oz and dace to 6oz fishing a home-made porcupine quill and balsa Avon – and using a fibreglass rod! – while Steve Sanders, myself and Terry Harrison all finished in the top 10. It was a fabulous final, one in which no one blanked – in fact, most anglers had double figures. And the venue fished even better the following year, when Oundle came out on top. In fact, every team in the 1982 final weighed in more than we did in 1981 – it's just a shame that Dorking didn't qualify for it!

On my way to 28lb 10oz, sixth place and a section win on the Skjern in 1981. I fished a 4AAA balsa, bulk-shotted to catch fish feeding on my upstream neighbour's loosefeed at the head of my swim as well as fish further down my peg. (Image courtesy of Angling Times*)*

All hands on deck – the Dorking squad returns home from the 1981 Winter League final with the spoils. From left, at the front are Keith Mills, Geoff Vallance, Terry Harrison, Rob Mittens, Steve Sanders and John Waples, in the middle John Larraman, Kenny Collings, myself, Dave Blanks, Nick Aplin and Andy Love, and at the back Mark Richardson, Pat Currie, Alan Wood and Dave Taylor. (Image courtesy of Angling Times*)*

After the 1981 Winter League final, Kenny was quoted in *Angling Times* as saying that Dorking would become the first southern team to win a Division One National. As it was, Essex achieved that feat later that year when they won on the Ancholme. Meanwhile we still had to get out of Division Two, and any hopes we had of that were dashed when we slumped to 38th place on the Leeds-Liverpool Canal. To make matters worse, Marazion one side of us came fourth, so they achieved what we failed to do – to climb from Division Four to Division One in successive seasons. On the other hand, Norwich on the other side of us were relegated, so you could say we got it half right on a day when Defiant Mobile and 279 also finished down the field.

When we went up to fish a 350-peg practice open on the venue, we were amazed how clear the water was. The bottom was strewn with rubbish as well as weed, and when the fish swam over a white plastic bag it was like looking into an aquarium. It was said that you could read a newspaper lying on the bottom, the water was that clear. In those days the canal was famously full of dark little tench, but there was a good head of roach to 1lb or more too. I reckon around three-quarters of the field in that open weighed in at least one tench. Alan McAtee won the match with nearly 20lb, and afterwards some of us went to look at his peg, but it looked no different from any other. We were all well impressed with the venue, despite the long drive to get there – and back! Sadly the canal declined drastically in subsequent years.

The evening before the National – which Southport won, ahead of two other local outfits, Rochdale Newtown and Liverpool – two barges were allowed through the match length to stir things up a bit, but the water was still painfully clear. With hindsight we should have fished to our strengths and used little wagglers – like the individual winner, Luton's Dave Sayce, did – especially as there was no movement on the water that day, but we tried to take on the locals at their own game and fished 10m poles. This was around the time of the first carbon poles, and some of the team had to 'beg, steal or borrow' one just for this match. In those days there were still basically only three grades of pole elastic – 'light', 'medium' and 'heavy', all solid of course – and the 'heavy' one was only about a number six. Anyway, I had a bit of fun on the day, catching three little tench, a couple of roach, a perch and some eels on caster for around 4lb, but I lost a couple of 2lb tench in the weed as well. It was 'hook and hold', but they were straight in there.

In 1981 for the first time Dorking entered match fishing's equivalent of the FA Cup, the Captain Morgan Cup, which had started life as the East Anglian Cup in 1978. The competition was notorious for stroke-pulling, like the time in 1981 when minnows Kings Arms drew at home to mighty Essex and took them to the infamous Heartbreak Pit, a big-tench or bust water, hoping for a giant-killing. Essex swamped their pegs with sweetcorn to try to fill the tench up and stop any being caught, but one tench for Kings Arms off their end peg saw them through to the next round. We were luckier when we drew Cove AS away and they sportingly took us to a bagging water, their lake at Theale, to ensure

Dave Sayce not only won the individual title in the Division Two National in 1981 with this 16lb 15oz bag of tench and roach, he gained promotion with Luton too. (Image courtesy of Angling Times*)*

a good match for everyone, even though they knew we were pretty much bound to beat them. Thanks to advice from Billy Makin we beat Birmingham away on the Staffs-Worcester Canal, then valuable advice from Wayne Swinscoe, Bob Stevens and Rex Camp helped us beat Robin Harris's Peterborough in our semi-final on the Trent at Shardlow. We were through to the final against Leeds on the roach-filled Bann at Portadown in Northern Ireland that October – *Angling Times* billed it as the 'Battle of the Bann' – but then I had a problem. I'd already used up all my annual holiday for that year fishing abroad and practising at home, and had to ask Jan, my boss, for an extra three days off at very short notice. Luckily he was obliging, but other anglers with full-time jobs in those days of high unemployment weren't so fortunate, I know. Indeed, after his triumph in the Winter League final we lost Rob Mittens, because he simply couldn't take the necessary time off from his job as the manager of an off-licence for serious team fishing any more.

In the final on the Bann most of the Dorking team fished 6–7m to hand with crunching gear – size 12 hooks and 3lb hooklengths – over an initial bombardment of groundbait, while Leeds, led by Jim Jordan, fed more cautiously and chopped and changed between pole and waggler. We would have done the same had it not been for local expat Pete Ottewill, the Croydon match angler who had moved to Sligo to run a guest house. In practice the day before on another stretch the roach wouldn't stay on the pole line, but he insisted that the Hoy's Meadow match length would be different – and how right he was. Every Leeds man had 40lb-plus of roach, but every Dorking man managed 50lb-plus

With the Captain Morgan Cup in 1981. From left, at the front are Geoff Vallance, John Waples, Steve Sanders, Keith Mills, Kenny Collings and myself, at the back John Larraman, Stewart Beresford, Gary Shotnik, Mark Richardson, Alan Wood, Andy Love, Terry Harrison and Nick Aplin. (Image courtesy of Angler's Mail*)*

to give us a comfortable win. I was lucky enough to pip captain Kenny by a mere 1½oz with 103lb 3¾oz of roach up to 1½lb for top weight – tremendous fishing – despite the bank giving way from underneath me at the start. I went straight down, feet first, and was clinging on for dear life when luckily Pete and bank runner Mark Richardson came along and hauled me out. All they could see of me was the top of my head! I was only wet up to my waist, so that wasn't too bad. I finished the match with a headache, not to mention arm ache, but my woes were as nothing compared with Kenny's, as Kenny somehow managed to stick at it despite having a migraine that left him almost unable to see his float. ITV covered the match for *World of Sport* but luckily missed filming me falling in.

One of these days I really must learn to swim, because I seem to have made a habit of falling in. One February in the 1990s – I forget the year – we were practising on the Cam for a Winter League semi-final on a day when the banks were swarming with university students cheering on hordes of rowing eights. I had lain my pole parallel to the water's edge to keep it from being trodden on when a gust of wind swung it around over the water. Just as I knelt down to retrieve it, the bank gave way and in I went, head first, breaking three pole sections in the process. Will and Richard Taylor were nearest to me and I remember saying to them, "Don't you dare laugh!", but of course they couldn't contain themselves. I had some spare clothes in the car, but to get there I had to walk past all these students looking like the proverbial drowned rat, frozen to the bone and feeling a right prat!

To return to the 1980s… In 1982 our Division Two National was on the Bristol Avon and while, once again, we failed to win, we at least gained promotion in fourth, behind local team Swindon, Defiant Mobile and 279, with Terry Harrison winning his section and nearly everyone else chipping in with solid scores. In fact it was a clean sweep of the top six places for southern teams, with Bathampton in fifth and Keith Arthur's Herts Fed in sixth. So in the end it was a dead heat between Dorking, 279 and Defiant Mobile for second place behind Marazion in our own little 'race' to get from Division Four to Division One in the shortest possible time.

It's at this point, with the team having arrived in Division One, that the story of Dorking in Nationals stalls, really, for amazingly it would not be until 2007 that we won our first National – and that was the Division Two

This barbel got Kim Milsom's Swindon Isis team mate Trevor Eckersall good points in the 1982 Division Two National, but his team fell well short of local winners and rivals Swindon, coming 29th. (Image courtesy of Angling Times)

event! To cut a long story short, what happened was basically this. After Kenny left in 1983, and under the captaincy of first Andy Love then Steve Champion and Steve Sanders, rightly or wrongly we prioritised other competitions, especially once we started fishing the Drennan Super League in the early 1990s, as that competition alone – six rounds plus six practice matches – took up more or less the whole summer. Then when the Super League finished each autumn our attention would turn to the Winter League. The Nationals were usually on venues so far away from the South that it was hard to justify the expense of practising for them properly, let alone find the time to do so. The exceptions were the Thames Nationals in 1988 and 1998, which we did practise for, the Thames being our home water, and we came sixth in both of those.

But even without practising properly, if at all, we had a number of top 10 placings over the years out of some pretty big fields, often of more than 80 teams – as well as a few blow-outs, admittedly, specifically 1983, when we were 54th on the upper Trent, 1985, when we were 29th on the Leeds-Liverpool Canal, 1996, when we were 65th on the Witham, and 1997, when we were 43rd on the Yorkshire canals. But we were sixth on the Nene in 1984, when the individual winner came from the same area I drew in 1975, and we were third on the Trent in 1987 – a match that Andy Love was probably right in saying we should have won, given that we drew end peg – the day before Durking won the Thames Championship for the first time ever.

Radcot's Trevor Bradley on the way to winning his section in the 1998 Division One National with some 20lb of bream from the famous groyne swim at Clifton Hampden. (Image courtesy of Angling Times*)*

Dorking's Simon Wheeler on his way to second in his section on the Thames in 1998 with over 20lb. (Image courtesy of Angling Times)

Unfortunately I missed that weekend, being away with the England team at the World Championship. (I missed quite a few Nationals over the years because they clashed with World Championships – three in the 1990s alone.) We were also ninth on the Severn in 1989, 10th on the Leeds-Liverpool Canal in 1993 and seventh on the Gloucester Canal in 1995.

In all these Nationals and others we generally just turned up on the day and gave it our best shot – frequently, some of our anglers would never have even seen the venue before, never mind fished it. And of course that's no way, really, to win, when you're up against good teams who do put the necessary practice in, no matter how talented your anglers are – and the Dorking team has got stronger and stronger over the years, as our record in Winter League and Super League finals clearly shows. We also had a bit of individual success along the way. I was eighth overall in 1983, on the upper Trent, after drawing a nice-looking peg and catching lots of little chub on the waggler, while Steve Sanders won his section and was sixth overall in 1984 and Will Raison won his section in 1995.

One National Steve won't forget in a hurry was the 1989 match on the Severn. We drew next to Isfield, and down on the Winnalls stretch all Steve could hear all day was splashing from Brian Wickens's peg next door. Steve put a creditable 6lb-odd on the scales for high section points, while Brian walked the match with 87lb 15¾oz of bream, a record weight at the time. Still, we beat Isfield that day – they were 28th. Champions on the day were Reading, who beat Barnsley by just six points, though Reading skipper Mick Craig was quoted as saying afterwards that the real satisfaction came from beating Dorking as we had their old captain, Robin Morley, in our ranks!

Things came to a head in 2000, when the Division One National was yet again on the Leeds-Liverpool Canal, which for a long time had been but a shadow of the venue it was back in 1981. We'd paid our pools and entry fee, but of the 12 anglers originally nominated, six simply didn't think it was worth the effort and expense of going when 'sport' for the vast majority of anglers taking part was guaranteed to be dire in the extreme. You were only allowed to make four team

All smiles as Billy Knott junior pays out Brian Wickens after the 1989 Division One National on the Severn. (Image courtesy of Angler's Mail*)*

changes, so if we *had* gone we'd have fished two men short anyway. So that was that, and Dorking didn't fish another National after 1999 until 2006. It was the same for many other clubs and match groups around this time, when the whole Nationals set-up was in decline. In truth, the glory days of the Nationals were long gone by 2000.

But then in 2006 the NFA made it much cheaper to fish a National – before, you had to belong to the NFA as a club, but now you could join as a team – so the Dorking team joined the NFA, starting again in the lowest of the three Divisions remaining at the time. National teams were now down from 12 to 10 anglers, though. Without my help – I was away again on England duty – Dorking came second on the Basingstoke Canal, a rare local venue where the team could put the necessary practice in. The following year, again with me away with England, Dorking anglers finally got their hands on winners' medals, in the Division Two National on the Fossdyke and Chesterfield Canals, Paul Holland winning his section and finishing third overall. I was away again with England on Dorking's return to the top flight in the Division One National on the Huntspill and Somerset drains in 2008, when the team finished a creditable fourth. In fact the first National I got to fish after 1999 was the 2010 Division One match on the Trent. But it was the two years after that when Dorking finally made their mark on Division One National history.

I'll come to that later, but first I want to take you back again to the 1980s, and the success we enjoyed in other competitions under the captaincy of Andy Love. Formerly the bass player in a 1960s band, The Pop Workshop – they released two singles, 'Fairyland' in 1968 and 'The Punch and Judy Man' in 1969 – Andy concentrated on match fishing in the 1970s, rapidly establishing himself as one of the top men in the South. Music's loss was undoubtedly Dorking's gain. In his highly amusing but always insightful monthly articles in David Hall's *Match Fishing* magazine, he was modest to a fault about his own contribution to our success, saying things like, "All I do is fill in the team sheet," but he did a hell of a lot more than that, and besides being a fine angler in his own right he had the great skill of being able to recruit new anglers while keeping existing squad members happy, even those not picked for the team. Andy never thought twice about dropping himself and running the bank if he reckoned someone else could do a better job than him. He commanded great respect and all of us who fished under him owe him a great deal.

Under Andy's command, Dorking got through to five Winter League finals, won four of them, and were second in the other – a phenomenal achievement on his part. Fishing-wise the final at Attenborough Lakes in June 1986 was a bit of a disaster. Everyone was expecting bumper nets of bream – everyone except Dorking, that is. When we walked around the lakes the day before, the bream were all thrashing around on the surface getting ready to spawn, so we knew it was going to be hard, and unlike most of the other teams we had a plan B, which was to switch to scratching on the float if the bream hadn't shown after a couple of hours. It turned out

Dorking celebrate winning the 1986 Winter League final. From left, at the front are Terry Harrison, Paul 'Tommy' Hiller, Dave Hurry, John Merritt, John Larraman, myself and Mark Richardson, at the back Steve Sanders, Andy Rogers, Andy Love, Tony Ruddle (MD of sponsors Ruddles), Lennie Goodwin, Gary Shotnik, Mark Gillard, Paul Greest and Stewart Beresford. (Dave Roberts)

even harder than we expected, and there were loads of blanks, me included. The night before the match, Lasher was sharing a room with Lennie Goodwin, whose snoring kept him awake, so at the crack of dawn Lasher went down to the lakes for a look and saw small shoals of roach on the surface in one area. As chance had it, he drew the same area in the match, fished up in the water with a waggler and caught 6lb 14oz of roach, skimmers and perch to win the individual title. With John Merritt, Andy Love, Terry Harrison, Mark Richardson, Andy Rogers and Gary Shotnik also weighing in, Dorking nearly doubled Oundle's second-placed weight with the grand total of 14lb 4¾oz. Afterwards, Shakespeare team captain Ken Giles – ever the gentleman – was quoted in *Angling Times* as saying that Dorking had won "with dignity and style"!

In 1987 we were second to the Trentman team in the Winter League final on the Warwickshire Avon at Twyford Farm, but by way of compensation we had the satisfaction of beating Barnsley, Keenets Swindon and Doncaster in the final of the Tuborg Cup (formerly the Captain Morgan Cup) on tranquil and beautiful Bygholm (Horsens) Lake, a skimmer venue, in Denmark. Barnsley had anglers over there practising beforehand, but we kept our powder dry. Essex had won there the year before, and Dennis Salmon had put us on to the Denmark team manager, Reyne Boon, who told us that while in practice you could catch close in on the waggler and pole, the lake was so shallow that as soon as the whistle went for the start of a match and everyone started feeding, the fish would back right off and could only be caught 70–90 yards out on the feeder or bomb. Dennis himself provided us with a detailed map of the venue showing not only the weights taken from each peg, but the distances out the fish were caught. Armed with all this information, we decided to do all our practising at home in the close season. Dennis suggested fishing the bomb, but Lasher was insistent we should at least start with Emmstat frame feeders. Designed by Edenbridge's Micky Emm and Ken Staton specifically for shallow lakes, these nose-weighted devices had streamlined hollow triangular frames that allowed you to mould fluffy groundbait around them without having to squeeze it on too hard, then cast them many a mile, the groundbait bursting into a cloud on impact with the water.

Down at Old Bury Hill, the team regularly practised casting frame feeders and bombs accurately at 90 yards and feeding with a groundbait catapult at the same range. Both take some doing, and though casting miles came easily to the likes of Lasher and Dave Hurry – Lasher favouring what was virtually a pendulum cast – most of the team found both long-range casting and catapulting far from easy.

One summer in the early 1970s Steve Sanders, Carole, Jeanette and I had a weekend in Bournemouth and fished the Hampshire Avon, where I had this chub.

My 'mentor', John Benham, practising for an Angling Times *Winter League final at Coombe Abbey Lake sometime in the 1970s. (Dave Roberts)*

*My dearest friend, Nick Aplin, who died in 1983 aged only 31. We grew up
together and had some great times together, and that's what I'll always remember.
(Dave Roberts)*

My old mate Kenny Collings, always laughing and joking, a very fine angler, and a great captain who took Dorking to Division One and Winter League final glory. (Dave Roberts)

Another old pal, Johnny Mac – 'The King' – seen here with his winning 15lb 10½oz bag from Laleham in the 1985 Lower Thames Championship. (Dave Roberts)

Jeanette and I on our wedding day, Saturday 17ᵗʰ July 1976. Forty years on, we're still happily married, with two children and six grandchildren.

*Taking it easy at beautiful Hever Castle Lake in Kent sometime in the 1980s.
Matches were always sell-outs there, with some good weights of bream and skimmers.
(Dave Roberts)*

*Getting to grips with the pole on the Rother in the mid-1980s. Terry Freeman
of Browning, who sponsored me for reels back then, kindly gave me this Spiral
Titanium. (Dave Roberts)*

Setting up a waggler rig on the Damme Canal in Belgium at the 1988 World Championship. This is when the butterflies start – but the nerves quickly settle once you begin fishing.

February 1991 was a good month! This is just part of my 42lb 9oz winning bag of roach in the Angling Times *Winter League semi-final on the Nene that month.*

*At Evesham with a small barbel that gave me a bit of fun on light pole tackle aimed
at roach, and gave the spectators a bit of a show. (Bob Taylor)*

Yes, Mark, we've won! With Mark Downes at the end of the 2001 World Championship in Paris. One of the greatest days of my life.
(Image courtesy of Angling Times*)*

Jean Desqué of France during the 2001 World Championship on the Seine. A great angler, a good friend, and a class act, always modest in victory and gracious in defeat. (Dave Roberts)

Will Raison plays a big eel at the 2001 World Championship in Paris. Will has the most natural ability of any angler I've ever seen. (Image courtesy of Angling Times*)*

This view from one of the bridges shows how close together and how high off the water we all were in the 2001 World Championship on the Seine. (Dave Roberts)

Netting a fish in the Angling Times *Winter League final on the Nene in 2004. Starlets won that year, but Dorking won the final there in 2006 and 2008. (Alain Urruty)*

With my old mucker Milo on the banks of the Spinadesco Canal at the 2008 World Championship. (Milo Colombo)

Steve Collins of Banstead fishing the pole, with Mal Fisher and his wife Megan in the foreground, on Lake Mead in practice one year for the Fort Myers fishing festival.

My good friend Steve O'Rourke with a redfish and me with a snook caught on lures from the shore at Fort Myers beach in Florida. (Liz O'Rourke)

At Evesham with my son James in the 1990s.

My granddaughter Alicia and my grandson Henry are both budding anglers. Young Henry had this mullet on holiday in Majorca, hooking and landing it all on his own.

With my daughter Victoria at the 2004 World Championship at Willebroek in Belgium, when she paid me a surprise visit! (Brian Gay)

Andy Love made himself a catty with a forearm grip, and got Dave to take him down to a local football pitch for practice sessions. Standing in one goal mouth, they took aim at the other, and according to Andy the place was soon overrun by rats!

All the practice paid off in the final, when Terry Harrison drew peg one for us. With Barnsley on peg four – their team looked like a 'who's who' of bream fishing, with the likes of Dick Clegg, Tommy Pickering, Denis White and Ivan Marks all fishing – all was set for a close battle. We took an early lead, then Barnsley clawed us back. Andy's peg began to fade, so he switched from feeder to bomb and started catching again. Lennie, our bank runner, soon spread the word, and we edged ahead for a narrow win. Andy Love rated it one of our best ever performances.

We practised four times on the Glen near Spalding for our Winter League semi-final in 1988, despite the long haul from Dorking to Lincolnshire and back, because we knew the venue for the final in June, Roy Marlow's carp- and skimmer-filled Mallory Park lakes, would suit us well. That was one final we could not afford to miss. Lady Luck smiled on Andy Love in the semi. Struggling for fish – the venue had taken too much stick from teams practising on it – he scaled down to a fine-wire 24 on an 8oz hooklength on his whip, the float buried and he lifted into what he thought was the bottom. The 'bottom' turned out to be a 5lb 10oz bream! At the end of the day we snatched the fourth and last qualifying place by a mere 10oz.

Netting a rare bonus fish in the 1988 Winter League semi-final on the Glen, where we just scraped through. (Dave Roberts)

The finalists weren't allowed to practise at Mallory in the close season, but Roy couldn't have been more helpful, giving us a detailed tour of the venue, explaining what was to be caught and how, not just in the different lakes but in each and every peg – I think he would have given us the names of the fish if he could! Roy advised us to feed hemp and caster, but we decided to stick with what we knew and feed heavily with maggots. The four favourites for the match were Barnsley, Oundle, ourselves and Shakespeare, and between us we drew pegs one to four in that order. Going into the last hour all four teams were in contention, and at the weigh-in no one knew who had won. For a while, all we knew for sure was that our man Stewart Beresford had taken the individual title with 43lb 13oz of carp on the waggler, nearly double the next best weight on 'the Concrete Bowl' lake. The team

results took a while to be totted up, so we had a few pints of Ruddles, the sponsors' beer, then finally it was confirmed that we had won with 149lb 3¼oz to Oundle's 126lb 13¾oz. That made it four Winter League titles for Dorking, equalling Cofton Hackett's record, their four victories having come in 1966, 1968, 1971 and 1976.

Winning the Winter League final in 1988 was just reward for the quiet and unassuming Stewart Beresford, a team mate throughout the 1980s. (Dave Roberts)

The squad after the 1988 Winter League final. From left, at the front are Terry Harrison, Dave Hurry, Steve Sanders, Lennie Goodwin, myself and Lasher, at the back Mark Richardson, Gary Shotnik, Robin Morley, Andy Love, Stewart Beresford, Mark Gillard, Chris James, John Merritt, a friend of John's, and Tony West. (Dave Roberts)

A year later we were back at a wind-lashed Mallory Park for an even more emphatic, record-breaking fifth victory, myself, Lasher, Lennie, Stewart and Dave Hurry all winning our sections as we beat Trev's Browning into second place with 152lb 11oz to their 114lb 15¾oz. Trev's had the individual winner in Pete Vasey, then we had the next three top individuals in Lasher – who only narrowly missed out on a second individual crown – John Merritt and Dave Hurry. It was a Dorking rout! Again, though, we weren't sure at any point in the match that we were actually winning, due to what Andy Love called 'the Dorking Lie Factor' – the tendency of every Dorking angler to underestimate his weight. After everyone had weighed in, we thought we might have done enough, but not until the results were confirmed did we know for sure. Ken Giles, who had fished for the great Cofton Hackett team whose record we had beaten, was one of the first to congratulate Andy, something Andy said he would always treasure.

We missed the chance of a hat trick of Winter League titles when we failed to reach the final in 1990, a year when Barnsley also beat us in the Scandinavian Seaways final on the picturesque River Storan near Vrigstad in Sweden in June. In fact we were last of the four teams on the Storan, the other finalists being Reading and Masterline Matchmen, while for Barnsley it was their third successive victory in the competition. I went over on the ferry with Lasher and Andy Love for a practice, and we would have stayed out there, but the sponsors understandably wanted all the teams to set sail from England together, so we had to come all the way home again, then go all the way back just a couple of days later! On the way over, Dick Clegg craftily accepted a £10 bet from Andy and Lennie that Dave Bird would get an MBE before he did, not letting on that he already knew

John Merritt was third overall in the 1989 Winter League final with this 20lb 12½oz bag of small carp caught on 'wag and mag' from 'the Lake in the Trees'. (Image courtesy of **Angling Times***)*

he was getting the gong! Anyway, in practice the river had been solid with bleak – we couldn't get through them to the skimmers below even with 8g rigs – but in the match itself the bleak didn't show and the barrage of groundbait that went in at the start seemed to drive all the fish downstream and out of the match length. Denis White duly bagged up on downstream end peg while most of the rest of us struggled. After all that travelling back and forth, I caught a staggering 3½oz! Mind you, Dick blanked.

That year, 1990, was also when Dorking finally signed a major sponsorship deal, with tackle manufacturer D.A.M., long after most other top teams had done the same. Keith Arthur called us 'Team Cockroach' after seeing our striking red and black outfits, and Pat Byrne, the head of D.A.M., must have wondered what he'd let himself in for when he approached Andy at his peg at Holme Pierrepont during the European Supercup to introduce himself, and Andy, not realising who he was, turned around and said, "Do us a favour, mate, and stay behind the bleedin' ropes." But later that year we repaid Pat's faith in us when we beat no fewer than 90 other teams of 12 to win the Thames Championship for the second time – a 1,092-pegger, from Lechlade to Medley – which was as good as winning a National in my book.

We did D.A.M. proud in 1991 too, in the Winter League, and the semi-final in February that year on the Nene above Peterborough is certainly one I'll never forget. The weather in the run-up was terrible and the fishing rubbish. With two weeks to go the river was frozen over. It thawed out with a few days to go, but we still thought we were in for a struggle and planned to feed very sparingly. For the first time the team result was to be decided on section points, not total weight, so it was vital not to rely on one or two weights but to have as many good section scores as possible. My draw put me on permanent peg 408 at Orton, in an area where people had been bagging up the previous few days, and straight away my old mate Kevin Wilmot of *Angling Times* and the organising Peterborough & District AA said I'd have 40lb and win the match, but I thought, yeah, right, we'll see, let's just get that first bite and take it from there. How often do we hear these things at the draw? You're always best advised to take them with a pinch of salt. And when I saw my peg there was nothing to make me get excited, it looked like every other peg around it, being on a long, barren straight – the sort of peg you'd walk right past as likely as not. Besides, there was every chance the fish had taken too much of a hammering and would shut up shop.

Believe it or not, the long pole didn't even feature in our team plan, which was to scratch with waggler, stick and straight lead, but looking at the water in front of me as I sat on my box I decided to set one up, because it was definitely pulling a bit. Plumbing up I found the bottom of the slope in around 10ft of water some 9m out, so that seemed a good bet. Besides, the lads either side of me hadn't got their poles out, so it looked like I'd have that line all to myself. I rummaged in my box for a suitable rig, found one with a 2g, round-bodied, wire-stemmed float – a Milo pattern, of course! – and thought, that looks just right. There was a bit of an upstream facing wind that might have stopped anything lighter going through properly.

The rig had been in my box unused for a while, I must confess, so to be safe I ripped off whatever hooklength was on there and put a fresh one on, a light one to a fine-wire 20. I had the rig on a fairly long line, with a couple of metres between the float and pole tip, so I could run it through on a straight course. I set the Olivette about 2½ft from the hook and spread out the six no.10 droppers in between. I was happy with the set-up, and thought I had every chance of catching a few if I took it nice and steady from the start and just trickled in the feed. It helped my confidence that we had some of the best bronze maggots I'd ever seen, really big, fresh, lively ones. I've got Lol Higgins to thank for that.

When the whistle went for the start I fed a pinch of hemp and the same of maggots, dropped in with a single maggot and began looking for that all-important first bite. I didn't have long to wait, as the float buried immediately and I netted a 3oz roach. As it turned out, that was the smallest fish I had all day. I went out again, the float buried once more and this time I had a chunky 6oz roach. It quickly became obvious that I was on a shedful – Steve Champion was running the bank for us, and he reckoned I put something like 6lb in the net in the first 20 minutes – but I didn't go mad with the feed, I took it steady, and I stuck to single maggot on

Another roach comes to the net for me in the Winter League semi-final on the Nene in 1991. Any one of the Dorking team would have won off that peg that day – I just happened to be the one lucky enough to draw it.

the hook. The lads either side of me soon had their poles out too, but by then I was way out in front, and no way was I going to be caught! I had a spell of lost fish about halfway through, so I changed up to an 18, which cured the problem. I bagged steadily for four hours, then inevitably, I suppose, things slowed down in the last hour as the shoal thinned out, and then it was a case of just keeping the odd fish going in the keepnet.

At the end I put 42lb 9oz on the scales, all roach bar a couple of skimmers, to more than double Mervyn 'Topper' Haskins's second-placed weight, and my day was made complete by Dorking winning the match too – the first time we'd actually won a semi-final, surprisingly – though the river fished patchily and there were the usual dire bits where everyone struggled for a bite. Poor Dave White suffered a blank from a no-hoper, but such was our strength in depth that it didn't matter. And Kevin had been spot-on before the match after all. I had drawn THE peg to have on the day, so you can't get any luckier than that, but having drawn it the key thing was that I didn't bust it by getting carried away and overfeeding. That's all too easy to do with river roach – one minute you're bagging, the next they're gone, and you realise too late that you've gone and overdone it.

The final in July that year was at John Raison's Willow Park lakes near Aldershot, a cracking mixed fishery in those days, and being a local venue it favoured us massively. All the Dorking lads were regulars there – it offered great sport in summer for all sorts, but crucians and tench especially, and also in winter for roach. In fact, when Steve Sanders took over from Kenny in the tackle shop in Sutton a few years later, John Raison generously hired Kenny and me to manage the fishery for him, and so for 10 years or so I divided my time between Willow Park and the shop.

Being expected to win at Willow Park in 1991 brought its own pressure, but we were determined not to fail and most of us practised hard there that spring. Some of those who didn't practise enough didn't make the team. That's how it was with Andy as captain, he was always scrupulously fair, and everyone in the squad knew where they stood. Anyway, we all went to our pegs on the day with a very good idea of how to fish them. Our main attack was caster and pole for the crucians, tench, roach and perch, but plan B was to try for bonus carp if we were struggling. I was lucky enough to finish second overall behind Oundle's Chris Cooper, and with good scores from Andy Love, John Merritt, Terry Harrison and Dave White – making up for his semi-final disappointment – we romped home ahead of Mark Downes's Starlets side. But it was the one and only Robin Morley who stole the show that day.

The closest I ever came to winning a Winter League final – 34lb 7oz of crucians, tench and roach in 1991, a couple of pounds short of Chris Cooper's total.

Robin was really struggling to catch much of anything – he'd had just one tench, in fact, from his only bite, on the pole – so with nothing to lose he started feeding floating dog biscuits over his feeder line and sure enough a few carp began swirling for them, attracting quite a crowd of spectators to his peg. He knew he couldn't afford to spend too long trying it, but out went a controller float with a dog biscuit attached to a size 8 hook to 4lb line – heavy gear in those days! – and all of a sudden a big carp wolfed it down and tore off across the lake to Robin's right. Unfortunately, when it ploughed through Starlet Steve Ashmore's peg it gave Steve an almighty liner on the feeder. Steve instinctively grabbed his rod and struck, and the fish was gone. To rub salt into the wound, the Team Tubertini guy to Robin's left nonchalantly tore a piece of crust off one of his sandwiches, cast it out and took a carp off the top straight away. Robin tried again, but typically the carp on the surface were taking every biscuit except the one with the hook attached, so he went back on the feeder to lull the fish into a false sense of security. All the time the crowd behind him – a couple of hundred strong by this point – were urging him to have another go with the floating bait, but Robin stayed ice-cool. Not until there were only 30 minutes left did he pick up his controller rig again. The ruse worked, another big carp took, and this time Robin piled on the pressure to show the fish who was boss. Only six minutes after hooking it – a spectator timed him – Robin was netting a near-20lb carp, a fish that propelled him at a stroke from last to first in his section.

The 1990s was a decade of major change for match fishing, the close season on still waters being abolished in 1995 and anglers then turning from natural to commercial venues, from silvers to carp, in their droves. The decade was also a time of great change for Dorking. Andy Love packed in fishing altogether at the end of the 1991/92 season to concentrate on a new business venture, and would not return to the scene for another three years. Steve Champion, who Andy had recruited from Banstead in 1990,

Who else but Robin Morley would have had the nerve to fish floating dog biscuits in a major final? This stunning 19lb 3oz common was his reward. (Image courtesy of Angling Times*)*

captained Dorking for a while until Steve Sanders assumed the role of team captain long term. It was around the same time, in 1992 to be exact, that Will Raison made his debut for the team aged 17. We were down on the Wallers at Boreham Street for a round of the Drennan Super League that summer, and for some reason Stewart Beresford hadn't been told he was fishing, so we found ourselves a man short when we got there. Will had only come along to run the bank and generally watch and learn, but we scraped some bits and pieces together for him and, sitting on an upturned groundbait bucket and fishing a whip, he scored good points for us that day. I had badgered Andy previously about signing him up, but Andy had thought him too young, yet we had missed out previously with Darren Davies in similar circumstances, when we waited too long and he joined Banstead instead, and I didn't want to see the same thing happen with Will, the most naturally talented angler I have ever seen. So we signed Will up, and his youthful enthusiasm rubbed off on the whole team. The rest is history, as they say, and he's been with the team ever since.

For its first two seasons, 1989/90 and 1990/91, the Super League was sponsored by Sundridge, but Dorking didn't enter it until Drennan started sponsoring it the following season and it became a major competition to challenge if not quite match the Winter League in stature. In the 1990s Dorking won it three times, in 1993/94, 1995/96 and then again in 1996/97, when we became the first team to win it in successive years. Highfield matched that feat in 1997/98 and 1998/99, then the 'noughties' saw our total dominance of the event in the new era of commercial carp fishing, Dorking winning it seven years in a row from 2002 through to 2009 under the captaincy of Steve Sanders and with a new generation of top-flight young anglers in the team – men like Des Shipp, Steve Mayo and Ben Leach, who all joined us in 1999, and Callum Dicks, Grant Albutt and Steve Hemingray. At least three of those finals were down at White Acres in Cornwall, a venue that for many of the Dorking team was like a second home! But we also won it when the final was way up North, at Woodlands near Thirsk, in 2005, mainly because, alongside runners-up Starlets and third-placed Essex, we put a solid week of practice in – and local finalists Barnsley and Goldthorpe didn't. Mark Downes predicted beforehand that it was a three-horse race, and he was right. Alain Urruty bravely wrote in Jim Baxter's sadly now defunct Sheffield paper, *The Angling Star*, that Dorking, Starlets and Essex "clearly wanted to win more than our northern teams, came to our doorstep, did their graft, worked out how to catch our fish and kicked our backsides big time". Poor Alain got a bit of stick from some of the Barnsley lads for that!

After 1991, frustratingly, Dorking didn't reach another Winter League final until 1996, and then after that we had to wait another five years before making the final again in 2001. On both occasions we 'hit the bar', just falling short in second place, though in 1996 – the year we signed the still on-going sponsorship deal with Daiwa – we had the individual champion on the Trent Embankment in Nottingham in the shape of the irrepressible Paul 'Tommy' Hiller, who has been a mainstay in the team ever since. From the point of view of attracting good crowds, that was always a great venue for a big match, but sadly the fishing deteriorated drastically and they stopped using it a few years later. Not that the venue used for the final every year in the final decade of the long life of the *Angling Times* Winter League – the Nene at Peterborough – was any great shakes!

Record crowds turned out in the sunshine in July 1996 for the Winter League final, and they witnessed a proper fishing match, with fish aplenty in the form of skimmers, hybrids and roach coming out on both feeder and pole. Mark Addy led Highfield to a narrow victory using both pole and feeder to great effect, though we gave them a good run for their money with section wins from myself and Pete Brownlow as well as 'Tommy'. When the results were totted up, Highfield's margin of victory over Dorking was just two penalty points, 41 to 43.

The steps on the Trent Embankment afforded the crowd a bird's-eye view of the skills on display in the 1996 Winter League final. (Image courtesy of Angling Times*)*

Paul 'Tommy' Hiller nets a hybrid on the maggot feeder from the section below Trent Bridge on his way to winning the 1996 Winter League final with 25lb 7oz. 'Tommy' had fished for Banstead when they, too, came second in the final on the venue in 1993. (Image courtesy of Angling Times*)*

It was the year after that, 1997, when 'Tommy' famously landed a 46lb catfish on the feeder on the first day of the Angloarc/NFA Team Challenge final on the Riba Roja reservoir part of the River Ebro in Catalonia in Spain. Unable to get the beast in his landing net, he grabbed it with both hands and threw it over his shoulder onto dry land. The next day, Dave Hurry thought he'd hooked a big catfish too, and said it was "fighting funny" as he carefully played whatever was on the end of his line towards his waiting landing net. It was certainly putting a healthy bend in his rod. When he finally got it in, it was an old kettle!

122

In the 'noughties', Dorking's strength in depth was such that we missed out on the Winter League final only three times, in 2000, 2002 and 2005, but we didn't taste victory again in the final – our first win since Willow Park back in 1991 – until 2006, when Simon Willsmore was also crowned individual champion after hauling in over 48lb of slabs on the feeder. Most anglers in those Nene finals could only dream of such catches, however – the fishing was crazy difficult, and in some sections, especially on the North Bank, it was a struggle to catch anything at all. In 2008 – "just weeks after Steve Sanders proclaimed his team to be the greatest ever," according to *Angling Times* – we won again, beating Barnsley by 13 penalty points, 30 to 43. We had a plan to stick it out for big fish on the North Bank come what may. I was drawn there myself, and with only 10 minutes to go I hooked into a big eel on worm over my chopped-worm line, a fish that propelled me from last in my section to third. Several of us caught late that day – we had the confidence in what we were doing. Tony Marti won individually for Image Van den Eynde, with 24lb 13oz of bream on the pole, but Ian Didcote and Will came second and third on another great day for Dorking.

In 2006 and 2008 we did the Winter League and Super League 'double'. Celebrating winning the 2006 Super League, from left, at the back are Paul Dicks (Callum's dad), Callum, Gary Pook, Steve Hemingray, Steve Sanders, Grant Albutt, Des Shipp, Steve Mayo, at the front myself, Paul Filmore, Gary Hamilton, Simon Willsmore, Mark Goddard, Will Raison, Paul 'Tommy' Hiller and Ben Leach. (Alain Urruty)

Will Raison swings in a small fish on his way to 8lb 10oz and third place in the 2008 Winter League final on the Nene. (Image courtesy of Angling Times)

By that time the standard of the top teams in the country was higher than it had ever been, and the increasing difficulty of beating the best teams was one reason that many of the smaller teams had lost interest in competitions like the *Angling Times* Winter League – another reason, sadly, was that by and large the anglers had all grown old together, and for many old-timers there was simply no longer the desire to compete, especially not against the youngsters coming through, because though there are very few of them, they are of such a high class. The *Angling Times* Winter League finally came to an end in 2011 when, fittingly for us, a Dorking team without me won the last ever final, at Furzton and Willen (Lodge and Teardrop) Lakes in Milton Keynes – Dorking's ninth victory in what for many decades was undoubtedly the top team competition in the land.

I may not have fished that last *Angling Times* Winter League final, but that same year, 2011, I was in the Dorking team for the Division One National on the New Junction Canal, on Barnsley's home patch – a match Barnsley were therefore somewhat keen to win! But we fancied our chances too, and practised on the venue hard, despite it being so far for us to go. I remember leaving home at half past four one Wednesday morning to drive all the way up for an open – a day trip to Doncaster!

Unlike in the old days, when the draw put each team member on the same peg number in the different sections, there was a random draw for each section, and on the day, Saturday 6th August, I was lucky enough to be on an end peg – A59 – and although the next section started below me there was a gap, so I had a bit more water to draw fish from, which always helps. Everything went to plan, and I caught mainly roach and a few perch steadily throughout on the pole. Come the end I thought no more than that I might have won my section when I put 4.380kg on the scales. After all, someone, somewhere nearly always finds a few bream or other big fish on big matches like that – there were 59 teams of 10 fishing that day. Back at the HQ comparing results we knew it was between ourselves and Barnsley for the title, and I didn't pay much attention to the individual results at first. It was only when they called out James Cameron of Clay Lane Tubertini in second place with 4.150kg that I realised I had won. I was flabbergasted. I mean, how many people can say they've won a National? It had never been my ambition to win one – it was always a team event first and foremost, as far as I was concerned – but having won one, I wasn't complaining, even though I was on halves as usual with Will! But even better was to come, when it was announced that we had beaten Barnsley into second place by 59 points – the equivalent of a whole section – to win our first ever Division One title.

It was an amazing team performance by any reckoning. Out of the 590 points available, we won 551 and therefore dropped only 39. Like me, Will and Dave Harpin both won their sections, and Des and Callum were second in theirs. We had formulated a clear plan in practice, and it worked like a dream for the whole team.

And then the following year Dorking proved once and for all – as if there was any doubt – that we were

England man Des Shipp with his catch in the Division One National in 2011, one that helped Dorking take the title. (Image courtesy of Angling Times)

a force to be reckoned with whatever the venue, be it a commercial fishery, a canal or a river, when, in my last ever National, with no real team plan other than for each angler to fish his peg as he saw it, to the best of his ability, we beat 50 other teams on the Bristol Avon to become only the second team since the great Birmingham side of 1976 to defend a Division One title.

It doesn't get much better than that.

Division One National Champion 2011 – I can live with that! But more importantly, we won as a team. From left, at top are Lee Edwards, Dave Harpin, Will Raison, Darren Davies and Des Shipp, at bottom Simon Willsmore, myself, Steve Sanders, Michael Buchwalder and Callum Dicks. (Images courtesy of Angling Times)

CHAPTER FOUR
On the World Stage

In the late 1970s and early 1980s I never consciously tried to get into the England team, despite all the talk in the angling press about my chances. I was just happy doing what I was doing on the open circuit and with Dorking. In September 1980, Kenny Collings and I did fish England manager Stan Smith's open 'trial' on the Warwickshire Avon at Luddington for the World Championship there a year later, but that was more out of curiosity, really, we knew we weren't in Stan's sights, and in fact it was obvious on the day that he already knew his team and was just testing the venue out. He certainly never stopped to watch either me or Kenny that day, or any other day for that matter. And if I had been picked earlier than I was, whether by Stan or by Dick Clegg, who knows what would have happened? I might not have been able to handle it, it might all have been too much for me. I could have been in one year and out the next, and that might have been that.

Dick took over from Stan in 1984, and in May 1985 I got a call from *Angling Times* telling me that Dick had picked me in a provisional 12-man England 'get together' squad. Sure enough I then heard from Dick himself and in July, by which time Dave Roper had been added to the original dozen, I met up with the rest of the lads for a pole-only work-out at Mallory Park. I remember I had to borrow a decent 13m pole for the day, because I only had an old 10m one. In the morning I caught a fair few bream, then in the afternoon we all had to swap around. I had to sit on Kevin Ashurst's box and fish with his gear, and he had to sit on my box and fish with my gear. So I thought, I'll just have a look inside his box and check out his other rigs. And there weren't any in there, not a single one. Later, not letting on that I'd looked, I asked him, "Kevin, did you bring many other rigs?" and he said, "Aye, plenty more in box!" That was Kevin all over – he was that good, he could make anything work.

Dick Clegg and his 'baker's dozen' at Mallory Park in July 1985. Standing, from left: Richard Borley, Bob Nudd, Tommy Pickering, Kevin Ashurst, Stan Piecha, Dave Roper and Alan McAtee. Seated, from left: Ian Heaps, Denis White, Yours truly, Dick Clegg, Dickie Carr, Ivan Marks and Alan Mayer. (Image courtesy of Angling Times*)*

I wasn't disappointed not to be picked for the World Championship squad that year, because I never expected to be. In August the following year, 1986, I was just one of several England section-winners in the Home International on the Trent Embankment in Nottingham – I caught on the waggler, as I recall – and again I wasn't surprised not to be in the World squad, as I knew I still had a lot to learn about pole fishing. Then one day in April 1987 I was out in my back garden doing something or other when Jeanette came out and said Dick Clegg was on the phone. I thought it might be a mate playing a prank, but there was no mistaking Dick's deep, gravelly voice as he told me that he wanted me to be in his six-man England squad for that year's World Championship on the River Mondego in Portugal, because it was likely to be a waggler match. As you can imagine, I was made up.

Getting the call from Dick Clegg to be in the England squad for the 1987 World Championship was my proudest moment in match fishing. (Image courtesy of Angler's Mail)

In practice one day on the Mondego that year we were all fishing away when Kevin decided for some reason that the inserts of his peacock wagglers were too short. I couldn't believe my eyes, but he cut them off with a pair of scissors, then jammed smaller whole straight wagglers down inside the main stems until the stems split, then whanged a load of Bostik around the splits, whipped over them with some silk – finishing each whipping off with a large knot – and smeared some more Bostik over the thread. I remember he had three or four of these monstrosities setting in the sun, all bent as bananas. I took one look at them and thought, Oh my God, Kevin, how can you fish with those? But again, Kevin could do things like that and get them to work.

I don't know if it was the shape of his wagglers that was to blame, but in practice that year Kevin kept casting left, and the rest of us – me, Ian Heaps, Bob Nudd, Tommy Pickering and Denis White – were all ribbing him about it. Back at the hotel, we were all paired up in adjacent rooms on the second floor, with balconies overlooking the swimming pool, and one day we thought we'd take the opportunity to shot up some waggler rigs, so there we were, casting into the pool from our balconies to test the shotting, and straight away Kevin got his float wrapped around the diving board to his left. A guest trying to enjoy a leisurely dip obligingly swam over and untangled it for him while the rest of us fell about laughing, saying "What did we tell you, Kevin!"

In our practice sessions we caught mainly little hand-sized barbel on the waggler and single maggot, but a few days before the team match – they had separate team and individual matches then – the heavens opened, it rained non-stop and the river came up about a metre and went a horrible orange colour, so we were apprehensive about whether our waggler tactics would work. Our feed was stickymag – I'd never used it before – and with yet more rain delaying the start of the match Dick gave us strict orders to keep our stickymag in bin liners and put our brollies up over it to make sure it didn't get wet. But when he got to Kevin during the match, Kevin was sitting there fishing away with his brolly nowhere to be seen. "Ashurst!" Dick said, "Where's your brolly?!" Kevin turned around and sheepishly pointed to where it was lying, unopened, several yards away. Meanwhile Dick could see that a small barbel had hooked itself and taken Kevin's rod tip round. "Right," Dick said, "Go and put it up now! And before you do, reel that fish in!"

The one section none of us wanted that day was A section, because they'd stocked some little carp in the river and that's where most of these carp were shoaled up – we'd found the best bait for them was treble maggot, a red one, a white one and a bronze one – but the carp, being carp, couldn't be relied on, because you were either on them or you weren't, you couldn't bring them to you. I duly drew A section and had Belgium ace Marcel Van den Eynde, of all people, on the peg to my right, so the pressure was on. To cap it all, Dick sat behind me at the start, so I was a little edgy to say the least. The match started, I cast out, the float ran through and went under, I struck and there was nothing there, but we'd had the same thing in practice, you got loads of phantom bites from the barbel. "Was that a bite?" Dick asked me. "I think so, Dick," I said. I chucked out again and caught a barbel, and Dick said, "Brilliant, we're going to be alright now," and left me to get on with it. The German guy to my left was on the little carp and beat me, but I caught a couple of dozen or so barbel to beat Marcel and finish third in the section, and we won gold, on my debut – incredible! And the next day Kevin and Denis showed their class by taking individual silver and bronze behind gold medal winner Clive Branson.

At this time I was still working for Jan Bohacek at JA & MF Engineering and only had three weeks paid holiday a year, and while Jan was delighted for me when I was chosen to represent my country he wasn't quite so happy about the amount of time off it entailed. So when, the following year, Dick selected me against all expectations for the World Championship squad for Belgium, and at the same time the

opportunity arose for me to join Kenny in his tackle shop business, it was like the gods had intervened in my favour. The shop was thriving, and that meant I could take all the time off I needed to fish properly for England. There was no falling out with Jan – we kept in touch, even after he later sold up and moved to Andorra – but there is no way

Sorting out the team bait with Kevin Ashurst at the World Championship at Holme Pierrepont in 1994. Every angler I ever fished with for England was hugely talented, but few had as much natural ability as Big Kev. (Image courtesy of Angling Times)

I could have combined an England career with carrying on my full-time job as a toolmaker.

Another key, massively important factor in my early England career was the influence of Bob. I learnt so much just by travelling with him to World Championships. Probably he was the first high-tech match angler, certainly he was the first one I knew. Ray Mumford had

In deep discussion with Dick Clegg in Belgium in 1988. Almost single-handedly, he made the England team the force it is today. (Image courtesy of **Angler's Mail***)*

started it, with his rows of immaculate rigs in the days of fibreglass poles with aluminium crooks, but Bob took it to another level. Everything had to be technically perfect. Lines had to be miked up, elastics tensioned perfectly, different groundbait mixes worked out for different applications, hook and hooklength combinations carefully pre-tied, stored and labelled for every conceivable situation – and not

Tackling up in the old days meant doing everything, even tying hooks, on the bank before the match. A far cry from today! (Image courtesy of **Angling Times***)*

just for pole fishing, either. We take all this sort of thing for granted now, but back in the 1980s it was all new to me – and it was Bob who showed us all the way forward. Before that, I might have had one or two rigs tied up for my short fibreglass pole, but when I fished with running line, which I did most of the time, I tied my hooks on the bank as I needed them, even for matches like Nationals – even for eels! We all did, we didn't know any better.

In 1988 the World Championship was in Belgium, and as usual the week before the two-day match was the official practice week, or 'training' week as the organising body calls it, the organising body being FIPSed – the *Fédération Internationale de la Pêche Sportive en eau douce* – which is itself part of an umbrella organisation called the *Confédération Internationale de la Pêche Sportive*, or CIPS. I had that week marked in my diary along with everyone else taking part, then out of the blue Bob asked me if I fancied going across the Channel with him even earlier for a few days to have a look at the venue – the Damme Canal – and have a bit of a fish, as it wasn't far to go, and I thought, yes, why not? And that set the trend, really, for the years to come, of putting early practice in, and we weren't the only country to do it, for we were all jostling one another to be ahead of the game. Whenever we could, as a squad we would go out a week ahead of the official practice week and familiarise ourselves with the venue as close to the match length as possible. (You aren't allowed on the match length beforehand.) Usually this meant exhausting journeys of hundreds of miles, but by taking a couple of vans and sharing the driving it wasn't so bad. And once you got there it was all worthwhile, because then we had a week to ourselves before the management team arrived, and it gave us the chance to sort a few things out before the really serious business of official practice, when as well as finalising tactics six or sometimes even seven of us would effectively be competing for five places in the team for day one. Often the first port of call would be the local tackle shop, as that way you can quickly find out the floats and, most importantly, the often unusual baits that the locals use. Having that unofficial week together also helped us bond as a unit, for sure, and you can't underestimate the importance of that. We took the week seriously to the extent that we all sat in a proper line, all started at the same time each day and all worked hard trying different things in order to get the right methods sorted, but we had a good few laughs too along the way.

Take the 1998 World Championship on the rowing course in Zagreb in Croatia. When we finally got there we walked the bank opposite the match length and straight away glimpsed the dark shape of a huge fish cruising just below the surface close in. We all wondered what the hell it was, but thought no more of it. Then, when we started fishing, we'd be catching bleak on the whip and all of a sudden the bites would stop and one of these enormous fish would glide through the cloud of groundbait with its mouth gaping. Sometimes one would foul-hook itself and tear off, taking your whole rig with it. This happened so many times that we started calling the creatures 'lostalots', as we didn't have a clue what they were, though it was clear they were filter feeders and were mistaking out cloudy groundbait for *Daphnia*. We were determined to catch one, so one day when one of these things appeared in my peg I quickly put together a Bolognese outfit with a light float and a 16 hook, fed some more groundbait and dropped a pinkie hookbait into the cloud. Sure enough this 'lostalot' slurped the whole lot in, I struck, and off it tore into the middle of the lake. Some of the Americans were practising nearby, including my old fellow 'CALPACian', Chicago-born Mick Thill, who had moved back to the USA by then. So, I had quite an audience, but calling on all my years of experience – alright then, luck – to a big cheer I finally got it in, all 20lb or more of it. Anyway, with the fish put back we adjourned to the lakeside restaurant for a well-deserved lunch. In Bob's case this included a couple of pints of local lager, and on our return to our pegs I had just sat down again when I heard a loud "Crack!" I turned around and there was Bob, staggering about and trampling all over his top kits. "You silly old b-----!" he said, and we all burst out laughing.

This was the year Will Raison made his debut, and on the second day of the actual match he hooked one of those 'lostalots' on the whip, but instead of tearing off it carried on cruising around as if nothing had happened. Realising that it didn't even know it was hooked, Will reached out with his landing net and was just about to scoop it in trademark fashion when it woke up, shot off and smashed him all ends up.

Me with the 'lostalot' I caught in practice in Zagreb in 1998. We later identified it as a bighead carp, a non-native, invasive species, and the local newspaper made quite a thing of me catching it. (Image © Mick Thill)

Fishing for your country in a World Championship involves much more than just rocking up at the venue a couple of weeks beforehand and hoping for the best. Months ahead, as soon as you know you are in the squad, you have to start doing your homework. How wide and deep is it, and, if it flows, how fast is it? What are the main species to target, and what size are they? What are the best ways of catching them? And what baits and groundbaits will we need? I was very fortunate during my England career because through my friend and sponsor Milo Colombo I made lots of contacts in different countries over the years – guys who most importantly speak good English. Organising a supply of bait in advance is critical. For the official practice week and for the actual match the organising body arranges an on-site bait supplier, but if you go out earlier you have to sort out a supply yourself. Then there's the question of what tackle you need to take. A lot of foreign venues are like nothing we have at home and require completely different set-ups.

You need to know in advance of a World Championship if you might be targeting unfamiliar fish like this little catfish, then plan your tackle and bait accordingly. (Image courtesy of Angling Times)

Tackle and bait sorted, you make all your travel arrangements with the rest of the squad and sort out some suitable accommodation. Tackle security wherever you are staying is a big issue, and more than one country's squad has had all its gear nicked in the past, which is just about the most calamitous thing that could happen, so you can't just book any old hotel. It has to be one where you can leave all your gear somewhere safe each night.

Travel arrangements and accommodation sorted, you then start getting your gear ready. In my case I liked to start preparing my tackle two months ahead of time. It's not like preparing for an ordinary match at home, you can't do it all the day before. Take float rods. Not only do you need a variety of rods – ones with different lengths and actions – you need to take several of each, to allow for duplicate set-ups in case of tangles or breakages during the actual matches. The same goes for reels, poles and top kits. Once I'd sorted the 'hardware', I'd start making up pole rigs, and tying up hooks, enough different kinds to cover every conceivable eventuality, and make sure I had multiple numbers of each. Meanwhile I would still be preparing for and fishing matches at home, so if ever you wanted to find me when I wasn't fishing, the first place to look would be in my tackle workshop. I'd spend hundreds of hours in there preparing for each World Championship, for the practice weeks at any rate, for I never took it for granted that I'd be in the actual team. No one in the England set-up ever does. You can be individual World Champion one year and bank runner the next, because every year the fishing is different, and it's the anglers who adapt best in practice who get picked, so each year every member of the squad has an equal chance at the start of the official practice week. And in the two weeks prior to going out for the unofficial practice week, I'd fish no matches at home at all. Instead I'd spend the time not just finalising my tackle preparations, but preparing myself mentally for the task ahead, getting myself 'in the zone'.

You can prepare as meticulously as you like, but unfortunately things don't always go quite to plan when you get there. In 2006 we got all the way out to the rowing course in Montemor in Portugal for a week of unofficial practice to find that they were using every last inch of the water for the match, so there was nowhere for us actually to fish. There was a bit of an offshoot from the main water that some of the less-fancied teams were practising on, but strictly speaking you aren't allowed to fish within 500m of the match length, never mind on it, and being one of the favourites we didn't dare risk it. Someone would undoubtedly have lodged an official complaint and tried to get us barred from the match. So that was that. We spent a few hours each day walking the match length and tying up rigs, but the rest of the time we just sat around, waiting for the start of the official practice week.

One thing you can't prepare for is the local insect life abroad, however much repellent you might take. In Bulgaria in 1989 when we got to the Plovdiv Canal – actually another rowing course – for the World Championship we found that the banks were swarming with wasps. There were always several in and around our groundbait bowls, attracted by the sweet smell, and we all got stung several times, usually between the fingers when reaching down without looking to squeeze a ball one-handed and grabbing hold of a wasp along with the groundbait. I had the brainwave of placing a jar with a few spoonfuls of local jam in water on the bank halfway between each of our pegs, to try to lure the wasps away to a syrupy death. I don't know what they put in their jam in Bulgaria, but the wasps never went near it and we carried on getting stung just the same as before. (I don't recall if it was to escape the wasps, or just to cool off, but one day at the end of practice there for the 2001 European Championship Bob plunged into the Plovdiv for a swim, and we had just got started with the groundbait catapults, using his bobbing head for a bit of target practice, when we heard the wail of a siren. A police car – a Lada, as I recall – screeched to a halt opposite, the local constabulary got out and Bob received loud and clear orders to desist what he was doing immediately.)

In Portugal on the Mondego in 2002 one spot we fished during the unofficial practice week must have been near an orange grove, I reckon, because it was infested with clouds of fruit flies. They settled in their thousands on our poles in particular, for some reason. The locals use fruit fly maggots to catch bleak, maggots so small – smaller than squatts, even – that some of the guests in our hotel didn't even notice they were swallowing a few of them each time they had a glass of freshly squeezed orange juice in the morning.

In Finland on the Saimaa Canal in 2005 there were big brown flies like the ones you see on cowpats, only these ones could bite right through your baseball cap and into your head. They snuck up on you from behind, so one minute you'd be sitting there merrily fishing away, the next you'd feel this sudden sharp pain like someone had stuck a needle in you.

We never had any trouble anywhere with any really dangerous creatures, but Will wasn't taking any chances on the banks of the Castrejon Canal in Spain in 1999 when he moved a rock so that he could level his seat box and a snake shot out from underneath. I've never seen anyone move so fast or go so white, it frightened the life out of him, but it gave the rest of us a good laugh. That was during the official practice week, so he didn't have the option of moving swims, and he kept a wary eye out for the creature the rest of the day.

They call it a canal, but the Castrejon actually hammers through. One day in practice, Bob hooked a carp and it flew off downstream, taking his top kit with it. We all thought that was the last he would see of that, when one of the Germany anglers practising nearby offered to go in after it. We thought he was mad, but he dived in, swam out and managed to grab hold of it. He then swam back against the current with the top kit in one hand like a sword, and the elastic stretched out behind him, for the carp was still on. So Bob not only got his top kit back, he got the fish into the bargain. It was obviously a lucky omen, because he went on to win his fourth individual gold medal on the canal a few days later.

The World Championship has just ended on the Castrejon Canal in 1999 and for Bob Nudd the reality of having won his fourth individual gold medal begins to sink in. It couldn't have happened to a nicer bloke, someone who has been a good friend to me as well as a massive influence on my approach to match fishing. (Stewart Cottingham)

As well as the wildlife and loony carp, there's sometimes extreme weather to contend with abroad, and that same year Will, Bob and I had already been out to the Castrejon a few months earlier, in July, but that was too early as it turned out, because it was like a furnace, and our pole sections and landing net handles got so hot in the sun that we couldn't even pick them up. The only time we could bear to fish was from about 6:30 to 10:30 in the morning. The rest of the day we spent back at the hotel, lounging by the side of the pool.

By contrast, one day in 2007, during our unofficial practice week on Lake Velence in Hungary – again, a rowing course – Alan Scotthorne and Stu Conroy decided to stay in the hotel and tie rigs while the rest of us, Will, Des Shipp, Sean Ashby and myself, went and fished. As we sat there fishing away, black clouds started gathering in the distance, and Will, Sean and I were all for packing up, but like a weatherwise old farmer Des declared in his broad West Country drawl that the clouds were moving away from us, so although dubious about this we carried on fishing. (I'm sure the fact that there was a topless girl swimming around in front of Des had no bearing on his pronouncement.) Moments later the heavens opened – I've never seen rain like it – and in seconds we were all drenched. Alan and Stu were in stitches when they saw the state we were in on our return to the hotel.

Unfamiliar food is something else you sometimes have to contend with abroad. One day during the official practice week on the River Vah in Slovakia in 2003, what looked like a burger van parked up behind us, its owner evidently hoping for plenty of hungry customers from among the hundreds of anglers lining the river bank. Feeling somewhat peckish myself, with thoughts of perhaps a nice burger to keep me going for the rest of the day, I strolled on over. There on the hot plate were griddled portions of local carp, each with a neat row of rib bones sticking out of it. Suddenly I didn't feel quite so hungry any more. (In Bulgaria in 1989, the hotel menu was all too familiar. You could have tomatoes, tomatoes or tomatoes.)

Bulgaria in 1989. The plastic bag on the right of this picture was for the fish to be put in to take to the scales, then they were put back in the bag and taken away to be eaten!

Coarse fish are a staple part of people's diets in many European countries, and that's something we're just not used to. In 1996, at the banquet at the end of the World Championship on the River Mincio at Peschiera del Garda in Italy, they served what looked like whitebait, but was in fact bleak caught by some of the competitors that day.

Over the years, as more and more countries joined the unofficial practice week bandwagon, competition for space on the bank became more and more intense. We joke about German holidaymakers bagging all the deck-chairs with their beach towels, but in 1996 on the Mincio – and I swear this is true – we got down to the pegs we wanted to fish one morning to find the Germany squad had tried to bag them by leaving an upturned groundbait bucket in each one the night before. So we stacked the buckets up, put them to one side and got tackled up, and there was nothing the Germans could do about it when they arrived a short while later – except collect their buckets.

Since 1994, I think it was, squads have been allocated pre-drawn zones during the official practice week, but before then that week was also 'first come, first served', and sometimes you had to get down to the bank at dawn to secure enough pegs in a line. I remember in Hungary in 1991 sharing a room with Bob and the two of us taking it in turns with the other guys in the squad to get up in the dark and get down to the rowing course in Szeged and bag swims each day. You then sat in the van bleary eyed and waited for the rest of the squad to finish their breakfast and join you a few hours later. It was the same in 1993 in Portugal, but there one country's squad – I won't say which – took things even further. To be sure of getting the swims they wanted, they forsook the comfort of a hotel and instead slept in a coach in a wood on the far bank of the Sorraia, swimming all their gear across the slow-flowing, 80m-wide river at first light on a home-made raft. Now that's dedication for you. Or maybe they just couldn't afford a hotel, I don't know.

In 2000, on the River Arno in Italy, we were told we weren't allowed to drive down to our first-day practice zone, so we parked as close to it as we could get, but that was some distance away, and we had to lug all our gear down to the river by hand, which took several journeys. The heat was intense, and we were knackered by the time we got started. Then at the end of the practice we had to lug it all back again. The next day, the host nation had the same zone and – surprise, surprise – drove straight down there.

The official practice week is hard enough work as it is, without that kind of extra hassle. You're up each morning at six to prepare the bait and load the van, then after two intense three-hour sessions, one in the morning and one in the afternoon, with a five-minute pre-baiting period before each, it's back to the hotel to tie rigs and mix groundbait for the next day, talk through the events of the day with each other and with the management team in a sit-down meeting, grab a quick meal and a drink, and then it's off to bed, ready to get up early and do it all again the next day. The management team aren't idle each day either – far from it. They have to watch all the other teams as well as watch and advise their own, and look after all the bloodworm, joker, maggots and other live bait. They also have the difficult tasks of, first, deciding who to leave out on day one, and second, telling that person that after all their hard work they're going to be running the bank. Being told you aren't fishing is a crushing disappointment, but there's no time to feel sorry for yourself, you have to gee yourself up, ready to do your utmost for the team the next day. Bank runners are assigned a section each, and play a vital role in passing on information to the England man in their section and to Mark Downes and Mark Addy, information that can determine crucial tactical decisions. As well as whoever is unfortunate enough to be left out of the team, England's runners include Will's dad, John, and anglers on the fringes of the World squad. They can make all the difference to the final result and are an essential part of the set-up.

The two actual days of the match are such hard work, take so much out of you, that as soon as they're over you feel spent. The nervous energy that's kept you going just drains away. When you've won you're obviously on a high straight afterwards, but that feeling sometimes doesn't even last until the presentation ceremony. You deflate so

Bank runner Dave Harrell and manager Dick Clegg assess the situation during the 1996 World Championship in Italy. The guys on the bank work as hard as those actually fishing, and have to be able to assess situations calmly and make crucial decisions about tactical changes that can alter the outcome of a match. (Image courtesy of Angling Times*)*

quickly, you feel totally flat, and all you want to do is get home as soon as possible – even if that means getting up at the crack of dawn again the next morning and driving all day and into the next night. And when you do get home, the last thing you want to do for the next week or more is fish a match anywhere. You need a complete break from the sport for a while, and if you do make the mistake of fishing a match too soon you find yourself going through the motions and longing just to be back home.

You're all thrown together when you fish for England, and there's great camaraderie, but you get different characters. You're bound to. There are always one or two who have their own thoughts on what to do in practice, and fish accordingly. Then at the end of the day they like to go back to their room on their own to think things over and prepare themselves mentally for the following day without any distractions. Kim Milsom was a really intense guy. Alan is a total perfectionist, and he doesn't rest in practice until he is satisfied that he has got everything absolutely right – his rigs, his bait presentation and his feeding. He's such a positive and confident angler, and sometimes he gets everything right straight away and shows everyone else the way to go from the very start. At other times he spends much longer trying out different things, always searching for a better way. But the fact is that by the end of practice he is always bang on the money. His record proves that, and no one can argue with it.

One day when we were practising for the European Championship on the River Raia in Portugal in 1998, we were all struggling, but Alan worst of all, so to wind him up I called down the bank, "Alan, have you tried using a smaller hook?" He came straight back at me, "Of course I f---ing have! And anyway, you've caught f--- all yourself!" Dave Harrell

Kim Milsom is a study in concentration as he decides his next move during the World Championship in Italy in 1996. No one put more effort into fishing for his country than the brilliant but single-minded Kim. (Image courtesy of Angling Times)

heard this, and at intervals throughout the rest of the day he would put on his best August Bank Holiday festival commentator's voice to call out, "Welcome to Evesham. And if you'd like to make your way down to peg 28, you'll find Steve Gardener, AND HE'S CAUGHT F--- ALL!"

Des is another fun guy, a really bubbly character, always cracking jokes and popping his head around your hotel room door to see what you're up to. Sometimes, though, the laugh is on him. In 2003, a year before his debut in the World squad, he came with us to Slovakia to run the bank on the Vah. On day two he was running my section, which he decided he could do best by sitting behind me and watching all my rivals through a pair of binoculars he had bought off a street seller for something like 20 Euros. Someone a few pegs away kept netting fish, but I couldn't tell what they were, and I wanted to know, because you caught bream running through with bloodworm over groundbait at the bottom of your peg, and barbel on maggots held back over stickymag and stones at the top. Each time I asked Des to find out, instead of bothering to scramble up the steep bank and go and look, he would peer through the binoculars then give his ruling. Afterwards it turned out it he had got it wrong every time – the binoculars were useless – and we ribbed him mercilessly about them.

Somewhere on the spectrum between guys like Kim and guys like Dave Harrrell and Des you get the likes of Bob and Will, each of whom I travelled with for many years on England duty, and both of whom like the occasional laugh but also like nothing better than talking tactics. One evening during the official practice week on the Mincio in 1996, Alan had a bit too much to drink and rather unwisely got into an argument with Bob about groundbait. Bob said to Alan, "I suppose you think I know f--- all about groundbait?" and Alan said straight back, "Yes, I suppose I do," at which moment the whole room went quiet. The next day, Bob was catching the best of all of us, and every time he landed another fish he shouted down to Alan, "I suppose I know f--- all about groundbait!" To his credit, Alan later told this story against himself in *Angling Times*.

Like Bob, Will is incredibly confident, and has been so from the very beginning. In 1998 on the Raia he was running the bank for me when I foul-hooked a barbel on the pole and it tore off into my downstream neighbour's box and leapt out of the water. Naturally enough my neighbour objected to this and called for the fish to be disqualified. No less a figure than the then President of the organising body, Fortune Jagulin, came down and asked what was going on. To our astonishment my steward said it was alright, it wasn't my barbel that had leapt out, it was another fish altogether, in fact a carp. Not knowing or particularly caring who he was talking to, Will – who bear in mind was still only 23 at the time – then turned to the President and said, "Anyway, mate, what's it got to do with you?"

I remember the more recent Italian President of the organising body, Claudio Matteoli, at a medal ceremony one time – I forget which year or event – good-humouredly announcing, "And in first place – *again!* – England!" which prompted as much laughter as it did applause. And that's one of the great things about the World Championships and other international competitions – the friendly nature of the rivalry between the anglers from different countries. Yes, you're all out to beat each other, and you try your hardest to do so, but there's also great respect between you all and there's always room for a joke or two and an arm around a shoulder, even in the heat of battle, and time for a drink together afterwards.

Some real friendships have been forged over the years. On his debut in Croatia, Will drew next to France's Jean Desqué, who apparently tried to psyche him out beforehand by telling him his floats were too big and his line too thick. But Will beat Jean that day – despite losing that 'lostalot' I told you about – and the two of them subsequently became good friends, and Sensas one of Will's sponsors as a result.

Then there's myself and Milo, who has sponsored me all these years since way back in 1990, and been my good friend for even longer, since 1987 in fact, when the England squad went over to Portugal a few months before the World Championship and won an unofficial European Championship, pipping Italy by just one point. In Belgium the following year we stood on the podium together at the end of the World Championship – I won silver and Milo won bronze – and we had a drink together one evening then again another night in Ostend with Bob. Even today, *non parlo molto italiano*, but Milo's English is pretty good, and anyway we share the common language of fishing. He's not without his eccentricities. At the 1990 World Championship on the River Drava in Maribor, a beautiful old city in what is now Slovenia, when Milo and I were only a few months into our sponsorship deal, the night before day one of the competition I was tucked up in bed in my room with my rigs all tied up ready for the next day and lovingly laid out beside me when Milo, having just arrived at the hotel, burst in to say hello. Seeing my rigs, he started examining them all with great interest, but when he found one with a float made by a rival Italian manufacturer he promptly ripped it off the winder and bit it in half.

When Simon Willsmore went to live and work in Italy in the early 1990s Milo couldn't have been friendlier or more helpful, and was soon taking him here, there and everywhere, but Simon wasn't getting any special treatment – Milo's like that with everyone. Simon, Milo and a few other top Italian match anglers, like Adriano Fumagalli and Giovanni

Always laughing, always joking, but don't let that fool you, for Milo Colombo has as sharp an angling brain as anyone I've ever known. (Milo Colombo)

Grisenti, would come over to England every year for a couple of weeks. One day they'd be on the Kennet wrestling chub and barbel on the pole, the next down the Thames at Hampton Court fishing the waggler for dace, the day after that scratching around in a match on the Forty Foot drain. It doesn't matter where you take Milo, he loves it, the banter and the competition. The first time he visited the tackle shop in Sutton, for a cup of tea and chat about the forthcoming Evesham festival – Milo is always a big draw there, and of course he won the individual championship in 2007 – Kenny stuck a picture of Milo in the toilet pan. (He did the same with a picture of me, once, in the loo at Willow Park!) Milo roared with laughter when he went to spend a penny and saw it – he's that kind of guy – and the two of them were soon good friends. Another time when Milo flew over to fish White Acres, I picked him up from Heathrow in the evening in my Ford RS Turbo and we set off on the long drive down to Cornwall. After an hour or two Milo could see I was in danger of nodding off and offered to take the wheel. So we swapped over and I quickly fell fast asleep. A little while later I woke up to find we were doing 120mph – on the A303 near Stonehenge!

Since the early 1990s, too, at Milo's invitation I have spent a lot of time each year fishing with him in matches in Italy, and I've loved every minute of it, the scenery, the food and drink, the venues, but above all the great company. Everyone is always so welcoming and friendly, and while some of the match rules can take a bit of getting used to at first, a match is a match in my book, and the experience gained and contacts made, as I've noted already, have proved invaluable over the years. Some sponsorship deals don't last, but the fact that I've been with Milo all these years tells you all you need to know. I've been very, very lucky to have him as a sponsor and friend. *Grazie* Milo!

Friendships aside, in the years since Dick first took over from Stan, Italy have probably been England's biggest rivals in World Championships, and we've had some mighty battles over the years. Italy won gold, silver or bronze every single year from 1985 to 2001 – roughly speaking, the period when Dick was England manager – but in the same period we missed out on a team medal only four times and won seven team golds to Italy's six and four team silvers to their five. Generally, venues in northern Europe suit England best, while venues in southern Europe favour Italy, mainly because of the different climate and different species to be caught, but as the years have passed both England and Italy have gained more experience of different climes.

On the Sorraia in Portugal in 1993, when Italy won and we finished only ninth – our worst result in all the years I fished for England – the main target fish were little barbel on the waggler, and in the ferocious heat our natural inclination was to cut back on the feed, which was balls of stickymag, but the Italians knew better and fed miles more than we did on day one, when they topped the field and we slumped to 17th. Dick was livid afterwards. He came stomping into the room and said, "We have NOT FED ENOUGH!" He turned to Tommy and Denis. "Right, you two, you're not fishing tomorrow!" Then he turned to Dave Harrell and Alan. "You two, get your gear ready!" He wasn't actually allowed to make two changes, but I don't think anyone dared challenge him, the mood he was in. (The only other time I saw him hit the roof was two years later, in Finland, when he thought we'd fed too *much*.) Dave didn't even have his gear with him. We'd changed hotels for the weekend of the match and he had to drive 20 miles back to our first hotel to fetch his kit. On day two I think we had something like three gallons of maggots each – I had stickymag everywhere – and we did much better, some of us beating the Italian on the next peg, in my case Ferruccio Gabba in his debut year. Jump forward to the European Championship on the same venue in 2010, and England finished behind only the host nation, which shows how much better we had become by then.

I'm not saying that any of the England anglers in years past weren't as good as those who came later – of course they were – but as a team England have got better and better year by year firstly by taking a more professional approach under three top-class anglers in their own right in Dick, Mark Downes and Mark Addy – with fantastic support since 1993 from Drennan and Sensas, and from Steade-fast and Leeda before that – and secondly by simply accumulating ever more knowledge and experience.

Dick's first goal when he took over was simply for England to win a World Championship for the first time, and he achieved that in only his second year. Once you taste victory you want to repeat it, and you keep raising the bar. After a couple more wins largely on the waggler, Dick wanted to show that we could win on the pole, and we did that for the first time in 1991. And so it goes on. Dick turned us into one of the most feared and respected teams in the world, and the two Marks have carried that on to this day.

Talking of 1991, on the first day that year I was fishing away and doing okay, catching a few fish on casters, then suddenly going into the last hour I couldn't get a bite, not a sniff, and I couldn't work out what I had done wrong. The hooter had just sounded, warning us we had five minutes left, when the float went. I struck, hooked into something and quickly unshipped, but the elastic was still right out there, and I thought, what on earth is that? With no time to lose – a fish doesn't count if it's still in the water when the final hooter sounds – I stuck another section back on and pulled as hard as I could. The next thing I knew, this massive grass carp with a head the size of a sheep's head was wallowing on the surface and rolling from side to side, then calamity, the top kit snapped clean in half. I stuck another section on and pulled like mad, but the jagged edges of the broken carbon sheared through the elastic and the fish was gone. That probably cost me an individual bronze medal. Not only had I lost the damn fish, but it was probably also the reason why my swim went dead for so long in the first place.

Getting back to the subject of how far England have progressed, bloodworm and joker were once a mystery to us, but there are no myths about them anymore. At one time we all thought the French had some secret ingredient in their groundbait, one with magical roach-attracting properties, when in reality it was the joker in the groundbait and the noise of the balling in that were key. Nine times out of 10 when you ball it in for roach they are straight on it, and when they find the joker they stay on it.

The only time I've thought it was the groundbait mix that made the difference was one occasion in the late 1990s when I was over in Paris with Dave Vincent, Will, Stu, Bob and Alan for a two-day match on a local water – Bob and Alan were fishing in a 'Superstars' team with Jean-Pierre Fougeat. In practice there were anglers every few yards, some shoulder to shoulder, and we were all struggling, even the French guys, then this local chap turned up, found a gap to squeeze into, put some groundbait in and promptly started bagging. Naturally we went over for a closer look, the upshot of which was that Dave asked him if he could get us some of whatever he was using. Later we found ourselves furtively meeting up with this guy in a car park somewhere, and he handed over a bucket of some horrible-looking stuff that was all lumpy and full of pigeon feathers. But it worked brilliantly, and in a match where there were 20 teams of four, Dave, Will, Stu and myself romped home, dropping only a couple of points between us. Trouble was, we only had enough of the mix for six balls each, and that left us none for the second day. We tried to replicate it as best we could, with pigeon droppings and what have you, but it wasn't the same and we struggled on day two. Whatever had been in that guy's mix, it was perfect for that particular water.

Alan Scotthorne squeezes another ball of groundbait ready for heavy pre-baiting on the Castrejon Canal in 1999. Much of the practice before a World Championship is spent experimenting with different mixes. (Stewart Cottingham)

A lot of people think bloodworm is bloodworm and joker is joker, but there's more to it than that, as we've learnt on our travels. In practice for the 2002 European Championship in his home country, that great Belgium angler Guido Nullens, who won the event that year – and other years – and who was later individual World Champion, in Finland in 2005, agreed to supply us with bait each day as well as his team mates, and one day when he opened a packet of joker and saw how lively it was, to our surprise he put it to one side, saying, "That'll do for so-and-so," then he opened another packet that looked half dead and put it carefully to one side for himself. We had always thought you needed your joker lively every time, but we learnt from Guido and others like him who have a lifetime's experience of the bait that in certain situations – when fishing for skimmers, bream or big roach, for example – inert joker is best. Most of the joker we get comes from Poland, but it's the same sort you find in the UK and elsewhere, and you can use it lively or inert depending on how you look after it. Russian joker, on the other hand, is much smaller – too small to put on the hook – and is naturally very slow-moving, which makes it better for feeding in certain situations. Likewise Russian bloodworm is very different from ordinary bloodworm, being much bigger and almost lifeless, so that's a good bait when you want to avoid nuisance small fish.

How to fish the slider properly is another thing we have now long since mastered, but it took us a while to get it right. At one time we had two different set-ups. One had the float sliding off the bulk, and this cast beautifully, but when the wind wasn't right it would sometimes tangle in the air or on landing, and so it wouldn't always slide, and was unreliable, and we'd reach instead for the second set-up. This had the float sliding off a shot a little way above the bulk, and never tangled, no matter which way the wind was blowing, and slid every time, but you simply couldn't cast it straight, no matter what. Bob called it the 'sack of shit' rig because of the way it tumbled through the air, intent on its own course. Not until 2000, when the World Championship was

Here I am about to net a bream hooked on the slider on the Willebroek rowing course in Belgium in the 2004 World Championship. (Stewart Cottingham)

on the deep River Arno in Florence and we came second behind Italy, did we finally master the slider, when Francesco Casini, who is based in Florence and won individual gold in the European Championship on the venue in 1997, showed us a few little things that allow you to fish a float sliding off the bulk without it ever tangling.

At the same time as England has improved, so have many of the other countries, including many of the so-called minnows. There are more countries than ever who are now a real threat. It started with the Hungarians, really. They made a conscious decision one year that they were no longer prepared just to make up the numbers, that they wanted to get good enough to be properly competitive with the likes of England, France and Italy. To this end they put the necessary extra effort in, doing things like videoing our practice sessions, then playing the tapes back in their evening squad meetings, studying and discussing in the minutest detail what they had seen. Their results got better, and now they're competing for medals. Other countries then followed suit. I heard that at Holme Pierrepont in 1994 the Russians didn't even have seat boxes, though I didn't see it myself. Now look at them, they're right up there and have had two individual World Champions in recent years. And the field gets bigger seemingly every year, as new countries enter the fray, not just new European countries, but countries from all four corners of the globe.

Improved technology has made it so much easier for all of us to learn. You don't need loads of bulky and expensive equipment any more to film someone fishing and watch it back – you can do it with a cheap handheld device and upload it straight onto a laptop. And whereas at one time there were a few magazine articles about this and that, but nothing of any real use, now if you want to find out about things like fishing the pole on a river whizzing past you at a hundred miles an hour, you can learn what tackle and techniques you need from in-depth articles in magazines and on fishing websites, and see it being done on YouTube.

With the competition so strong, with so many of the countries so closely matched, then to win a World Championship in recent years you have often needed an edge – either something that only you as the host nation already knows about, or else something that only you as one of the 'away' teams discovers in practice and manages to keep secret from all your watching rivals.

Take Italy and the 1996 event on the Mincio. Milo lives only an hour and a half away from Peschiera del Garda, where the river flows out of Lake Garda, and earlier in the year he asked me if I fancied a recce, so I went out for a week's fishing with him. It's a fantastic place to visit, with stunning scenery and gorgeous summer weather. Lined with poplars on the far bank, the river is deep, fast and crystal clear, so clear that on a cloudless day it's as blue as the sky. It isn't hard to see why Milo rates it his favourite venue. You can see the bleak swimming around some six feet down. Besides the bleak, which you can catch on the long whip, the main target fish are scardola, which are like rudd and feed on top of the thick streamer weed that grows up to four feet off the bottom and waves in the current. The best method for the scardola the week I went with Milo seemed to be the Bolo at range. There are also chub to be caught, mainly in the first 30 minutes on the Bolo when they can be straight on your feed, but occasionally also later in the match when they're cruising around near the surface and can sometimes be caught on the shallow waggler, though they're ultra-wary then and very difficult to tempt. One day that week, Milo and I fished a 100-peg open on the river. It was one of those complicated affairs with so many points per gramme and so many points per fish. I snared four chub at the start on the Bolo, then had something like 358 bleak, and that was enough for first place. (I've still got the Bolo rod I won that day somewhere, a Tubertini one I think. I've never dared use it in case Milo found out!)

Not once during that week did Milo pick up a pole.

Come the practice for the World Championship, all of us in the England squad – myself, Dave Harrell, Kim, Bob, Tommy, Alan and Denis – worked hard to hone our tactics, which were based around the whip for the bleak and the Bolo about 20–25m out for the scardola. Streams of floating weed coming down caused problems for everyone, though, and you had to wait for gaps in the weed before casting your Bolo rig in, otherwise it just got swamped. Likewise, when you hooked a fish you had fun and games getting it in with weed festooned around the float, shot and fish. (Before each day of the actual match they placed a boom across the river above the match length to try to reduce the problem of floating weed, but it was only partially effective.) The way to gather the scardola was to feed heavy groundbait that sank straight through the streamer weed then released a stream of floating casters and other particles as the balls broke down. The scardola took the casters as they emerged from the weed. When I say floating casters, I don't mean just ordinary ones, but also blackfly casters, which stick together in small clumps. The groundbait also contained sweetcorn, and as a change bait for the hook, besides the sweetcorn and the two different types of casters, we had whole dried *crisalidi del baco da seta*, or silkworm cocoons. Imagine trying to find those in a tackle shop in England. For the bleak, meanwhile, we fed a different groundbait and threaded a specially bred, hard-skinned kind of pinkie up the shank of the hook so that you could catch up to 20 or so fish on the same pinkie before you had to rebait.

Bob Nudd prepares his groundbait in the World Championship on the Mincio in 1996. We knew from what the Italians use that it had to include a cheese additive and crushed up, dried silkworm cocoons. (Image courtesy of Angling Times*)*

Mark Addy, who was there that year as a bank runner, spent the official practice week watching the Italians, and they fished much the same as we did, until the very last day when they started fishing long poles for the scardola for the first time. They also fished lighter Bolo rigs on the same 14.5m line that day, and Mark spotted that they were basically stret-pegging. They would swing the Bolo rod around so that it pointed downstream and dragged the float in toward the bank slightly faster than the current – and therefore ahead of the hookbait for a few feet   then swing the rod back the other way to slow the float, and that would sometimes tempt a bite, because then your hookbait looked to the scardola as if it had just emerged from the weed with the particles popping up out of your groundbait. It was a great bit of observation by Mark. Everything still had to be just so to get a bite. You could put your float through 19 times, and you knew each time the way the water was swirling that it wasn't going to happen, then on the 20th cast the water would smooth out a bit and you'd just know the float was going to go under.

On the basis of what the Italians were doing we modified our Bolo plans somewhat, but we still regarded the whip for the bleak as an important method.

With Mark Addy on England duty abroad. Mark's greatest strength is his tactical astuteness, as he has demonstrated on numerous occasions.

Unluckily for Dave and Denis they caught the fewest bleak in practice and so were the two men left out of the team. One day in practice, Dick asked us all to count our bleak. Denis never really liked fishing for bleak and when Dick asked him how many he had caught he made up a number on the spot. Unluckily for Denis, Dick decided to count his fish to see how many they went to the pound, and wasn't too pleased when he found Denis was 50 or more fish out with his 'count'.

On day one I managed fourth in my section with whip and Bolo, but Italy caught so well by essentially ignoring the bleak and groundbaiting really heavily at intervals throughout the three-hour match that by the end of the day they had an unassailable three section wins and two section seconds – an incredible score, when you consider there were 32 anglers in each section – with England in second place but too far behind to catch them up.

Netting a fish on the Bolo on day one of the World Championship on the Mincio in 1996. (Image courtesy of Angling Times)

Netting a fish, on the pole this time, on day two of the World Championship on the Mincio in 1996. (Image courtesy of Angling Times)

On day two there was a mix-up that somehow resulted in me being dropped off at the wrong end of the match length, so I had to borrow a bicycle and pedal a couple of miles along the bank as fast as I could to get to the right end, where my tackle was waiting for me. (At nearly every World Championship there are plenty of bicycles around, because they make it so much easier for team managers, their support staff and spectators alike to cover the match length.) As you can imagine, the sight of me pedalling past caused much merriment among the other competitors already at their pegs. Anyway, we fed more heavily and fished more positively this time – I fished mainly long pole and won my section – and we managed to beat Italy on the day by one point and claim silver, but we were never going to overhaul them overall, and they took gold as expected and had the individual silver and bronze medal winners in Claudio Guicciardi and Milo. To round off a memorable World Championship for England, Alan won the first of his five individual gold medals. I think he got thrown in three times at the end.

As host nation, Italy were confident all along what the best way to fish would be, but kept it under wraps until the last day of practice, when they had to try it out just to be sure. Some of their guys, like Roberto Trabucco, who pipped me for fourth individual place overall, had fished the river since they were kids. We had a few weeks to try to master what was a very challenging venue. Italy had had a lifetime.

France did not have quite such an advantage as host nation on the River Seine in 2001, because the match was held on the river in the middle of Paris, so the venue was almost as foreign to them as it was to everyone else. Mark Downes and Mark Addy took over from Dick that year, and the squad was Sean and Stu, making their World

Roberto Trabucco serenely watches his Dolo float on the Mincio in 1996, knowing his Italy team had the venue mastered. (Image courtesy of Angling Times*)*

Championship debuts, plus myself, Bob, Will and Alan. In practice we found, like everyone else, that there wasn't much of anything at all to be caught on any method from the venue (another deep one with a heavy flow), just a few bleak and the odd big bonus fish here and there. We had the odd big bream, Sean had a 5lb tench, Will had double-figure catfish and carp, and I had a 3lb roach, the fish of a lifetime – but bites from fish you normally expect to rely on catching, like small roach, were very few and far between. Crucially, however, we early on worked out a way to catch big eels, something we realised would give us a massive edge.

The method was to add chopped worm to our top-up groundbait, which contained heavy soil to take it straight down, and which had to be fed accurately by hand. (Pole cups weren't allowed in those days, and bait-droppers have never been allowed by the governing body.) You then held a worm hookbait dead still over the top of the feed on a biggish hook, around a 12, and a strong hooklength, of around 0.18

diameter – these were big fish, and could easily bite you off or snap you up if you weren't careful – fishing a couple of feet overdepth with a 40g flat float we nicknamed 'Big Bertha', with the bulk just off bottom. The method also sometimes caught you bonus perch or bream. As soon as we had it taped we stopped doing it, to keep it secret from prying eyes and save it for the match.

The French were confident of winning on their own patch, but they didn't reckon on eels and were caught out when I had one late on day one, plus two perch – after fishing for two hours for one bleak – to rocket me up my section. On day two I drew only a few pegs away from where I'd been on day one, in front of the Tuileries garden, and again made sure to avoid a blank by first catching a lone bleak before going on 'Big Bertha'. Then, when Will and I both started catching eels, some of the guys in the French team entourage thought that we might be breaking the rules with our 'Big Bertha' rigs. They suspected that we had the main bulk of our shotting touching the bottom and so were float-legering. But we weren't. At one time the rules didn't allow what the governing body called 'impeding the flow', meaning you couldn't hold your rig back in any way, but then they were amended to allow you to have up to 10% of your float's shotting capacity touching the bottom. So with our 40g 'Big Berthas' we could have had 4g of droppers on the bottom had we wanted to, but we didn't even have that much, and our bulks were set well clear of the bottom. We were therefore well within the rules, and Will got the right hump with one bloke about it.

On both days in Paris in 2001 I was drawn opposite the Musée d'Orsay, and on both days 'Big Bertha' got me good section points. (Dave Roberts)

A fish comes to my net on day one in Paris. (Stewart Cottingham)

About halfway through the match that second day, when I'd already had one eel, the French steward in charge of the whole of my section came along and checked the rig of the Dutch guy to my left, then Mark Downes said, "He wants to see yours as well, Steve, either now or after the match, he wants to see what you're up to." I had no complaint – he was well within his rights – so I said, "Fine, he can look at it now," and lifted it out for the man. There was nothing he could object to – he could see from the distance between my float and bulk, and from the shotting below the bulk, that I was well within the rules, and declined Mark's kind offer to let him sit on my box and try it for himself – so I carried on fishing. But now he was there, right behind me, and this is where my real troubles began, when I hooked another eel while he was watching and it charged off downstream.

I should explain at this point that normally in World Championships your box is 10m wide, with a 1m 'neutral' zone either side. But to

Fish on! Action from day two in Paris. Note the second keepnet jammed down inside the first. (Image courtesy of Angling Times)

squeeze everyone in that year – there were 36 countries taking part – the boxes were only around 9m wide. Because of this, we were assured beforehand, the box stewards had been instructed to be lenient about fish swimming out. But now, as well as my box steward, I had the main section steward watching me.

Not only did we have smaller than usual boxes to contend with, but we were perched some 4m off the river with a steep stone slope between us and the water's edge, so the tapes marking the boundaries of the boxes didn't even reach the water, which made it impossible to tell exactly where the boundaries actually were. It was blowing a Hooley too that day, plus we were under trees, so when I hooked this second eel and off it went, pulling miles of elastic out, I put as much pressure on it as I could, holding the pole high over my head among the overhanging branches, and when Mark called out, "Steve, it's going out of your box!" all I could say is, "Well, I can't pull any harder!" Because of the long drop to the water, we all had 6m landing net handles, and when they get to that length you have to have a small net head otherwise you'd never be able to manoeuvre it properly, so netting anything, never mind a big eel, was tricky, but eventually I had the eel, which was slightly bigger than the first, safely landed. "It's alright, Steve," Mark said, "Put it in your net."

Well, that's when it all kicked off, with some of the French team entourage saying they were going to object to the fish and get it disqualified – I remember thinking, so much for leniency! – so when I then hooked and landed a third and even bigger eel, one of nearly 2lb (without any trouble this time, ironically), Mark said, "Whatever you do, Steve, don't put that in your net, put it in a bucket!" because if I put it in the keepnet with the others and the objection to my second eel was upheld, it would be the biggest of the three eels in the net that would be ruled out. So now, with the eel still in the landing net, I had to sort out a bucket and some rope and scoop some water out the river, but the French guys objected to this as well, so Mark said he'd go and find me a second keepnet. He found one alright, but it wasn't an official one, so he consulted Dick, who was there that year for the first time in his new role as 'overseer'. Dick said that I should put the eel in the second net then ram that down inside my official net. The French couldn't object to that, he said, because he'd seen Jean Desqué do exactly the same thing the day before in case the wash from the many boats on the river rubbed the official net against the sloping stone bank and tore it open. Ramming the second net down inside the first was easier said than done, and I remember thinking, I don't need any of this, not now, not in a World Championship, but I just about managed it with my long landing net handle. Eventually I was able to resume fishing, had a nice perch, and that was the end of my match. They weighed my catch twice, once with my second eel and once without. Then, when Dick went to the post-match meeting and saw that with or without the disputed fish we had won the team gold, he told the French, "You can have the eel," even though having it ruled out cost me the section.

But what a result, and what a venue. I know it was criticised for a lack of fish, a lack of action for the spectators, and I'll admit it was a nightmare place to practise on – it took something like two hours each morning to drive the two miles or so from our hotel to the river, such was the traffic – but fishing a World Championship in such a setting, in the heart of such a great old capital city, was an unforgettable experience, one made all the more memorable when at the

Stu Conroy had a great debut for England in a World Championship, winning his section on day two in Paris with 1.040kg of bleak. (Dave Roberts)

opening ceremony at the Hôtel de Ville the USA team received a standing ovation in the wake of the '9/11' terrorist attack in New York a few days earlier. Having the World Championship in the centre of Paris only came about because the guy who organised it, Raphael Faraggi, the owner of Fishabil in Brittany, had clout in high places. As for the fishing, I love hard venues like that, I relish the challenge, because when you get a bite, and catch something – anything – it's a real sense of achievement, a much greater one than when you're on a bagging water and sack up. Will is of the same mind, I know – in fact he probably got that mentality from me in the first place.

Will Raison and I have just had confirmation that England are the 2001 World Champions. I think our faces say it all!

Bridges over the River Seine were closed for spectators in Paris in 2001. Can you imagine that happening in the centre of London? (Dave Roberts)

Our win in Paris demonstrated that England could compete on any type of venue. Dick and the two Marks declared it England's greatest ever victory at the time, and beating the French on their home patch was certainly a fantastic feeling. But all of the France team are good friends of mine, and they were all gracious in defeat – Jean Desqué especially so. It was all the more special for me personally because Jeanette was able to be there to see it, and to see us go up for our medals in front of thousands of people in the Trocadéro gardens by the Pont d'Iéna on one side of the river under the backdrop of the Eiffel Tower on the other side.

Some 15 years on, Sean, Alan and Will are still at the heart of the squad. They and all the other guys who have fished for England since Dick became manager in 1984 stand out like sore thumbs now, they've that much experience on venues the like of which you just don't see

at home. Where in England do you need to fish the pole with 60g, 80g, even 100g flat floats, like they did in Croatia in 2014? And where at home do you need to be able to fish a waggler at 70m, like you do on the Ostellato Canal, or fish a slider for carp?

That's why the next generation of England anglers will come from within the ranks of

With Jeanette under the Eiffel Tower at the end of the World Championship in 2001 – a priceless memory.

the junior and intermediate set-ups managed by Steve Sanders and Mark Downes. They aren't going to come from anywhere else. You simply can't gain the necessary experience here in England, fishing commercials. And there's not such a kudos to fishing for England as there used to be, because commercials dominate the domestic scene and anglers brought up on them can't relate to any other kind of fishing, unlike young anglers of the past who were brought up on a variety of waters and could appreciate things like scratching for a few pounds of gudgeon or ruffe. Fishing for England requires experience of different countries, different techniques and different fish. How many youngsters fish the Irish festivals these days? In the days before commercials, when there was a close season on canals and still waters as well as rivers in England, the likes of Denis, Bob, Kevin and Tommy all gained invaluable experience in Ireland, in Denmark, in Sweden, in Holland. Now, sadly, the interest just isn't there. Why go abroad, when you can bag up on a commercial down the road? The anglers coming through the young England ranks are therefore a select band, and some of them are very, very good indeed. Whether they all end up in the full England team is another matter, because it isn't easy, and in the coming years some of them at least will get married and have children, and that's when you have to ask yourself, do I really want this? So I'm not going to name names. I don't want to jinx any of them.

It isn't just experience abroad that you need to fish for your country. You need that little bit something extra. When I see someone fishing, I can tell at a glance if they've got what it takes. It's hard to put your finger on exactly what it is, they just stand out from the crowd. There are anglers who when they're on their particular method are unbeatable, there are old hands who know from years of experience just what to do on any given day, and there are those who are good all-round anglers who regularly win matches, but you need that indefinable star quality – that 'X' factor, if you like – to make the grade.

Luck plays a huge part, too. There are a lot of anglers who can consider themselves unlucky never to have been picked for England, but then you can't pick everyone, can you? It's not like the England cricket team in the 1990s, there's been no 'revolving door' selection policy under Dick and the two Marks, thank goodness. And then there are those anglers who do get picked, but who don't have that little bit of luck you need to stay in. In my own time with England I fished with some brilliant anglers who just didn't get the breaks you need. Paul 'Tommy' Hiller had a dream debut for England in the home international in Cardiff in 1993, but never really got the chance after that. Dave Vincent can consider himself very unlucky not to have been picked for the team more often in World Championships given the number of times he was in the squad. And who could possibly question Dave Harrell's ability? No one. Then there was Darren Davies, another great angler. But it never went right for him either. In 1994 he fished alongside myself, Bob, Kim, Dave Vincent and Vinnie Smith in a two-day match against France, in France, on the River Sevre at Niort – it was pole-only the first day, waggler-only the second – and struggled on the first day on a horribly shallow peg. Then when picked for the World Championship squad in Portugal in 2002 he had no luck either. There were seven of us in the squad that year, not the usual six, and in the official practice week we had such small zones that we were all sitting on each other's shoulders, and it was hopeless, he had no chance to shine.

Dave Vincent (above) was one of the unsung heroes of the England set-up for many years, working tirelessly for the cause.

Paul 'Tommy' Hiller (left) and Darren Davies (right) both knocked hard on the England door. (Dave Roberts)

It was the same for Vinnie, another great angler. Vinnie got picked for Belgium in 1988 on the strength of his bloodworm and joker skills at a time when he and the other top canal men in the North West were years ahead of everyone else at that game. He did really well in practice, got picked for the team, then drew the worst of all of us. To cap it all, he was heckled by some so-called England 'supporters' opposite him. That was unforgivable in my book. But he showed great character, fished his heart out, and went home with a gold medal.

There's another factor everybody forgets. You could be the best angler ever individually, but not a good team man. That's something the management has to weigh up. Will he be good or bad for team spirit and unity? In 2001, Sean got his first call-up to the England squad for Paris at only a couple of weeks' notice when Kim pulled out at the last minute. Sean worked so hard in practice, he nodded off at our first team meeting! He ran the bank on day one, but when offered the chance to fish on day two in place of our lowest day-one points scorer, Alan, he magnanimously declined, because he reckoned the experience gained from having fished on day one meant Alan was the better bet for the team's chances of claiming gold. That's the kind of angler I'm talking about.

The final thing is, it's alright winning competitions on your local venues when you've got no one watching you, but what about when the England manager is sitting behind you scrutinising your every move, or a whole crowd of expectant England supporters? This was one of my biggest concerns when I was first picked, whether I could handle the pressure, because there is a lot of pressure, believe me. But it's only pressure that you apply to yourself. You don't want to make yourself look stupid, you don't want to let the team down, and, in the back of your mind, you can't help wondering, am I good enough? You might be the best angler in the world, but that counts for nothing if you crumble. You can have hundreds of people watching you, and it isn't easy sometimes because they're quite close, but you have to be able to deal with it. Usually the crowd is behind you, so once you start fishing you can blank them out, but sometimes they're opposite you as well. In the World Championship in Belgium in 1988, the venue, the Damme Canal, was only about 30m wide, and the far bank was lined with spectators. Some anglers are exhibitionists, they love to perform in front of a crowd. Look at Ian, when he won the individual title in a similar situation in Poland back in 1975. I've never liked even one person watching me fish, but I think I proved I could handle it. It must have been the masochist in me.

I reckon the far-bank spectators on the Damme Canal in Belgium in 1988 could see my waggler better than I could – especially as I'm colour blind! (Image courtesy of Angler's Mail*)*

I once asked Bob if he ever gets nervous, and he said, "Never," but I don't believe that, I think everyone who fishes for England gets nervous, even Alan or Will, even now. I know Will was nervous the night before his debut, because we were sharing a hotel room and he never slept a wink. He spent the whole night sitting out on the balcony, preparing himself.

As for me, I was always nervous at the start of each day of a World Championship, but by far the most nerve-racking day of my career was day one of the 1994 match at Holme Pierrepont. Fishing a World Championship on foreign soil is one thing, but the pressure you're under when you're the host nation and anything less than team gold is considered a failure is quite another. And there was even more pressure at Holme Pierrepont because the once-prolific venue had become gin-clear and rock-hard and we knew there would be loads of blanks, with large areas of the rowing course seemingly devoid of fish. Gone were the days when you could bag up with roach, skimmers and even bream on the pole. It was now a case of fishing for a bite, with perch the main target in the clear water. The England squad that year was Kevin, me, Kim, Bob, Alan and Denis, and Kevin was the unlucky one left out of the team. Bloodworm and joker were the baits, but fishing sliders at range, and clipping up for accuracy – credit goes to Alan for coming up with that idea – was our main attack, with the long pole as back-up.

Come the first day, a huge crowd gathered at each England angler's peg, so when I got off my section coach – this being an NFA-run event, we weren't allowed to drive to our pegs ourselves – I had to carry my gear through the middle of a seething mass of England supporters. I wasn't used to strangers calling out, "Alright, Steve?" and "Good luck, Steve!" so every time it happened I couldn't help turning around and looking to see who it was, as if it must be someone I knew. This carried on all the time while I was tackling up and trying to get myself mentally prepared, and it was very hard to blank out. Denis was so distracted tackling up that first day that he forgot to set up his landing net, and had to beach his first fish. As for me, when the whistle went, my heart was thumping like mad and I couldn't stop my hands shaking. A friend who was watching told me later that when I catapulted out my first ball of feed and it landed bang on top of my slider, he thought, "Bloody Hell!" but that when my next ball went nowhere near it he began to have his doubts. Once I caught my first fish – to great applause from the crowd behind me – I settled down, and caught a few more. The crowd cheered each one, and indeed you could hear loud cheering every time an England man caught a fish. The Dutch guy one side of me blanked, while Jean Desqué the other side found a few skimmers to beat me. I finished 12th in my section and England ended the day in third place with all to play for.

Day one at Holme Pierrepont in 1994. Not like fishing an ordinary match quietly on your own! Some people blamed the clarity of the water partly on the barley straw bales, like the one you can see here. They were put in the water's edge all around the rowing course to prevent a bloom of toxic blue algae. (Image courtesy of Angling Times*)*

Roberto Trabucco was one of the few anglers to catch a skimmer on day one at Holme Pierrepont. Luck deserted him on day two. (Image courtesy of Angling Times*)*

On the second day there were thousands of people behind us again, and I was fishing away, but it was a really tough section and I was blanking. Then Dick came along and asked me how it was going. I was on the pole at the time and just as I said to him, "No, nothing, I ain't had a bite," the float slid away and I clonked into a small perch. At the sight of the elastic coming out the crowd behind me went deadly quiet – as did Dick – but when I netted the fish, Jesus, they roared like I'd scored the winning goal at Wembley. Dick said, "Go on, put that in your net, but then turn round and wave to them!" Talk about theatre.

I sat back down, shipped out again and hooked another perch, but it came off, and I never had another bite all match. But it didn't matter. That one little perch I did catch got me fourth in a section in which only five other anglers caught. All around me loads of people blanked, including, at the next peg, Roberto Trabucco, who had been fourth in my section the day before. Without that perch, we would have finished second behind France – none of us would have liked that – and I wouldn't have the fantastic memory of going up with the other lads to be crowned champions of the world, with Bob winning his third individual title as well, on home soil in front of thousands of cheering England supporters.

Job done at Holme Pierrepont, it's time for a well-earned cuppa! (Image courtesy of Angling Times)

Time to celebrate! Victory on home soil in 1994 tasted even sweeter than that tea!

It's so often the case that saving a blank on a rock-hard venue is the difference between silver and gold, bronze and silver. In the European Championship on the Trent Embankment in Nottingham in 2000, Will caught a miniscule perch on day two to save his blank and help give us victory over Hungary by one point. Without Alan's single roach on day one in Paris in 2001, we wouldn't have won gold. On day one on the Drava in 1990 – a deep, powerful river, over 100m wide – near the end of the three hours I hadn't had a bite, not a sign. The French angler below me had caught one roach, but other than that there was nothing happening around me. Then Dick came up to me and said, "Steve, stick a pinkie on with your bloodworm, I've just been watching Marcel Van den Eynde and that's what he's catching on." I thought, okay, I'll try it. First run down the float went under and I had a little 'cigar' – a sterlet, a kind of small sturgeon. I couldn't believe it, what a relief! Next day, first run down I had a roach and went on to come second in the section. That's what it can be like, and it's when you can't get a bite, no matter what you do, that you have to be able to stay cool, show character and tough it out.

Dick Clegg checks on how I'm doing in the 1990 World Championship on the Drava, where he saved me from blanking on day one. (Image courtesy of Angler's Mail)

On day one in Paris in 2001, Alan Scotthorne had a priceless 235g roach to avoid a blank. (Images courtesy of Angling Times)

In 1992 on the Erne, where the target fish were roach and bream, we had three blanks over the two days, which was one blank too many – we finished fourth – but there was nothing you could do if there weren't any fish in front of you. This was certainly one venue where no team had an edge. The only line you could catch on was about 30m out, but the fish were in pockets, and you were either on them or you weren't. England's main approach was the slider, with the Bolo as back-up. I 'got out of jail' on day one. In practice we had discovered that there was one swim with a massive boulder, the size of a car, under the water on the 30m line, and while I was tackling up on the first day Alan came along – he was there that year to run the bank and gain experience – and said, "You know what, Steve, I think you're on that rock." Sure enough, when I tried to run a float through, it only went a couple of yards before it folded over. I was bang on the boulder, and I thought, what I am going to do now? I was on the outside of a sweeping bend, so I went to each side of my box and looked along the tapes to see where they pointed. As I feared, they both pointed at the same spot, the 'e' of the Sensas hoarding on the far bank. That meant I couldn't fish past the rock, because if I did, the stewards were sure to call me up for fishing outside my box. There was nothing for it but to fish short, at 20m, where in practice we hadn't had a bite. But as it happened I had one bite for one 10oz roach, and after I netted it I had to scramble up the bank for my keepnet, which in all the bother beforehand I had forgotten about. All around me that day anglers were walking up and down their boxes with little whips searching for fry just to try to save a blank. It didn't work for them, but it did work for Denis in his section, and that at least kept us in contention for day two.

I can't leave the subject of my England career without addressing the elephant in the room, the question I always get asked, whether it bothers me that I never won an individual World title. I can honestly say that it has never bothered me at all. For me, as for most of the lads I fished with, it was the team result that mattered, every time. From a selfish point of view, the best way to stay involved was to ensure I was part of a successful unit. Then they couldn't drop me, could they? I didn't consciously think like that, but that's how it was.

I had my chances to win individual gold, but funnily enough I don't really think of Belgium in 1988, when I won individual silver, as one of them. It's always easy with hindsight after any match to think you could have done something different, but I don't look back at that one with any regrets. I look back and remember that we won team gold!

Trying the Bolo in the 1992 World Championship on the Erne. Note the Sensas hoardings along the far bank. (Image courtesy of Angling Times*)*

The Saimaa Canal in Finland in 2005 was another matter. We were fishing double joker or a small bloodworm for skimmers and roach, and because the bed of the canal was rocky I felt sure we should be able to catch a few off bottom, but although I kept trying it in practice I couldn't make it work. On day one I fished at depth and had a 2lb bream on really light gear – it took 20 minutes to land, the longest I've played a bream in my life! But it helped me to a section second, so I was right up there. On day two I fished at depth again for not much, then with 15 minutes to go shallowed up and had two skimmers and a roach. All I needed for individual gold was another 600g or so, and I know I would have caught that if I had made the switch sooner. I should have listened to that voice in my head, the one that says, "Do it now!" But – and it's a big but – again, the important thing is that we won team gold.

The following year, in 2006, in Portugal, where the target fish were mullet, I did so well on the first two official practice days that at the end of the second day the two Marks said to me, "Steve, you're fishing," something that was almost unheard of. On day one I was second in my section and second overall on weight, but on day two I drew a difficult bit. Stu had fished there the first day and he warned me, "They're bigger fish there, Steve," but I didn't listen to him. Anyway, I was fishing away, not much was happening, when all of a sudden I started getting mullet liners. Then I hooked one and off it went, but I got it back and was just about to net it when the hook pulled. I went out again, hooked another one, and it rocketed away, ripping the hook off the line. Third time lucky? No, I hooked another one, and that one snapped me up good and proper. Maybe it was foul-hooked, I don't know. I finished right down near the bottom of the section, when the individual title was there for the taking. You can call it bad luck – I was certainly cursing it myself – but also I should have taken heed of Stu's warning. Again, though – and I suppose I really can't stress this enough – the most important thing is that we won team gold.

Bad luck was definitely to blame on the Arno in 2000. I won my section the first day, but on day two it all went wrong for me from the start. For the five-minute pre-baiting period the plan for the long pole line was to ball it in with the pole in the rest, but instead of just aiming at a bare pole tip we decided to lay the rig in the water, to see how the float sat, then use the float as our target. I had about a dozen balls of groundbait plus two great balls of stickymag and stones made up, and I had just thrown in the fifth ball of groundbait and picked up the sixth when a carp foul-hooked itself and tore off, dragging the pole down into the water. I had no choice but to stop feeding and deal with the fish, which I played in as fast as I could, but just as I netted it – it was about 10lb – the hooter went for the start of the match. So now I couldn't use two hands to feed as you can in the pre-baiting period, so I couldn't put the other balls of groundbait in. Nor could I use both hands to squeeze the two big balls of stickymag – though they've since changed the rules on this one – and I really needed to, but I thought, I've got to put them in. Well, that was a disaster, because they broke up on impact, when the idea was for the stones inside to take them straight down to the bottom some 10ft below. I never settled after that, my peg was all over the place, and my head, because I knew my initial feed wasn't right. I never caught a carp, and then to really make my day the guy next to me foul-hooked one and it ploughed straight through my swim. I finished 10th in my section when the chance was there at the start of the day to win it.

Oh dear! While all around me carry on feeding their swims during the five-minute pre-baiting period on day two on the Arno in 2000, I have to stop feeding mine to deal with a rogue foul-hooked carp. (Stewart Cottingham)

The weird thing is, almost exactly the same thing had happened to me in 1993 on the same stretch of river, in the match we used to fish at the beginning of every year against Italy, France and San Marino, a match tied in with the Nautex Tackle Exhibition in Rimini. The event was usually held on the Ostellato Canal, but this particular year the canal was frozen over, so we had a three-hour coach journey through the snow to the Arno. At the beginning of the pre-baiting period I chucked my slider out as a target for my groundbait and was about to fire in the first ball when the float shot away and I found myself playing a foul-hooked carp. That one, too, I netted just as the hooter sounded for the start of the match. I ended up second that day, beaten by Roberto Trabucco at the next peg. So, it was a real case of déjà vu when much the same thing happened on the same venue in 2000.

My final chance to win individual gold was on the Spinadesco Canal near Cremona in Italy in 2008. This was another time when we went into day one with an edge, something even the host nation didn't seem to know about, despite us being put on to it in the first place through our Italian contacts. The target fish were carassio, carp, skimmers and bream, and the long pole the main method, but we'd been tipped off that bonus big fish could be caught very close in. The canal has a concrete side that slopes down into the water, and sure enough in practice we found that by feeding maggots just past our keepnets and fishing against the side of the slope we could catch bonus asp as well as the occasional carp and bream. As soon as we discovered this we put it in the locker. On day one of the match Italy slumped to eighth while our close-in edge helped us to take a commanding lead. I was third in my section and pulled out of a good fish that almost certainly cost me a section win. Italy fought back to win day two, but could only finish third overall, behind San Marino in second and England, who took gold. I won my section to finish third individually overall, so that lost fish on day one probably cost me the individual title, which Will claimed instead with a section win on day one and a section second on day two. But that's fishing, we all lose fish from time to time, and I still had the pleasure of standing on the podium alongside Will as he was crowned individual World Champion. But, again, by far the most important thing for both of us was the team result. Beating Italy in a World Championship in their own back yard for the first time since 1985, after we'd come so close in 1996 and 2000, was very special indeed. Of all the 11 team golds I won with England in World Championships, that one was right up there with Portugal in 1987, Holme Pierrepont in 1994 and Paris in 2001.

Individual glory is but the icing on the cake in World Championships. Here Will Raison and I celebrate helping England beat Italy in their own country in 2008. (Image courtesy of Angling Times*)*

CHAPTER FIVE
As I Please...

It pains me to have to say it, but I can't help feeling that fishing is a dying sport in this country. There simply aren't the number of youngsters taking it up that there were when I was young. Someone was telling me recently that he met a lad fishing on the Thames and the boy told him he doesn't tell his mates at school he goes because they would take the mickey out of him about it if he did. It's not fashionable, you see. And of course there are so many other things for young people to do these days. When I was a lad you had no computers, no mobile phones, no internet, no DVDs, no computer games. You could read a book or magazine, you could go to the cinema occasionally, you could listen to the radio or watch a bit of TV, but otherwise you made your own entertainment, indoors or out.

Light lure fishing may well be one way of getting young people to take up the sport. Jigging and drop-shotting for perch is growing in popularity, and that's all to the good if it gets more young people to pick up a fishing rod, for they may then branch out into other areas, like match fishing. Lure fishing's such a simple way of fishing, you travel light, roving about with just one rod. It would be even more popular if we saw reservoirs and other enclosed waters in this country being stocked with black bass, both largemouth and smallmouth. Can you imagine having the first black bass fishery here? You'd make a killing. Go to the USA and you'll see how massive lure fishing for black bass is there. But it isn't just the USA. I've been to Spain and caught bass in the reservoirs there.

As for match fishing, I would like to see some matches with a 13m limit for poles, the same as in the World and European Championships. There used to be no length limit for poles in these events. Then they brought in a 14.5m limit – that's what it was in Paris in 2001, for instance – and now it's down to 13m. This makes it much fairer for those countries who can't afford the best long poles, especially when you consider that each angler in the squad needs two of them, in case of breakages. But you can get two decent 13m poles for the price of one decent 16m one. Most of the rest of Europe – Belgium, Holland, Italy – has a 13m limit for poles in their domestic matches, and manufacturers have started reducing the diameter of their poles again as a result, because a slimmer pole is easier to handle when it's windy. Balance is not such an issue at 13m, so funnily enough the manufacturers have also slightly increased the weight of their 13m poles, to make them stronger and therefore more versatile. We could follow the example set by these other countries by having a 13m limit ourselves in some matches at least. Such matches would give more anglers a chance to compete and learn.

Another thing I'd like to see tried, at least, on commercials is a few pole-only matches, again with a limit on the length of pole allowed, because what with method feeders, pellet wagglers and 16m poles, the pressure the carp are put under from the start of a match can be colossal. Often the fish have nowhere to hide, and to get away from us they all go to one end of the lake or other, or to the middle of the widest part.

John Raison used to run silverfish-only matches at Gold Valley, with so many points per fish and so many points per ounce or whatever. The first three hours would be brilliant, but in the last two hours everyone would get mullered by carp. What was happening was that at the start of the match all the carp would back off to the middle of the lake, thinking they were being fished for, but then, because everyone was fishing on the pole for the silvers, the carp would feel safe and move back in close to the bank to chomp on all the feed going in. And once that happened you couldn't fish for the silvers properly anymore, because you kept hooking carp instead.

Ever since then I've realised what a massive part angling pressure can put on carp in commercial fisheries. You want somewhere in your peg where there's sanctuary, where the carp can settle and not be bothered, where you can just pick them off until going after them at the end. Many anglers now go for a walk when they're not catching, because they know that by resting their peg there's a good chance they'll catch straight away when they go back to it. I've seen that a lot. If we had a few pole-only matches, with a limit on the length of pole allowed, maybe they wouldn't need to do that, maybe we'd see more carp spread out around the lake.

People are surprised when they hear that the majority of matches I fish now – and I still fish three matches a week when I can – are only 20- or 30-peggers, often smaller, but I'm not out to impress anybody by trying to win big matches for the sake of it. I do as I please, and that means fishing small matches on some really nice local venues – like Passies Pond and Old Bury Hill in winter, and More House Farm and Willinghurst all year round – where the fishing is as fair as possible and you have half a chance from most of the pegs. They aren't lucky dips where most of the time you're beaten before you even start. And even when there's only a handful of you, you can learn something on the day that gives you an edge the next time there's a full house. If I don't bother to fish just because only half a dozen other anglers turn up, those anglers are going to have an advantage over me the next time – and I don't want that!

If I lived nearer the upper Thames, I'd be tempted by some of those matches for sure, but there are too many problems on the lower river. There's hardly anywhere to park, for a start. I did fish Dave Harper's revived Lower Thames Championship, but the sad fact is that the general public aren't used to seeing anglers on the lower river anymore, so when we all turn up out of the blue with our long poles – and you have to fish the long pole nine times out of 10, because we know now that most of the time it beats the waggler or stick float hands down – it's us the anglers who are getting in the way of the cyclists and dog walkers, who've long since claimed the river bank as their own. I can't be doing with all the hassle you get there nowadays.

The other thing to consider is that, given all the gear we need to take to fish the long pole properly – the modern seat boxes with foot platforms and all the various attachments, the pole rollers and so on – then you've got to have ease of access to your pegs. In France, Spain, Italy, where believe it or not they take even more gear than we do, they only fish rivers and canals where they can park near their pegs, like we can on commercials here in the UK. If they can't do so, they don't fish there, it's as simple as that. There aren't many rivers or canals where you can park close to your peg in this country – not in the South, at least, though I know there are a few up North, like parts of the Trent and Newark Dyke.

Do I miss fishing rivers? Yes I do, but I don't dwell on it, there's no point. I enjoy the company and the competition on the venues I fish now as much as I've ever enjoyed my match fishing, because the competition is the most important thing to me, not the venue. And I put just as much effort into my match fishing now as I ever did, because otherwise what would be the point? I still spend hours in my workshop preparing my gear, tying rigs, making sure I've got every bait option covered. I probably spend a full day each week working on my kit – often more. If I went to bed the night before a match not satisfied that I'd done everything I needed to, I wouldn't be able to sleep, I'd lie there thinking I should have done this, I should have done that. I can't think of anything worse than turning up for a match ill-prepared.

More and more in recent years I've erred on the side of caution when I fish a match. With bream as well as carp on commercials, it's all too easy to ruin your peg by being too positive at the start and putting too much pressure on the fish straight away. You catch a few early, then the rest become unsettled, and those fish will then likely move. So again I like to leave a safe haven in my peg that they can back off to and settle in, rather than risk having them vacate the swim.

As well as trying always to be aware how the fish are responding to what I'm doing, I like to keep tabs on how they're responding to what the other anglers on the lake are doing. I might start a match with a certain plan, but if I think someone else doing something else is getting a better response, I'm not too proud to change tack. Far from it! It's like I said before, if I think I should change something, I will, straight away. I'm well known for constantly looking up and down and asking out aloud to find out who's catching what and how. I always have been. If someone's catching a certain way, then I want to know about it! That's why if someone asks me, "What did you get that on?" or "What was that you just had?" or whatever, I'll always tell them – unless it's a team match, of course – because then (hopefully!) they'll tell *me* when it's me asking *them*! You need to know how you're doing at all stages of a match, so that you can make the right tactical decisions. It may be that you don't need to change anything, which is fine, but if you don't *know* that then you can't make an informed decision. Mobile phones are a great help to the modern-day match angler, where allowed. When you see a mate on the other side of the lake catching, you can ring him up straight away and ask him what he's doing!

I spend a lot of time on the phone in between matches, too, because you've got to have your finger on the pulse. Say I fish a match somewhere on the Sunday then there's a match on the same venue on the Wednesday when I'm not there, but I'm planning to go back there again the following Sunday. Then I need to know what happens in that midweek match. Someone might catch on an unexpected bait, and if so, I want to know in advance, so that I can cover that option. It's common sense, part of my pre-match preparation. I could never just turn up blind.

Much of the time, too, I'm on the phone going over what happened in a match with a mate – picking the bones out of it, if you like. Will Raison's the same, he just thinks fishing, fishing, fishing. We have the same mindset. We constantly analyse what we did, where we went wrong, what we did right, what we might do differently next time. It's a never-ending learning process. In recent years I've also started jotting things down in a diary – just things like who caught what, and where, and anything I think I should have done different on the day – so that I can refer back to what happened in the same place at the same time next year. It's uncanny how patterns repeat themselves, how you can go back to a place at the same time of the year and the fish are in the same areas and taking the same baits, for example. It's such a simple thing, but writing things down ensures that you don't forget them – especially when you get to my age and your memory starts going!

With us match anglers all growing older together, the veterans match scene is burgeoning, not just here, but across Europe. I was honoured when Joe Roberts asked me if I would like to fish for the England veterans national team, but the truth is I had 27 years of fishing for my country and I don't want to have to commit myself to all that all over again. My priorities now are my family, my friends and my own fishing.

I still fish a lot with Milo, especially in pairs matches. These aren't like pairs matches here in the UK, where you have one man from each pairing in separate sections. You and your pairs partner fish the same peg! So you have to work as a team, and it's great fun. Depending on the event and the nature of your swim, sometimes you sit side by side, and sometimes you sit a few yards apart. Milo and I fished a pairs match on the Mincio a couple of years ago, and Milo very kindly 'let' me sit on the downstream side. I spent most of the match waiting for him to lift his rig out so that I could have a go! Not surprisingly he more or less trebled my weight.

Earlier this year Milo and I won the Milo Red Tetragon Pairs on what has become one of my favourite venues in recent years, the River Arno at Pisa. Being close to the sea, the Arno there is very different to what it is in Florence. It is deep and wide, and the flow varies so much depending on the amount of rain that's been falling that you can need a 5g float one year and a 40g float the next. The fishing's always good, though – this year Milo and I had combined weights of 35kg on day one and 52kg on day two. But more importantly, the competition, while serious, is friendly. The event is held over two days, with one five-hour match on each day, and anglers come from all over Europe to take part. Each pair gets a 20m-long peg, so you've plenty of room to work with. The main fish to be caught are catfish up to about 6lb, but there are carp, carassio, bream and hard-fighting mullet too. Milo and I use proper gear – heavy hollow elastic, 0.20 hooklengths and forged size 10 hooks – and you have to feed heavily to attract and hold the fish.

This year I've also been to Holland as the non-fishing *capitano* of a team that Milo put together to represent Italy in a two-day six-nations match against teams from the host country, Germany, Switzerland, Austria and Luxembourg. That was on the Lage Vaart Canal, where I fished for England in the 2009 World Championship and where Wales won this year's European Championship. Milo's team fished brilliantly to win, and also had the individual winner in young Alberto Italiano, but I had to miss the prize ceremony to catch my flight home.

The bream run big on the Lage Vaart Canal! (Milo Colombo)

I live only five minutes from Gatwick, but after a mix up at the airport I found myself on a flight to Luton instead, from where I had to get a taxi all the way home. That hit the wallet, I can tell you!

Milo and I have also been to Belgium this year, for a two-day pairs match on some fabulous commercial carp lakes. There were five lakes, with 34 anglers on each, so it was a big event. On the second day Milo and I fished a lake called Palais du Pêche! If I tell you that we had 183kg between us that day but only came third, you'll get some idea of how good the fishing was. Like on many matches abroad, they had 'half time' each day, when everyone downs poles and gathers in a hospitality area for something to eat and drink. Very civilised! Some of the carp were proper big, and Milo had me in stitches with his attempts to deal with one of over 20lb once he had it in the net. It looked like he was trying to either wrestle it or dance with it!

Milo's mad. He came all the way over to the UK this year just to represent his country in a six-peg, four-hour Fish'O'Mania match at Cudmore. I went along and ran the bank for him, and he came second with over 20kg of mainly ide. He loved it!

With Milo and his catch at this year's Fish'O'Mania. (Milo Colombo)

Every October Milo and I also meet up at his festival on Tensi Lakes in Novara west of Milan. The lakes are full of carp, the pegs are only a few metres apart, and once again the atmosphere is really friendly. But with great company, beautiful scenery, loads of colourful gear on display and up for grabs, and good food and drink as well as good fishing, what's not to like?

One day is a teams of three match, and in 2014 myself, Andy Neal of the Wales team and Claudio Guicciardi won that one. It's great to win such events, but the main thing about them is that they are such huge fun, and it's that, more than anything, that makes all the travelling involved so worthwhile.

At one time, for about six or seven years in a row in the 'noughties', along with quite a few other match anglers from the South, I used to go even further afield, to the Nevada desert in the USA, to fish the annual Las Vegas festivals that fellow UK matchmen Tony Troth and Steve O'Rourke used to hold on Lake Mead, a vast reservoir, like an inland sea, covering hundreds of square miles and swarming with carp. One year when we went the lake was full to the brim and I lost dozens of feeders in submerged bushes, so the next year I took something like 100 feeders to find there'd been a drought and the level

Love thy neighbour! Fishing Milo's festival at Tensi. (Milo Colombo)

was right down, as a result of which I only lost two or three hooks – and no feeders at all – in the whole week I was there.

Such trips are never just about the fishing, of course, and are as much family holidays as anything else. When the kids were young Jeanette and I took them to Florida for the first time on holiday, and we liked it so much that we've been back almost every year since. I knew from talking to Steve O'Rourke in Las Vegas that he holidayed in Florida too, and one year we happened to bump into each other out there, the upshot of which is that Jeanette and I have teamed up on holiday with Steve and his wife Liz every year since, not just in Florida, but in Antigua in the Caribbean too. Then just the other year in Antigua I got chatting in hotel reception to a guy called Andy Hale and it turned out he'd moved from London to a small town in Italy I'd happened to have been in only a week earlier. Talk about a small world! He'd never been fishing before, so I said why not come along and try it? And he absolutely loved it! So now there are six of us in the Florida/Antigua gang – Andy and his wife Pat, Steve and Liz, and myself and Jeanette.

In Antigua we all do a bit of kayaking, and in Florida we play a bit of tennis, but inevitably we do plenty of fishing too. Some mornings Steve and I fish with lures off the beach, or from an outcrop or jetty, while Jeanette and Liz go off walking or cycling, and some days all six of us in the gang go out boat fishing. We've had some big grouper and sharks, all of which are unhooked and released at the side of the boat, but half the enjoyment is simply being out in a boat in the sun on deep blue seas for the day. We take a few small fish for the pot, but the rest go back alive.

Every year in Antigua we meet up with a really fun local guy called Corn, who's become a good friend to us all, and he comes out with us on some of our boat fishing trips too. I say he's called Corn, but one time he had a T-shirt on that said Captain Amos and a bracelet that said Delroy, and when we asked him what other names he went by, he said, "It depends! 'Honey', 'Darling', 'Sweetheart'…!"

In Antigua, without leaving dry land you can catch tarpon that come in to feed on the fish scraps discarded from the dock by the local fishermen, and we always return those – those that we get in, that is! Hook a tarpon of any size and you know all about it, they fight incredibly hard, and with their bony mouths can easily throw the hook when they make their spectacular leaps. It's quite something the first time you hook a fish that looks like

An early morning snook from a beach in Florida.

Those Antigua nights! Steve, Liz, Jeanette and I get ready to rumble. (Liz O'Rourke)

On the highs seas with Andy, Corn and Pat. (Liz O'Rourke)

a giant bleak and it strips line off your reel at a hundred mph and repeatedly leaps clear of the water in a shower of spray – in fact it's quite something *every* time it happens. When they jump, you have to lower your rod, otherwise they'll smash you – it's called 'bowing to the king'!

We hooked this tarpon close to shore and had to follow it in the boat a mile or two out to sea, otherwise it would have snapped us! (Liz O'Rourke)

Back in 2000 I teamed up with Jack Harness – another old match fishing pal – Simon Willsmore, Milo and five of Milo's Italian chums for a 'boys own' adventure in Madagascar, in the Indian Ocean. We weren't exactly roughing it, but the local transport was a few old chairs in the back of an open-top truck! Most days we went out fishing in a couple of boats, catching all sorts, like bright green and yellow mahi-mahi, or dorado, and 'GTs' – giant trevally – and trolling for sailfish. A guy in the boat would stand up top and scan the water, and when he saw a sailfish following the surface lure would call out, "Sailie! Sailie!" The local people were as friendly as they are poor, and welcomed us with open arms. The smallest kindness meant the world to them. So there was no putting fish back here – they all went to feed local families and their children. Evenings with Milo and co were pretty raucous affairs, as you can imagine, and helped make it the experience of a lifetime. When it came to getting the internal flight back to Ivato International Airport in the capital, Antananarivo, we found it had been cancelled because the plane had a broken rudder, so we had no choice but to charter a small private plane to make it in time for our main flight back to Europe. It was only an eight-seater and there were nine of us, so we had to commandeer the seat next to the pilot as well.

Your carriage awaits, sirs! Our transport in Madagascar.

Milo supervises the loading of a fishing boat in Madagascar.

Trolling for sailfish in the Indian Ocean Milo Colombo style.

Boys will be boys – Milo and Jack larking around in Madagascar.

I can't believe Milo and I haven't had the opportunity to go on another foreign sea fishing holiday together since – he loves sea fishing as much as I do – but it's like anything else, it's finding the time. Sea fishing here in the UK is something else I don't do enough of, though only this summer I did go one day with a friend to Selsey to fish off the beach. I hadn't done that in years, and though we didn't catch much apart from weed I thoroughly enjoyed it. I'd like to do more boat fishing here, too. Just about the last time I went out in a boat in the UK was back in the mid-1990s, when myself, Dick Clegg, Kim Milsom, Tommy Pickering and Wayne Swinscoe did a couple of day's filming with Pauline Quirke and Linda Robson of *Birds of a Feather* fame for an episode of a TV series called *Jobs for the Girls* in which Pauline and Linda learnt to fish. We had one day at Mallory Park – Kim couldn't work out why he was being pestered by geese all the time, not noticing that Wayne was loosefeeding the grass behind him with his catapult – and then another day on Dave Pitt's boat *Wight Warrior* off the Isle of Wight. Pauline and Linda couldn't have been nicer – they were great fun – but the night before the boat trip, at the hotel, they were fretting about being seasick the next day. The water was pretty choppy when we went out, but as it turned out both Pauline and Linda were absolutely fine. Not so, however, Dick and Wayne. I was chatting away with Dick when all of a sudden he went very quiet – and very green. Luckily for him they had an inflatable rescue boat on standby, but as it pulled up alongside, before anyone else could move, Wayne – who no one had realised was also feeling somewhat queasy – launched himself into it headfirst! By the time the rest of us got back to shore Dick and Wayne had both made a full recovery and were propping up the hotel bar together, happy as Larry.

Match fishing has given me a lifetime of such memories, and I look forward to acquiring many more in the years to come. I may no longer be fishing on the world stage, but all the while I have my health, my family and my friends I shall carry on enjoying my fishing and my life as much as I have ever done. For that I feel blessed.

FROM THE *ANGLING TIMES* ARCHIVE –

Steve Gardener's
Best Eleven

I n 1975/76 and 1981/82, *Angling Times* published a fair few pieces on the match fishing scene as viewed through the eyes of young southern star Steve Gardener. Picking up my copy of the paper from the newsagents every Wednesday on my way to school and then college was something I looked forward to each week in those far-off days. It was my weekly fix. There was something special about *Angling Times* then, something that was later lost, and I know that some of my friends think the same. Whatever it was – and maybe it was just that we were young and impressionable – it was enough to make a few of us keep our old copies for all these years. Anyway, here is my 'Steve Gardener's Best Eleven', selected on the basis of the common theme of how best to feed a swim, and they are pieces in which, it seems to me, much of his advice is as sound today as it was way back then. They are reproduced here, with their original illustrations, with the kind permission of *Angling Times*, whose copyright they remain. (And in case you're interested, *Angling Times* cost 10p when the first of these pieces was published, and 30p when the last of them was printed.)

Pat Newman

How to Beat the Block-end

(*Angling Times*, 19th November 1975)

Londoners who travel far afield for their fishing don't realise the potential of their home water – the Thames. The tidal river from Richmond to Teddington is without doubt the best water in the South for match and pleasure anglers alike ... but to get those herring-sized dace and big roach on song demands a special approach.

The great majority of summer matches on the 'Tidal' are won with the block-end swimfeeder, and it used to grieve me to see top-notch float anglers being pushed out of the prize money by such crude, makeshift tactics. But until I really studied the water, I could see no other way of concentrating feed where the fish wanted it ... out in the main current.

Now, however, I've come up with the answer, and with my revised float tactics I can beat the swimfeeder brigade at their own game. To understand how I do it, you need to know a little about the rise and fall of the tide.

Most contests on this part of the Thames are timed to start while the river is still rising, and in this early stage I don't really fish seriously – just trotting a maggot close in in the hope of the odd dace. But then comes the top of the tide, when there is no flow at all. It's only a matter of five minutes or so before the level starts dropping again, but during this short period I play my trump card.

After plumbing the depth of the water – usually around 10ft past the marginal shelf – I catapult six heaped pouchfuls of hemp and casters into my swim. And I mean heaped. Then out goes the float. I use an Avon carrying a no.4 shot immediately below it for anchorage, five AAAs a couple of feet from the hook, and a no.4

A favourite swim on the tidal Thames opposite Richmond ice rink. (Image courtesy of Angling Times*)*

or a couple of no.6s pinched on 15 inches below that. The object is to get the caster hookbait down quickly before the bleak get a chance to shell it.

I like to chop a little off the stem of my float, because my experience is that the shorter it is, the easier it is to control at long range.

It's interesting to note the reactions of anglers either side when you suddenly release this barrage of feed. But with no flow, it goes to the bottom and gets the fishes' heads down.

When the tide begins to run out again, it does so very rapidly. To put more feed in at this stage would be suicide – the fish you have drawn from adjoining swims would disperse. But after 20 minutes or so, the flow slackens. This is when I introduce phase two of my heavy feeding technique. Every trot I bang in a pouchful – you can judge how much when I tell you I get through five pints of casters and three of hemp in a five-hour contest.

Some of the feed inevitably gets carried downstream, but enough gets down to draw fish from the neighbouring swims. Now, if you wish, is the time to bring the shoal in closer. It's quite simple – just feed nearer and nearer to your rod end. The last match I won on the Tidal, I succeeded in getting the fish out of the main flow, over the marginal ledge and right under my feet. At this range, nobody stood a chance – not even those using swimfeeders.

This year, however, the Tidal has remained in summer trim much later than usual, and provided it remains dry there is no reason why my method of fishing shouldn't work.* But when the extra water comes it pays to come in closer, though keeping the seed going in. A 4BB balsa is about right, though I'll always go lighter if possible.

Steve Gardener was talking to Nick Fletcher.

The summer of 1975 was a famously hot one.

Be Nice and Easy Down on the Mole

(*Angling Times*, 26th November 1975)

The River Mole is my home water, and it's been good to me – this season I've won five opens on it and have been runner-up twice.

But it's not what I'd term an easy river, because the swims vary so much. In the five-mile stretch controlled by the Dorking club, for example, there are medium-paced runs, fast shallow glides and a deep weirpool … all demanding a different approach.

But two rules apply wherever you fish. Keep it light … and don't overfeed. You may have gathered from last week's article on the tidal Thames that I am an advocate of filling in the swim, but try that on the Mole and you'll be on a hiding to nothing.

Let's look first at those medium-paced swims. They are between two and four feet deep and contain most species … roach, dace, chub and even carp. These fish tend to congregate either side of the main flow, and it's a mistake to trot the middle when you'd do better under your rod tip.

When I'm drawn on a swim of this type, I introduce around 40 casters and a couple of hundred grains of hemp in the first quarter of an hour and try to assess what fish I have in front of me.

My aim is to pick fish off gradually, so I don't feed more than four casters on each trot down. It's much better to get a fish every 10 minutes throughout the day than get one a chuck for the first six casts and then have the swim die on you. Overfeed, and your swim will very soon 'boil' – fish come up into the surface layer, you start getting drop bites and then you're in trouble. It annoys me to hear anglers patting themselves on the back for getting 4lb of fish out of a 10lb swim.

So save extra feed for later. On a recent [six-hour] match I won, I had 5lb in the first four hours … on a minimum of feed. With these fish in the net, I felt I could afford to step up the feed, and in the next one and a quarter hours I added 7lb to my total. Sure enough, in the last three-quarters of an hour I had nothing, but I'd probably got the maximum number of fish possible.

The float I use for this style of fishing carries 2½BB, and consists of a 1½-inch balsa body with a crow quill tip the same length. It's home-made, like most of the others in my box. I call my floats 'animals', because some of them look a bit odd. But animals can be trained. In the slower swims I attach the float top and bottom, and aim to hold

The River Mole – overfeed here and you'll be on a hiding to nothing. (Image courtesy of Angling Times)

all my line off the water for maximum control. On the shallower, streamy swims, however, I fish bottom ring only. This is so that, on the strike, the float disappears quietly.

The weirpool at Dorking is one of the few places where I'd advocate using the swimfeeder. You can win matches here with bream – but there's one swim called the 'Stump' that can hold its own on the strength of the roach fishing, provided your fellow anglers don't lump in too much groundbait.

There's a dead slack ahead of you, with about 10ft of water. I cast over this, and draw my float back until I can hold the caster bait stationary. The Stump can take heavier feeding than most Mole swims, but don't use cereal [breadcrumb]. The aim is to fish as light as possible and I never go above a 4BB float.

Now a bit about the smaller fish. When there's a good flow on, you can win matches with gudgeon. Use tiny pinches of bread on the hook, feeding small balls of cereal. This is leger fishing, and I opt for a running bomb rather than a link, which I find picks up loose weed.

A dodge I find pays off is to attach one or two small shot along the hooklength, below the lead – these stop the weed building up around the hook by intercepting it. Sometimes you'll get a sharper bite than the usual gudgeon tap, and if you then switch to a small redworm you're guaranteed a roach or a dace.

Going down the size scale still further, you may be surprised to hear that minnows can be match winners on the Mole. My best score is 4½lb, but I'm slow compared with my colleague Johnny Errett, who once knocked out 900 for 7lb – bleak bashers take note. The time to go for these small fish is when they are shoaling in the weed and taking baits intended for better things. The aim is to draw them in towards your feet with a pinkie on a size 22 barbless hook. Build your weight with them, and when they're preoccupied, go across for the dace. You can often get half a dozen sizeable fish like this, by removing competition for the bait.

Finally a tip if your swim dies on you for no apparent reason. Don't fish on – if the rules permit, go for a short walk. The break gives the fish time to reassemble and it refreshes you, too. It works for me on the Mole, but when I fish Nationals for CALPAC I have to curb my wanderlust.

A Favourite Water on My Doorstep

(*Angling Times*, 3rd December 1975)

Strange, isn't it, how anglers neglect waters on their own patch. Until a couple of years ago, I'd paid only casual visits to Old Bury Hill Lake in Dorking, even though I lived almost on top of it. Now it's possibly my favourite still-water match venue – though I've yet to win there.

Nobody can deny that the lake is overstocked … least of all fishery manager Graham Rowles. He believes in giving the matchmen what they want, and if anything the high density of fish has improved the sport at this Surrey Lake. The grubbings of carp and tench stir up the bottom and keep the water coloured, so that you can catch on nine days out of 10.

Besides these sizeable fish, the lake contains bream, roach, rudd and hybrids. In a match I want to have a reasonable chance of landing anything that comes along, so I fish a 1.7lb line straight through to the [size 18] hook.

Plumbing the depth here is vitally important. There's a shelf running round the lake, but its distance from the bank can vary from a few feet up to 20 yards.

And this year the level of the water has been raised, so that you might find yourself fishing over what used to be dry land. My plumbing is done with a swan shot pinched on the hook – commercial plummets are too heavy for my tastes.

The bait that scores best for me at Bury Hill is casters, and I usually take a minimum of three pints for a five-hour contest. But maggots – especially pinkies and big chrysoidines [bronze maggots] – can also be useful. During last summer's maggot shortage [caused by the hot weather] I fished here behind the island with just one pint of casters, and when they ran out I was forced to switch to those bronze maggots. To my surprise I got a bream a chuck.

I use a peacock float for all my matches – one carrying four no.4s below the ring and locked on with a no.8. The only other lead is a no.6 down the line, about nine inches from the hook.

My first action after the starting whistle is to throw in four balls of cereal laced with casters and pinkies. I always start with a caster hookbait, only changing if things are slow. From then on I loosefeed casters every chuck.

If you are pegged near lilies, never fish over them or to the side – if you hook a tench he'll go straight for them. Better to cast this side of the obstruction – as long as you are over the shelf, you'll catch. Bury Hill is fished so heavily that the fish are at their least shy before a match, when the water has had a chance to settle. They'll often be right under your feet.

Normally I shot my float down so that only a dimple shows above the water. But sometimes, especially in the shallow swims, you'll get line bites, or the bait will be messed around without being taken firmly.

I'd say that more fish are lost through striking too quickly than through any other cause, so if the line bites become too frequent, I take off a no.4 shot and substitute a no.6. That makes the float that bit less sensitive.

Having said that, I'd point out that the crucian carp at Bury Hill are very shy biters. If I've been having a slow time, I sometimes throw in an extra ball of cereal and the float pops under. A crucian has been mouthing the bait, but it's only when the fish is alarmed that it moves off and registers a bite.

Matches have been won with these little carp, and pinkies probably sort them out better than anything else.

Sometimes I'm pestered by small roach which boil in my swim. Then the answer is to come in closer than the baited area. Large fish often hang around the edge of the carpet, away from the centre of the commotion, and can be picked off.

For really close-range fishing, I opt for a 14ft pole, with an elastic shock absorber. With a conventional rod, fish tend to bounce off the hook at the strike. I've had a 3lb tench out of Bury Hill on the pole, so it's not purely a small fish weapon.

There are five pegs … 27–31 … where Bury Hill matches can be won on bream. The shoal patrols right along this bank – on your left as you approach the lake – but only at these pegs do they come in really close.

If I'm drawn on these pegs, I like to put in a pint of casters straight away, and use a couple on the hook. I don't believe in baiting too small an area, bearing in mind the size of the shoal.

Now a few tips that have proved their worth for me at Bury Hill.

Keep the float moving – just twitch it a couple of inches every 10 seconds or so.

Strike sideways – in a shallow water, this stops the fish coming to the surface and scaring the shoal.

Watch for tench bubbles. Then take off one shot, push the float up the line and cast to the area.

If sport is slow, change down to a 20 hook. But make sure it's a forged pattern.

Steve Gardener was talking to Nick Fletcher.

Canal We Don't Fish Enough
(*Angling Times*, 17ᵗʰ December 1975)

We're very short of good match waters in the South, so it's a pity when those available aren't used to full capacity. I'm thinking especially of the Wey Navigation Canal.

This fishery, situated between Weybridge and Pyrford in Surrey, is capable of holding 500 anglers – yet summer and autumn matches are few and far between. And by the time the season of winter contests gets under way, the water is past its best.

The canal is only about 15 yards wide and 2-4ft deep. Boats have cut a deeper channel, but this varies in position, especially on the bends. It's important to locate this channel by plumbing, especially if you're going for gudgeon. There are plenty of small fish over the marginal ledge, but the better ones – ounce samples – are picked up further out.

The Wey Navigation Canal – a shallow water but the home of good numbers of chub. (Image courtesy of Angling Times*)*

Early in the season, the gudgeon will take maggots and casters, but now the best bait is bloodworm – fished on the pole. We can't get fresh supplies down here, and have to rely on mail order for our bloodworm and jokers. It's the most expensive way of buying peat I know!

When baiting the swim for this style of fishing I use a bait dropper for economy. I just load the dropper with the jokers and peat mixture, and this usually gets the fish going straight away. From then on I throw in small balls of the same stuff, mixed with a little white groundbait to ensure it gets to the bottom.

Don't get the idea that the Wey Navigation is a gudgeon-only water … far from it. The water also contains chub from 6oz to an alleged 5lb – I never believe anything until I see it – isolated roach shoals, and a few dace and bream.

The gudgeon technique I have described comes into its own when the water is 'off' – and that's usually when there's extra colour in the canal. Unlike most venues, the Wey Navigation fishes best when it's clear. Under these circumstances I always go for the chub – they win nine out of 10 contests.

The chub tend to hang on the far side, even if there is only a foot of water. I think this is because a lot of the opposite bank is private and the fish don't get disturbed. If boats are moored up, so much the better – they are noted holding spots.

In summer, the chub will take casters, floatfished just off the bottom. But at this time of year you can flog away for hours on the float without a touch – the fish are reluctant to move for their food in the colder water, and a legered maggot is more productive.

If the flow is not too strong, I use a springtip. This device has only been on the market for about 18 months, but I've been using a home-made version for the past four years. It consists of a length of cane and a Terry spring, and I've several ready made up in various lengths.

When there's a bit of a push on, I resort to the quivertip. It may be just me, but I've never got on with the screw-in version. For an all-through action, I favour a 9½ft rod with the tip permanently spliced in.

End tackle consists of a 2½ft tail, a nine-inch link and just enough AAA shot pinched on to hold bottom. A bomb creates too much disturbance. If the wind isn't too strong, I like to keep my rod well up in the air – this leaves less line submerged and creates less resistance on the strike.

A word of warning – the chub here take a bait quite decisively, and it's a temptation to respond with a hefty strike. Don't do it – only the slightest movement will make contact with a fish.

Now a few general tips I've picked up on the 'Navigation'.

At the Weybridge end of the canal there are good shoals of summer bleak. These have won matches.

Occasionally you'll pick up quantities of postage-stamp sized skimmers on bloodworm. I once fished with pinkies on a 24 – fruitlessly – but the little bream came on as soon as I changed to an even smaller bait.

Only go on the pole when it's hard to get bigger fish. Too many anglers are preoccupied with the French style of fishing, but it's by no means a magic success formula.

Feed your swim little and often. Fish can be 'drawn' on this canal. But don't always cast to the same spot, or you'll scare your shoal.

Don't be surprised if you pleasure fish the canal and hit a 'goldmine'. This autumn, my pal Bob Evans had 31 chub to 3¼lb in one session.

If you go on the float, fix it bottom only. There's less disturbance on the strike.

I'm Not Afraid to Feed

(*Angling Times*, 7th January 1976)

If any angler can be said to have a 'style', mine is centred around feeding the swim. A lot of people pay great attention to tackle presentation, but while this is important, I feel that getting the fish taking at a uniform depth is the first thing to consider.

My feeding is heavy by any standards, but I don't just lump it in. I feed according to the swim and the fish I expect to catch. And by feeding in a smooth rhythm, I get the maximum weight from my peg.

Nowhere is this rhythm more important than when bleak fishing. I use this species as an example because no other fish is more prone to move up and down in the swim if the feed is not properly introduced. When I begin a bleak match, I throw in 10 large maggots every cast until I have gained information on the quantity of fish in the swim.

Having established how many maggots are necessary to produce the most number of bites, I introduce the same number every cast. The fish have by now taken up a feeding spot and should be biting regularly. Now is the time to decide bait presentation and the depth you should fish.

Many anglers believe that 'regular' feeding means introducing 50 maggots every five casts, rather than 10 every trot down. But these tactics, which involve less hard work, don't get the best results.

What happens is that the bleak come up to feed on the sudden influx of bait and then drop back down. So over those five casts, you won't be fishing at the best taking depth. 'Regular' means just that, even if as sometimes happens the fish go right off and I feed a single maggot every cast.

Generally I feed heavily because I'm out to win matches and not merely to get a section placing. With this in mind, particularly on waters like the Thames – which are virtually impossible to overfeed – I decide before the match the weight needed to win on the day and gear my feeding accordingly.

It sometimes pays to keep your hand in the groundbait bowl – no matter what neighbouring anglers may say. (Image courtesy of Angling Times*)*

Sometimes this can be a nerve-racking business. I've often sat for hours without a bite, feeding constantly while anglers around me mutter, "The water won't take it". Invariably when the fish come on, they arrive in quantity. Only a couple of weeks ago I won a match on the tidal Thames with 20lb of dace, after being fishless for the first 1½ hours!

I always prefer loosefeeding to the use of cereal. The only time I'm happy with breadcrumb is in really deep water when I feel that it gets the bait down quickly with the minimum 'spread'.

Whether I feed casters or maggots my style is the same. I take the bait in my left hand, place my closed fist on my chest, then give a sudden flick so that the feed is shot out underarm.

I'm naturally right-handed, and I find this is the best way to ensure uniform feeding … though after a five-hour match I feel the pain for up to three days. If groundbait is needed, there is nothing for it but to put the rod in a rest – or simply between the knees – and throw right-handed.

I go through frightening quantities of casters during the season, but if they are necessary to my success and keep me in the prizes they can be seen as an investment. For loosefeeding I favour them fairly light-coloured, and save the darker ones for the hook.

Finally, a tip about hooking casters. I used to find that when I was using light float tackle and had to 'punch' the bait out, the caster would be forced down the hook. Now, having buried the hook in the bait, I hold the line just behind the caster and give it a slight twist. I don't know why it works, but now my casters stay firmly put.

Fenland Tactics – in Surrey

(*Angling Times*, 14th January 1976)

In the South there are few waters where swingtipping is a worthwhile method. But it's the accepted medicine in the Fens and on many venues where bream take the prizes. So the southerner wishing to be an all-rounder must practise where he can.

A place I find ideal is a pit on the side of the A3 at Wisley, in Surrey. It isn't heavily fished, and being on National Trust land it's a free water. Maximum depth is only 3½ft, yet it produces well all year round. The main species are bream – skimmers in the 4–10oz range plus a fair head of larger fish, together with roach, perch and pike.

While you can catch round the margins, the best policy is to fish at long range. A cast of 40 yards should put you over the deepest spots, wherever you sit.

I tackle this water with a 10ft hollow glass rod and a fixed-spool reel loaded with 3lb line. My swingtips, which I make myself from cane, are as light as possible and usually adequate for this lake – though if there's surface draw, I

(Image courtesy of Angling Times)

just wind lead wire round them until they hang vertically. My method is the link leger, with an 8–12 inch link and quarter or three eighths ounce bomb.

The hook tail can vary between three and six feet. If the fish are feeding well a size 18 hook will be small enough, though I have gone down to a 22. In either case I like to use a short shank or fine wire pattern.

My hookbait is either one or two pinkies or a large white maggot tipped with a pinkie. This combination, I find, tends to spin less on the retrieve than a simple double maggot bait.

On arrival at the lake I put in half a washing-up bowl of groundbait laced with squats and a few pinkies. The cereal is mainly brown, with just enough white crumb to hold it together. I prefer to catapult it into the swim in about 20 sausage-shaped pellets, firing low.

While this may take 10 minutes, it doesn't disturb the fish and the bait breaks up on contact with the water.

My normal rod position is not quite parallel to the bank … if you imagine the hands of a watch, the rod is at two o'clock. But the longer the tail of the hooklength the more I tilt the rod towards the baited area. This is to ensure that I take up all the slack on the strike.

Sometimes I give the reel a couple of turns at the same time, finding the hook goes home at the very end of the strike – this happened to me in my last two Nationals.*

If I'm getting few bites I use one rod rest and place the butt on the corner of my basket, putting the anti-reverse lever on the reel into the engaged position. If things hot up I hold the handle of the rod. On windy days I position my umbrella in the water to protect the tip – I find this also flattens out the waves.

Oddly enough, the best bites come on the roughest of days when the bigger bream also tend to feed well. But in calm conditions, particularly in winter, I'm lucky if the tip moves more than a fraction. Indeed, until I began to hit these bites I was sure my eyes were deceiving me – for the fish were not even bursting the maggot.

It goes without saying that it's imperative to sink the line. I soak mine overnight in washing-up liquid to speed the process, and since I never use a line for more than two outings it doesn't have a chance to deteriorate. On calm days it can still be difficult to bury all the line, and a slightly heavier bomb is the answer. It's important to get a tight line between bomb and tip as soon as possible, for bites very often develop while the bait is settling. To get the most from these drop bites I lengthen the hook tail.

Twitching the bait is sometimes a sure fire way of getting a bonus fish, especially on cold days. Then the bream often stay put until something induces them to grab the maggot.

If I haven't had a bite in the first 15 minutes I repeat my initial groundbaiting pattern. I know the fish in this lake can take any amount of feed – how it is introduced is what matters.

My final advice to swingtippers – as an angler who has a lot to learn about the method himself – is to take it easy in the strike. A smooth pull back is all that's needed to hook fish, but all too often I see people tearing out with a fearsome swipe.

This happens particularly if the fish has given the tip a good pull round. It's as if the angler is trying to match the vigour of his quarry.

Steve Gardener was talking to Nick Fletcher.

*The 1974 match on the Welland and the 1975 match on the Nene.
But see Chapter Three, where Steve recalls catching on the float,
not the tip, in the 1974 National.

Let's Not Be Hasty

(Angling Times, 24th June 1981)

Having just started on my 14th [actually 13th] season on the open circuit, I can look back in all honesty and say that I've had more than my share of flyers when it comes to plum pegs.

By flyers, I mean pegs from where I should have won with one hand tied behind my back. They really were that good. However, as is so often the case, not all of these pegs have turned out to be winners, and if you can't win from a hot peg, then you've got to stop and think very carefully about your fishing.

I've had a lot of good pegs as well as the real plums, and after five hours of match fishing I've always ended the day with the same thought in my mind. Did I get the best from the swim that I've just fished?

Because of the swims that I've drawn, especially the really good ones, I've had the chance to put them through their paces under tough match conditions. It's no good confusing match and pleasure catches because the two simply aren't alike.

Anyway, under match situations, I'm faced with working out either how I could have caught more fish or what I did wrong if I didn't have enough. From these thoughts come two prime questions. Was my approach wrong in terms of tackle required for that particular swim, or did I expect too much from it and attack it all wrong?

In a situation like this you must be completely honest with yourself, otherwise you'll end up with the wrong analysis. How often have we heard an angler say, "I really had the fish going mad and then they just stopped coming. I must have overfed." In all honesty that angler just doesn't know what he did to kill his swim.

It is my belief, in a situation like this, that one of two things has happened. The angler has either overfed his swim, which frightened the fish, or he caught too many too soon, which had exactly the same effect. Either way, the fish have been frightened off feeding.

How often have you caught 3lb of fish from a swim in the first hour of a match, and then just when you're thinking of winning the swim dies? More to the point, how many times have you tried to catch fish at a slower rate?

I admit that it might sound strange advice to try and catch slowly, but a more careful approach won't alarm the fish as much. In a situation like this, you could spread your weight over the full five hours, which might have allowed you to either sneak a place or even win the match outright.

The true art of match fishing is to keep the fish feeding steadily throughout the time allowed, and the better you do this without frightening the shoal, then the better your catches will be.

My experiences have shown me a great deal about the feeding habits of fish and the ways in which they react to being caught. There may be overriding factors as well on the waters you use. Perhaps boat traffic or changes in currents may restrict your actual catching time to just a couple of hours. In these cases I've found that the careful approach still works.

Over the next few weeks I'll be telling you how I've managed to keep fish feeding and the reasons behind my thoughts. Meanwhile, if you get the chance, try and catch a little slower while you're practising and see what ideas you come up with. We'll start comparing notes next week.

Divide to Conquer
(*Angling Times*, 1st July 1981)

I touched briefly last week on what I consider to be one of the main problems which arises when you find yourself drawn on a shoal of feeding fish ... and that it is the damage which alarmed or frightened fish can do to a productive peg.

I want to explain how I overcome the problem.

Let's assume that you've drawn a swim on a steadily moving water with an even bottom and a depth of between five and 12 feet. It's a peg which you can either fish with a waggler or a stick float and the predominant species are roach and dace.

Look carefully at the swim you've drawn and select the spot where you are going to concentrate your fish. As you don't want the fish to feed too close to you, this will be a spot downstream of the peg. Having chosen the line, then your main catching area will be about a rod length inside this.

Having done this, you have not only created a definite feeding area, but you are providing a sanctuary as well. This sanctuary is the banker, if you need it, later in the match. When the whistle goes, start feeding the first choice as if you were building up a main swim. This will attract those fish which were in the area already and the sight of these fish feeding happily and undisturbed will attract others until you've built up a fair sized shoal.

What you won't be doing at this stage is fishing this main area. You'll be feeding much lighter on that inside line, which will be your main catching area. Although this might sound a bit cockeyed, I'll tell you what my own observations have shown.

Having watched the reactions of shoals of roach and dace when they are being fed and fished for, I've found that the fish tend to group themselves roughly into the shape of a fan, with the widest end furthest away from you, which, in effect, means that there are more fish at the end of the shoal.

Because of this fan shape, you can see quite clearly that, if I set out to catch all of my fish from this one shoal, then I would begin to pick up the fish at the head of the fan which will be in full view of the rest of the group. Although I would catch from the front initially, it wouldn't take long to spook the rest of the shoal, which would either move away out of danger or even stop feeding altogether.

I know that a lot of anglers have already worked this out for themselves and now fish inside their feed line. Even so, they're still catching from the main body and, if they get frightened, the effect will be much the same.

How often, for instance, have you suddenly caught half a dozen fish on the trot only to have the swim go off just as quickly? What happens is that the fish scatter and you'll have trouble getting them back again.

So, I continue to feed the main shoal and, by feeding lighter on my second choice of line, I can create a second shoal. These are fish which will have moved out of the back of the fan-shaped group and started feeding independently of the rest. This group might only be a dozen fish, but at least now I can concentrate on catching them without worrying the rest.

In any case, if I do startle these fish, they'll only dash back into the main shoal, which, because I haven't disturbed them, should still be feeding quite happily. Because these fish are undisturbed, they seem to have a soothing effect on the escapees from my other line and, hopefully, it won't be long before they drift back out and start feeding again. Meanwhile I'm still feeding the main shoal.

Hopefully, I can keep sneaking fish out of the secondary line throughout the match, but at times there will be a need to plunder the main shoal. This can only be determined by either the amount of fish you've caught already, or how many fish you'll need to win the match. Obviously, the longer you leave the main shoal, the better it will be, because it means that you've been catching steadily enough not to worry about the rest.

The object of the exercise is to time it or pace yourself, so that your swim stays alive to as near the end of the match as possible, and if that's what happens you can justifiably say that you've just fished a good match.

However, if you need to get on that main shoal for that extra pound or so which is going to put you in a winning position, then don't leave it too late. There's nothing worse than changing lines and taking fish one after the other to find that the whistle goes while you're still half a pound light. I know, because it's happened to me.

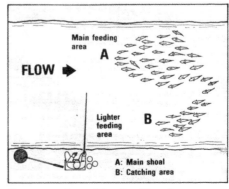

(Image courtesy of Angling Times*)*

Go Steady on that Stodge!

(*Angling Times*, 8th July 1981)

When it comes to catching still-water bream I doubt that there's another species which demands so much care and attention when it comes to feeding.

The problem is how and when to feed in order to catch fish in the 2–4lb bracket which are likely to be shoaled up, and this is a particular problem where the water is relatively shallow.

A lot of anglers get groundbait mania when they're after bream, and we've all experienced situations where a bombardment can do a lot more harm than good. So I have one hard and fast rule. When you're in doubt as to what the fish want then loosefeed whenever possible. If you can't do this because of distance or wind, then use the maximum amount of bait packed into the minimum of groundbait. I always start the same way on bream waters by fishing without feeding for the first 10 minutes or so. I do this to see what's about. I might get a bite or a line bite which shows that there are fish already in the swim, but 99 times out of 100 nothing happens at all. But at least I'm starting with a clear picture of what's in my swim.

If nothing happens then I'll put in a dozen golf ball sized offerings packed with feed, and I'm not too concerned where they land, within reason. You'll discover why I'm more particular about accurate casting rather than accurate baiting later on.

My feeding pattern is spread over a wider area on the theory that very few anglers actually catch bream all day long. They probably catch two or three relatively quickly, but then the shoal moves on for some reason, sometimes never to return.

On other occasions the bream are always on the move on a constant patrol where anglers sitting in a line will take a couple of fish each and then wait until they come back on patrol later on. In a situation like this, it's the angler who nails them down who'll win the match. For this reason I feel that if I can feed an area but not actually fish it, then the fish which move over the feed will stay happier for a lot longer.

My main aim, therefore, is to spread the fish out by putting my feed over a larger area. By doing this, I'm giving a shoal of perhaps 30 fish the chance to root around quite happily rather than having half a dozen fish fighting it out to grab groundbait that's been put on a sixpence while the rest of the shoal moves on.

So, having created a large feeding area and hopefully attracted a shoal, I want to catch as many as possible without frightening them off. Of course I could lose a fish which might well spook them, but as far as the actual catching is concerned I've got my attack planned.

I think that bream will arrive at the edge of a baited area and then spread out over that area from the sides. They won't all dash into the middle of the feed and work their way out, so I'd expect to catch firstly at the front of the baited area. Catching here offers me three big advantages. One, if I catch there then I know I'm on the edge of the shoal. Two, I won't get any line bites if I'm legering because the bulk of the fish are beyond my hook, and if I do get line bites then I simply come a bit closer. And three, I won't be pulling hooked fish through the main shoal and frightening them.

If I do slow down, then I still have the sides of the baited area, which I can fish with ease, or, as a last resort, the back, where there might still be the odd fish feeding after the rest of the shoal has stopped because they won't have been disturbed at all.

I'm pretty certain that there will be fish at all of these points because although I've been catching at the front, I've still been feeding regularly with small offerings through the rest of the area to keep the shoal spread out.

Of course the question of how much, how often, can only be answered by experience and a certain amount of 'feel' for the situation.

You'll have noticed that I haven't mentioned skimmers in this article – and that's because an entirely different approach is needed …

Clouds with Silver Lining

(*Angling Times*, 15ᵗʰ July 1981)

Now that we've got some really warm weather with us, the one species of fish which we really look forward to catching fairly regularly is skimmers.

When it's hot, these fish seem to show up all over the place. And there's nothing more satisfying than a match on a still water where there's a fair head of these juvenile bream.

For some reason, perhaps their age, ignorance and greed, skimmers tend to be more co-operative than the adult bream, and for this reason, up to a point, you can almost make a shoal of skimmers do what you want them to.

There will always be those days when the skimmers are going to stay on the bottom come what may, and this will generally mean finicky nudges at the bait and a float which almost has a will of its own as it dips and bobs.

However, nine times out of 10, a good regular offering of very finely sieved, cloudy groundbait will bring the fish up to feed … and that's when to score. For me, skimmer fishing is all about groundbaiting, because these fish tend to want a continual cloud in the water which contains the food they're looking for.

To create this cloud your groundbait must be as fine as you can get it and you might want to add dried milk or some other concoction to make sure that the water colours up. If you've done your homework on the water you'll know which bait is working best and this, either mixed into the groundbait or loosefed, should have the fish heading up towards the surface.

When you've got the skimmers rising in the water, you're almost certainly on for a good weight.

If you've started fishing close to the bottom and, after a couple of fish the bites have stopped, then come up a few inches. Keep on switching your depth until you find the fish, and then stick at it until things change again.

Even though you might be getting the odd fish from the bottom, keep checking to find the bulk of the shoal. If they've moved up then you won't be helping matters by dragging a hooked fish upwards through the rest of the shoal.

When you have got the shoal feeding, your feeding pattern becomes doubly important. Keep it sloppy to maintain the cloud and keep it going in regularly. If you alter the mix of the groundbait or you leave gaps between feeding, then you'll find that the fish are going up and down like yo-yos and you'll be doing the same with your gear in trying to maintain contact. Even in shallow water I will still use the cloud as my main attractor, and there have been occasions when I've got through quite a bit of groundbait in a swim that's just a few feet deep.

When I know that a water holds a fair amount of these fish then I keep on trying different depths, baits and feeding patterns until they come, and most of the time they'll come to that big light-coloured cloud in the water.

Because shoals of skimmers tend to be fairly large, the bigger the cloud the better. And, when they're on the feed, it doesn't matter whether your groundbait goes in right on top of your float or five feet in the wrong direction.

Bear in mind also that you might even end up fishing within a couple of feet of the surface, but the cloud goes in just the same.

These points are very much a generalisation on skimmer fishing because some waters react totally differently. On some very heavily match fished waters I've found that the skimmers won't react to this method any more.

Now they want big balls filled with bloodworms which the anglers put in at the start of the match and then wait until the fish arrive.

Positive Way to Success

(*Angling Times*, 2nd June 1982)

There was a time when I used to worry about what was going on around me instead of worrying about what was winning the match. Now, however, my outlook has changed.

Some anglers believe that to be beaten on the adjacent swim is an acute embarrassment, and they fish to beat just the anglers either side, instead of trying to win the match. This is a negative approach to match fishing.

I never worry about what's going on next door unless I am competing for first place with them. That's because I always fish to win.

There are some anglers who are quite happy to win their sections each week and walk away with a few pounds for their efforts, but this is not my approach. A look at my results over the years shows that I either win, get well placed …or come nowhere! There are no half measures when I start to fish.

Most matches today are won within the first few hours of the contest unless conditions are so bad that you're fishing for just one big fish which will win the match, and which could come at any time.

The only way to assess how well you're doing is to keep your ears and eyes open. Even if I'm catching I always try to be aware of what's on around me as I'm casting or reeling in. If it's a bad day generally, then the sight of an angler nearby with a fish can give an indication of what's going on. If, however, there's nothing happening and you know that you haven't got a bad draw, then maybe it's time to start thinking about a change of tactics.

This can often apply in Sunday matches when the water has been used the day before. Because the expected fish are a bit shy, or disturbed, it's worth thinking about a secondary line of attack. This happens a lot on waters like the Thames, when an overnight frost can also kill the fishing.

For example, a match on the Saturday could be won with 10lb on the stick float, but on the following day, after the disturbance, early indications could be that despite what happened 24 hours earlier, the same method is not going to fool the fish again. In this instance, you could be looking for a low winning weight, and a couple of chub on the feeder could well be enough to win. Once again, keep your ears open and listen to the bankside grapevine. Although at times it can be misleading, it can also give you a good idea as to what's going on.

Because I always fish for a win, I don't like waters which don't offer me an alternative to my original plan of attack. This often rules out canals and small rivers because I like plenty of room to try out all possible methods if the fish don't come quickly. I invariably have my tactics worked out before the match, so I know what I'll do before I arrive at the peg, under normal conditions.

Take the River Medway at Teston, for instance. This venue invariably starts with a bang because, in recent years, chub have dominated on this stretch. I'll go to the far bank straight away on the waggler, using maggot or caster, and I expect to catch a couple of chub within the first 10 minutes. Yes, that quickly! These could be between 8oz and 1½lb, and if I'm lucky I'll get another half a dozen within the next hour or two. If this doesn't happen, then it's time for a change. I'll keep on feeding the far side, but I'll switch my attack to the middle with maggot in the hope of finding the roach. Then I'll give myself an hour of alternating between the two lines, and if this doesn't bring any response it's time for another positive change.

Although there aren't a lot of them here, my last hope of winning the match will be with bream, which will mean using groundbait and possibly going on the lead.

On a good day, I often know within the first quarter of an hour whether I've got a winning peg or not. This isn't unique – most experienced matchmen will tell you the same. If I know that I can't win, then I'll try for second place, and only when all else fails will I go for a section win.

In team events it's obviously different, but I treat my section in exactly the same way, looking on it as a mini match in itself which I'm trying to win. I have won the Surrey [winter] league individual points championship twice, and last year I won four sections out of the five matches I fished. I blew out completely on one event, but that's not unusual for me.

What I do consider on team events is the harm I could do by going all out to win the match individually. I have to curb my tendencies to try for a win and set out just to concentrate on catching enough to win the section. There have even been instances where big fish have shown on the far side, yet the near swims are producing plenty of fish on the stick float. Although I'll admit to having a couple of chucks across, I still have to keep in touch with the anglers in my section, so I don't spend too much time trying unless I get a fish or two quickly.

This brings me back to the start. There's no shame in being beaten off the next peg if you can't win the match. Some anglers get so involved in peg-to-peg fishing that they lose sight of the overall victory. If you're in with a chance of winning, then by all means consider your neighbour, but if neither of you have a chance then don't be drawn into a scratching contest. Stick with the method that you think might bring you a couple of big fish which could win the match, and if you don't catch them then don't worry. There's always next time.

You will have given yourself the chance of winning by being positive in your approach. Often, the scratchers will miss out on the opportunities which you have created for yourself.

On the other hand, don't forget your neighbour, he could always set you on the path to victory by choosing the right approach, or a method which you might not normally have considered.

Appendix A

Steve Gardener's record in World Championships

(Points are penalty points: 1pt for a section win *etc.*)

Year	Country	Venue	Day 1	Day 2	Individual	Team
1987	Portugal	River Mondego, Coimbra	2.510kg 3pts	1.085kg –	13th	Gold

Squad: Kevin Ashurst, Steve Gardener, Ian Heaps, Bob Nudd, Tommy Pickering, Denis White (Day 1 team match, Day 2 individual)
Kevin Ashurst won individual silver, Denis White individual bronze

| 1988 | Belgium | Damme Canal | 3.040kg 2pts | 2.230kg 1pt | 2nd | Gold |

Squad: Kevin Ashurst, Steve Gardener, Alan McAtee, Bob Nudd, Dave Roper, Vinnie Smith, Dave Vincent
Steve Gardener won individual silver

| 1989 | Bulgaria | Plovdiv Canal | 3.010kg 14pts | 9.700kg 2pts | 22nd | Bronze |

Squad: Kevin Ashurst, Steve Gardener, Bob Nudd, Tommy Pickering, Dave Roper, Denis White
Tommy Pickering won individual gold

| 1990 | Yugoslavia | River Drava, Maribor | 0.090kg 15pts | 1.190kg 2pts | ? | Silver |

Squad: Kevin Ashurst, Mark Downes, Steve Gardener, Bob Nudd, Tommy Pickering, Denis White
Bob Nudd won individual gold, Kevin Ashurst individual silver

| 1991 | Hungary | Rowing Course, Szeged | 2.585kg 5pts | 3.695kg 2pts | 13th | Gold |

Squad: Kevin Ashurst, Mark Downes, Steve Gardener, Bob Nudd, Tommy Pickering, Denis White
Bob Nudd won individual gold, Kevin Ashurst individual silver

| 1992 | Northern Ireland | River Erne, Belleek | 0.310kg 10pts | 6.060kg 4pts | 18th | 4th |

Squad: Kevin Ashurst, Mark Downes, Steve Gardener, Bob Nudd, Tommy Pickering, Denis White

| 1993 | Portugal | River Sorraia, Coruche | 1.400kg 15pts | 4.440kg 4pts | 36th | 9th |

Squad: Kevin Ashurst, Steve Gardener, Dave Harrell, Bob Nudd, Alan Scotthorne, Tommy Pickering, Denis White

| 1994 | England | Holme Pierrepont, Nottingham | 1.090kg 12pts | 0.130kg 4pts | 22nd | Gold |

Squad: Kevin Ashurst, Steve Gardener, Kim Milsom, Bob Nudd, Alan Scotthorne, Denis White
Bob Nudd won individual gold

Year	Country	Venue	Day 1	Day 2	Individual	Team
1995	Finland	Saimaa Canal, Lappeenranta	0.464kg 13pts	1.019kg 7pts	39th	4th

Squad: *Mark Addy, Kevin Ashurst, Steve Gardener, Kim Milsom, Bob Nudd, Alan Scotthorne, Dave Vincent, Denis White*

| 1996 | Italy | River Mincio, Peschiera del Garda | 1.642kg 4pts | 2.894kg 1pt | 5th | Silver |

Squad: *Steve Gardener, Dave Harrell, Kim Milsom, Bob Nudd, Tommy Pickering, Alan Scotthorne, Denis White*
Alan Scotthorne won individual gold

| 1997 | Hungary | Lake Velence | 3.490kg 5pts | 4.130kg 13pts | 33rd | Silver |

Squad: *Mark Addy, Steve Gardener, Kim Milsom, Bob Nudd, Alan Scotthorne, Dave Vincent*
Alan Scotthorne won individual gold, Kim Milsom individual bronze

| 1998 | Croatia | Jarun Rowing Course, Zagreb | 1.172kg 5pts | 3.456kg 3pts | 10th | Gold |

Squad: *Steve Gardener, Kim Milsom, Bob Nudd, Will Raison, Alan Scotthorne, Dave Vincent*
Alan Scotthorne won individual gold

| 1999 | Spain | Castrejon Canal, Toledo | DNF – | 30.010kg 4pts | – | Bronze |

Squad: *Steve Gardener, Kim Milsom, Bob Nudd, Tommy Pickering, Will Raison, Alan Scotthorne*
Bob Nudd won individual gold

| 2000 | Italy | River Arno, Florence | 16.040kg 1pt | 6.060kg 10pts | 14th | Silver |

Squad: *Steve Gardener, Kim Milsom, Bob Nudd, Tommy Pickering, Will Raison, Alan Scotthorne*
Will Raison won individual silver

| 2001 | France | River Seine, Paris | 1.335kg 7pts | 1.880kg 2pts | 9th | Gold |

Squad: *Sean Ashby, Stu Conroy, Steve Gardener, Bob Nudd, Will Raison, Alan Scotthorne*

| 2002 | Portugal | River Mondego Coimbra | 4.160kg 5pts | 5.740kg 2pts | 10th | 4th |

Squad: *Sean Ashby, Stu Conroy, Darren Davies, Steve Gardener, Bob Nudd, Will Raison, Alan Scotthorne*
Stu Conroy won individual bronze

| 2003 | Slovakia | River Vah, Madunice | 1.600kg 12pts | 4.550kg 3pts | 25th | 5th |

Squad: *Sean Ashby, Stu Conroy, Steve Gardener, Bob Nudd, Will Raison, Alan Scotthorne*
Alan Scotthorne won individual gold

| 2004 | Belgium | Rowing Course, Willebroek | 1.820kg 6pts | 3.775kg 6pts | 17th | Silver |

Squad: *Sean Ashby, Stu Conroy, Steve Gardener, Will Raison, Alan Scotthorne, Des Shipp*

Appendix A

Year	Country	Venue	Day 1	Day 2	Individual	Team
2005	Finland	Saimaa Canal Lappeenranta	1.560kg 2pts	1.625kg 4pts	6th	Gold

Squad: Sean Ashby, Stu Conroy, Steve Gardener, Will Raison, Alan Scotthorne, Des Shipp
Will Raison won individual bronze

2006	Portugal	Montemor Rowing Course, Coimbra	6.375kg 2pts	0.580kg 28pts	58th	Gold

Squad: Sean Ashby, Stu Conroy, Steve Gardener, Will Raison, Alan Scotthorne, Des Shipp
Sean Ashby won individual bronze

2007	Hungary	Lake Velence	4.100kg 4pts	3.550kg 5pts	10th	5th

Squad: Sean Ashby, Stu Conroy, Steve Gardener, Will Raison, Alan Scotthorne, Des Shipp
Alan Scotthorne won individual gold

2008	Italy	Spinadesco Canal, Cremona	7.510kg 3pts	8.020kg 1pt	3rd	Gold

Squad: Sean Ashby, Stu Conroy, Steve Gardener, Will Raison, Alan Scotthorne, Des Shipp
Will Raison won individual gold, Steve Gardener individual bronze

2009	Holland	Lage Vaart Canal Almere	3.974kg 1pt	0.975kg 8.5pts	51st	5th

Squad: Sean Ashby, Stu Conroy, Steve Gardener, Will Raison, Alan Scotthorne, Des Shipp
Will Raison won individual silver

2010	Spain	River Guadiana, Merida	8.775kg 4pts	14.060kg 2pts	9th	Gold

Squad: Sean Ashby, Stu Conroy, Steve Gardener, Will Raison, Alan Scotthorne, Des Shipp

2011	Italy	Ostellato Canal, Ferrara	DNF –	8.720kg 4pts	–	5th

Squad: Sean Ashby, Stu Conroy, Steve Gardener, Will Raison, Alan Scotthorne, Des Shipp

2012	Czech Republic	River Morava, Uherske	4.788kg 2pts	1.047kg 14pts	64th	6th

Squad: Sean Ashby, Stu Conroy, Steve Gardener, Will Raison, Alan Scotthorne, Des Shipp
Sean Ashby won individual gold

2013	Poland	Zeranski Channel, Warsaw	DNF –	DNF –	–	Gold

Squad: Sean Ashby, Steve Gardener, Steve Hemingray, Will Raison, Alan Scotthorne, Des Shipp
Steve Hemingray won individual silver, Alan Scotthorne individual bronze

Appendix B
Steve Gardener's record in European Championships

The first official European Championship was in 1995, when England (without Steve Gardener) came fifth on the River Vienne at Availles-Limouzine in France. The following year, 1996, the European Championship was on the River Maas at Liege in Belgium, where England (again without Steve Gardener) again came fifth. (Points are penalty points: 1 for a section win *etc.*)

Year	Country	Venue	Day 1	Day 2	Individual	Team
1997	Italy	River Arno, Florence	5.000kg 2pts	4.800kg 3pts	4th	6th
		Squad: Steve Gardener, Dave Harrell, Bob Nudd, Tommy Pickering, Alan Scotthorne, Denis White				
1998	Portugal	River Raia, Cabecao	3.560kg 7pts	2.880kg 3pts	17th	Gold
		Squad: Steve Gardener, Dave Harrell, Bob Nudd, Tommy Pickering Will Raison, Alan Scotthorne Tommy Pickering won individual bronze				
1999	Ireland	Lough Muckno, Castleblaney	1.79kg 1pt	1.89kg 11pts	24th	8th
		Squad: Stu Conroy, Steve Gardener, Bob Nudd, Will Raison, Alan Scotthorne, Dave Vincent				
2000	England	River Trent, Nottingham	0.090kg 10.5pts	DNF –	–	Gold
		Squad: Stu Conroy, Steve Gardener, Kim Milsom, Bob Nudd, Will Raison, Alan Scotthorne				
2001	Bulgaria	Plovdiv Canal	?kg 9pts	?kg 3pts	23rd	Silver
		Squad: Stu Conroy, Steve Gardener, Bob Nudd, Tommy Pickering, Will Raison, Alan Scotthorne				
2002	Belgium	Albert Canal, Liege	1.270kg 4pts	2.920kg 2pts	8th	5th
		Squad: Sean Ashby, Stu Conroy, Steve Gardener, Bob Nudd, Will Raison, Alan Scotthorne				
2003	Holland	Nord Willem Canal	(3.200kg total) 2pts	6pts	10th	Gold
		Squad: Sean Ashby, Stu Conroy, Steve Gardener, Will Raison, Alan Scotthorne, Des Shipp Alan Scotthorne won individual bronze				
2004	Hungary	Lake Velence	DNF –	9.240kg 1pt	–	Gold
		Squad: Sean Ashby, Stu Conroy, Steve Gardener, Will Raison, Alan Scotthorne, Des Shipp Will Raison won individual silver				

Year	Country	Venue	Day 1	Day 2	Individual	Team
2005	Slovakia	River Vah, Madunice	1.870kg 1pt	2.78kg 6pt	9th	Silver

Squad: Stu Conroy, Darren Cox, Steve Gardener, Steve Hemingray, Will Raison, Alan Scotthorne
Will Raison won individual gold

Year	Country	Venue	Day 1	Day 2	Individual	Team
2006	France	River Vilaine, Brittany	(10.230kg total) 11pts	10pts	42nd	Bronze

Squad: Stu Conroy, Darren Cox, Steve Gardener, Steve Hemingray, Will Raison, Alan Scotthorne

Year	Country	Venue	Day 1	Day 2	Individual	Team
2007	Italy	River Cavo Lama, Novi di Modena	9.490kg 1pt	8.220kg 2pts	5th	Silver

Squad: Stu Conroy, Darren Cox, Steve Gardener, Steve Hemingray, Will Raison, Alan Scotthorne

Year	Country	Venue	Day 1	Day 2	Individual	Team
2008	Czech Republic	River Morava, Uherske	5.430kg 6pts	3.990kg 8pts	18th	5th

Squad: Stu Conroy, Darren Cox, Steve Gardener, Steve Hemingray, Will Raison, Alan Scotthorne

Year	Country	Venue	Day 1	Day 2	Individual	Team
2009	Slovenia	River Sava, Radece	7.810kg 4.5pts	6.460kg 1pt	15th	Bronze

Squad: Sean Ashby, Darren Cox, Steve Gardener, Steve Hemingray, Will Raison, Alan Scotthorne
Steve Hemingray won individual gold

Year	Country	Venue	Day 1	Day 2	Individual	Team
2010	Portugal	River Sorraia, Coruche	2.235kg 3pts	5.135kg 1pt	7th	Silver

Squad: Sean Ashby, Darren Cox, Steve Gardener, Steve Hemingray, Will Raison, Alan Scotthorne
Alan Scotthorne won individual gold, Will Raison individual silver

Year	Country	Venue	Day 1	Day 2	Individual	Team
2011	Poland	Ulgi Canal, Opole	0.073kg 1pt	0.856kg 3pts	4th	4th

Squad: Sean Ashby, Darren Cox, Steve Gardener, Steve Hemingray, Will Raison, Alan Scotthorne

Year	Country	Venue	Day 1	Day 2	Individual	Team
2012	Spain	River Guadiana, Merida	14.741kg 3pts	13.058kg 12pts	26th	Silver

Squad: Sean Ashby, Steve Gardener, Steve Hemingray, Will Raison, Alan Scotthorne, Des Shipp

Appendix C
Steve Gardener's record in Nationals with CALPAC

Year	Division	Venue	Weight	Points	Team
1970	All England	Middle Level	1lb 5½oz	–	38th out of 114

Team: John Benham, Peter Burton, Kenny Collings, Les Collins, Bob Evans, Steve Gardener,
John McCarthy, Ray Mumford, Pete Patman, John Russell, Dave Southall, Dickie Vetterlein
(Team positions were decided on total team weight, not on points)

| 1974 | One | Welland | 20lb 13¼oz | 79 out of 80 | 7th |

Team: Ted Allen, John Benham, Kenny Collings, Reg Cook, Steve Gardener, Freddie Gladwin,
Peter Knight, Dick Lloyd, Chris Love, Ray Mumford, Dickie Vetterlein, Dennis Wells
Steve Gardener was eighth overall

| 1975 | One | Nene | 35lb 4½oz | 78 out of 78 | 22nd |

Team: Ted Allen, Maureen Anderson, John Benham, Kenny Collings, Steve Gardener,
Freddie Gladwin, Peter Knight, Dick Lloyd, Chris Love, Ray Mumford, Dickie Vetterlein,
Dennis Wells
Steve Gardener won his section and was fourth overall

| 1976 | One | Trent | 3lb 7oz | 70 out of 79 | 38th |

Team: John Benham, Les Collins, Reg Cook, Steve Gardener, Billy Hughes, Peter Knight,
Chris Love, John McCarthy, Rob Mittens, Ray Mumford, Andy Partridge, Steve Sanders

1977 and 1978, Steve Gardener did not fish a National

Appendix D
Steve Gardener's record in Nationals with Dorking

The years in square brackets are Nationals that Steve Gardener did not fish, usually because he was on England duty

Year	Division	Venue	Weight	Points	Team
1979	Four	Trent	13lb 7oz	56 out of 56	3rd

Team: Nick Aplin, John Benham, Kenny Collings, Pat Currie, Steve Gardener, Terry Harrison, John Larraman, Bob Leadbetter, Mark Richardson, Steve Sanders, John Waples, Alan Wood
Steve Gardener won his section and was seventh overall

1980	Three	Ancholme	9lb 11½oz	68 out of 68	4th

Team: Kenny Collings, Steve Gardener, Terry Harrison, John Larraman, Rob Mittens, Andy Love, Mark Richardson, Steve Sanders, David Taylor, John Waples, Alan Wood, Kevin Zanocelli
Steve Gardener won his section and was third overall

1981	Two	Leeds/L'pool Canal	4lb 1½oz	56 out of 73	38th

Team: Nick Aplin, Stewart Beresford, Kenny Collings, Steve Gardener, Terry Harrison, John Larraman, Andy Love, Keith Mills, Steve Sanders, Gary Shotnik, John Waples, Alan Wood

1982	Two	Bristol Avon	4lb ¼oz	62 out of 74	4th

Team: Stewart Beresford, Kenny Collings, Steve Gardener, Terry Harrison, Andy Love, Mark Richardson, Steve Sanders, Gary Shotnik, Charlie Taylor, Geoff Vallance, John Waples, Alan Wood
Terry Harrison won his section

1983	One	Upper Trent	12.75kg	75 out of 79	54th

Team: Stewart Beresford, Steve Gardener, Terry Harrison, John Larraman, Andy Love, John Merritt, Mark Richardson, Andy Rogers, Steve Sanders, Gary Shotnik, Geoff Vallance, John Waples
Steve Gardener was eighth overall

1984	One	Nene	2.02kg	74 out of 77	6th

Team: Stewart Beresford, Steve Gardener, Paul Hiller, John Larraman, Andy Love, John Merritt, Mark Richardson, Andy Rogers, Steve Sanders, Gary Shotnik, Charlie Taylor, Alan Wood
Steve Sanders won his section and was sixth overall

1985	One	Leeds/L'pool Canal	0.09kg	13 out of 79	29th

Team: Stewart Beresford, Steve Gardener, Terry Harrison, Paul Hiller, John Larraman, Andy Love, John Merritt, Mark Richardson, Andy Rogers, Steve Sanders, Gary Shotnik, Geoff Vallance

1986	One	Oxford Canal	1.20kg	64 out of 78	14th

Team: Steve Gardener, Mark Gillard, Lennie Goodwin, Terry Harrison, Dave Hurry, John Larraman, Andy Love, John Merritt, Mark Richardson, Andy Rogers, Steve Sanders, Gary Shotnik

[1987	One	Trent	–	–	3rd out of 80]

Year	Division	Venue	Weight	Points	Team
1988	One	Thames	1.16kg	44 out of 78	6th

Team: *Stewart Beresford, Steve Gardener, Mark Gillard, Lennie Goodwin, Terry Harrison, Dave Hurry, John Larraman, Andy Love, John Merritt, Robin Morley, Steve Sanders, Tony West*

Year	Division	Venue	Weight	Points	Team
1989	One	Severn	2.45kg	57 out of 76	9th

Team: *Stewart Beresford, Steve Gardener, Lennie Goodwin, Terry Harrison, Pete Hawley, Dave Hurry, John Larraman, Andy Love, John Merritt, Robin Morley, Steve Sanders, Gary Shotnik*

Year	Division	Venue	Weight	Points	Team
1990	One	Witham	2.32kg	55 out of 89	20th

Team: *Stewart Beresford, Steve Gardener, Lennie Goodwin, Terry Harrison, Pete Hawley, Dave Hurry, Andy Love, Robin Morley, Steve Sanders, Gary Shotnik, Simon Wheeler, Dave White*

Year	Division	Venue	Weight	Points	Team
1991	One	Trent/Mersey Canal	0.36kg	20 out of 86	14th

Team: *Steve Bush, Steve Champion, Glen Fleet, Steve Gardener, Terry Harrison, Pete Hawley, Andy Love, Robin Morley, Steve Sanders, Gary Shotnik, Simon Wheeler, Dave White*

Year	Division	Venue	Weight	Points	Team
1992	One	Trent	4.22kg	73 out of 88	17th

Team: *Stewart Beresford, Steve Bush, Glen Fleet, Steve Gardener, Terry Harrison, Pete Hawley, Dave Hurry, John Merritt, Robin Morley, Steve Sanders, Gary Shotnik, Dave White*

Year	Division	Venue	Weight	Points	Team
[1993	One	Leeds/L'pool Canal	–	–	10th out of 84]

Year	Division	Venue	Weight	Points	Team
1994	One	Ouse and Cam	1.76kg	81 out of 85	14th

Team: *Ben Bray, Pete Brownlow, Glen Fleet, Steve Gardener, Pete Hawley, Nick Howell, Mark Hoye, Robin Morley, Will Raison, Steve Sanders, Kevin Stack, Dave White*

Year	Division	Venue	Weight	Points	Team
1995	One	Gloucester Canal	0.65kg	49 out of 85	7th

Team: *Russ Ackers, Ben Bray, Pete Brownlow, Steve Champion, Glen Fleet, Steve Gardener, Terry Harrison, Paul Hiller, Dave Hurry, John Merritt, Will Raison, Simon Wheeler*
Will Raison won his section

Year	Division	Venue	Weight	Points	Team
[1996	One	Witham	–	–	65th out of 84]

Year	Division	Venue	Weight	Points	Team
[1997	One	Yorkshire canals	–	–	43rd out of 84]

Year	Division	Venue	Weight	Points	Team
1998	One	Thames	2.30kg	42 out of 81	6th

Team: *Pete Brownlow, Glen Fleet, Steve Gardener, Terry Harrison, Paul Hiller, Dave Hurry, John Merritt, Robin Morley, Gary Pook, Will Raison, Steve Sanders, Simon Wheeler*

Year	Division	Venue	Weight	Points	Team
1999	One	Huntspill & drains	0.06kg	34 out of 81	19th

Team: *Pete Brownlow, Glen Fleet, Steve Gardener, Paul Hiller, Ben Leach, Steve Mayo, Gary Pook, Will Raison, Michael Sanders, Steve Sanders, Des Shipp, Simon Willsmore*

2000 – 2005 inclusive, neither Dorking nor Steve Gardener fished a National

Year	Division	Venue	Weight	Points	Team
[2006	Three	Basingstoke Canal	–	–	2nd out of 47]

Appendix D

Year	Division	Venue	Weight	Points	Team
[2007	Two	Fossdyke and Chesterfield Canals	–	–	1st out of 46

Team: Callum Dicks, Ian Didcote, Mark Goddard, Gary Hamilton, Terry Harrison, Steve Hemingray, Paul Holland, Gary Pook, Steve Sanders, Simon Willsmore
Paul Holland won his section and was third overall, and Dorking won the team title]

| [2008 | One | Huntspill & drains | – | – | 4th out of 63] |

| [2009 | One | Shropshire Union, Trent/Mersey, Staffs-Worcester Canals | – | – | 14th out of 69] |

| 2010 | One | Trent | 2.04kg | 51 out of 67 | 15th |

Team: Callum Dicks, Ian Didcote, Steve Gardener, Dave Harpin, Steve Hemingray, Ben Leach, Gary Pook, Will Raison, Steve Sanders, Simon Willsmore

| 2011 | One | New Junction Canal | 4.380kg | 59 out of 59 | 1st |

Team: Michael Buchwalder, Darren Davies, Callum Dicks, Lee Edwards, Steve Gardener, Dave Harpin, Will Raison, Steve Sanders, Des Shipp, Simon Willsmore
Steve Gardener won his section and the individual title, Dave Harpin and Will Raison won their sections, and Dorking won the team title

| 2012 | One | Bristol Avon | 2.56kg | 41 out of 51 | 1st |

Team: Michael Buchwalder, Darren Davies, Callum Dicks, Ian Didcote, Lee Edwards, Steve Gardener, Gary Pook, Will Raison, Des Shipp, Simon Willsmore
Dorking became only the second team (after Birmingham in 1976) to win successive Division One titles

| [2013 | One | Trent/Mersey Canal | – | – | 3rd out of 56] |

Appendix E
Dorking's record in *Angling Times* League finals

The Surrey Winter League started in 1970 and from 1971 was part of the *Angling Times* League, which ran until 2011. Dorking won the Surrey Winter League every year except 1973/74, when they were third behind winners Leatherhead and runners-up Twickenham, and 1992/93, when they were second to Banstead. This table shows that Dorking won a record nine finals.

Year	Venue	Position
1972	Great Ouse	3rd
1973	River Blackwater (Ireland)	5th
1975	Coombe Abbey	2nd
1977	Coombe Abbey	6th
1978	Coombe Abbey	1st
	Squad: Nick Aplin, Mike Bartlett, John Benham, Kenny Collings, Les Collins, Steve Gardener, Peter Knight, Bob Leadbetter, John McCarthy, Keith Mills, Rob Mittens, Mark Richardson, Dave Roberts, Steve Sanders, Dave Taylor, Alan Wood, Terry Wright	
1981	River Skjern (Denmark)	1st
	Squad: Nick Aplin, Dave Blanks, Pat Currie, Kenny Collings, Steve Gardener, Terry Harrison, John Larraman, Andy Love, Keith Mills, Rob Mittens, Mark Richardson, Steve Sanders, Dave Taylor, Geoff Vallance, John Waples, Alan Wood Rob Mittens won the individual title	
1986	Attenborough Lakes	1st
	Squad: Stewart Beresford, Steve Gardener, Mark Gillard, Lennie Goodwin, Paul Greest, Terry Harrison, Paul Hiller, Dave Hurry, John Larraman, Andy Love, John Merritt, Mark Richardson, Andy Rogers, Steve Sanders, Gary Shotnik John Larraman won the individual title	
1987	Warwickshire Avon, Twyford	2nd
1988	Mallory Park	1st
	Squad: Stewart Beresford, Steve Gardener, Mark Gillard, Lennie Goodwin, Terry Harrison, Dave Hurry, Chris James, John Larraman, Andy Love, John Merritt, Robin Morley, Mark Richardson, Steve Sanders, Gary Shotnik, Tony West Stewart Beresford won the individual title	

Appendix E

Year	Venue	Position
1989	Mallory Park	1st

Squad: Stewart Beresford, Steve Gardener, Mark Gillard, Lennie Goodwin, Terry Harrison, Pete Hawley, Dave Hurry, Chris James, John Larraman, Andy Love, John Merritt, Robin Morley, Mark Richardson, Steve Sanders, Gary Shotnik, Tony West

1991	Willow Park	1st

Squad: Stewart Beresford, Steve Bush, Steve Champion, Glen Fleet, Steve Gardener, Mark Gillard, Terry Harrison, Pete Hawley, Dave Hurry, Chris James, Andy Love, John Merritt, Robin Morley, Steve Sanders, Gary Shotnik, Simon Wheeler, Dave White

1996	Trent (Nottingham)	2nd

Dorking's Paul Hiller won the individual title

2001	Nene	2nd
2003	Nene	5th
2004	Nene	3rd
2006	Nene	1st

Squad: Grant Albutt, Callum Dicks, Paul Filmore, Steve Gardener, Mark Goddard, Gary Hamilton, Steve Hemingray, Paul Hiller, Ben Leach, Steve Mayo, Gary Pook, Will Raison, Steve Sanders, Des Shipp, Simon Willsmore

Simon Willsmore won the individual title

2007	Nene	3rd
2008	Nene	1st

Squad: Callum Dicks, Ian Didcote, Paul Filmore, Steve Gardener, Gary Hamilton, Terry Harrison, Steve Hemingray, Paul Hiller, Paul Holland, Ben Leach, Gary Pook, Will Raison, Michael Sanders, Steve Sanders, Des Shipp, Simon Willsmore

2009	Nene	6th
2010	Nene	3rd
2011	Milton Keynes Lakes	1st

Team: Michael Buchwalder, Callum Dicks, Ian Didcote, Mark Goddard, Dave Harpin, Paul Hiller, Gary Pook, Will Raison, Des Shipp, Simon Willsmore